He Works
She Works

Successful Strategies for Working Couples

Jaine Carter, Ph.D.
James D. Carter, Ph.D.

amacom
American Management Association
New York • Atlanta • Boston • Chicago • Kansas City • San Francisco • Washington, D.C.
Brussels • Mexico City • Tokyo • Toronto

This book is available at a special
discount when ordered in bulk quantities.
For information, contact Special Sales Department,
AMACOM, a division of American Management Association,
135 West 50th Street, New York, NY 10020.

This publication is designed to provide accurate and authoritative information in regard to the subject matter covered. It is sold with the
understanding that the publisher is not engaged in rendering legal,
accounting, or other professional service. If legal advice or other expert
assistance is required, the services of a competent professional person
should be sought.

Library of Congress Cataloging-in-Publication Data

Carter, Jaine.
    He works, she works : successful strategies for working couples /
Jaine Carter, James D. Carter.
        p.   cm.
    Includes bibliographical references and index.
    ISBN 0-8144-7896-4
    1. Dual-career families—United States.   2. Work and family—
United States.   3. Marriage—United States.   I. Carter, James, D.
II. Title.
HQ536.C377   1995
646.7'8—dc20   95-24721
                                                                CIP

Printing number

10   9   8   7   6   5   4   3   2   1

To
Paul Stewart Carter and **Todd Douglas Carter,**
who have contributed volumes to our couples heritage
and who have developed into such wonderful adults
that they make us look good as parents.

Thanks for the memories and the laughter and for
allowing us
to share your lives.

Contents

Acknowledgments   vii

Foreword: Susan Sarfati, CEO, Greater Washington
    Society of Association Executives   ix

Introduction   xi

**Section One—Working Couples: Identifying the
Challenges**   **1**

  1   Working Couple Challenges   3
  2   She Works: Wonder Woman Is Weary (From the
      Woman's Perspective)   16
  3   He Works: The Discounted Gender (From the Man's
      Perspective)   31
  4   You Work: Self-Worth for Value Added   42
  5   Why Partnerships Fail   56

Section Two—The Power of Partnerships   **71**

  6   We Work: Making Partnerships Work   73
  7   Making Workable Decisions   88
  8   Making Stress Work for You   100
  9   They Work: Gaining the Support You Need   118
10   Working With What You Have   136

**Section Three—Success Strategies for Working
Couples**   **151**

11 Managing Career Challenges   153
12 Working Realities: Resolving Critical Issues   168
13 Working Together: Co-preneurs   185
14 Ways the Partnership Can Help Achieve Greater
    Success   198
15 Work, Work, Work: Enjoying Life While Pursuing
    Your Goals   208

Bibliography   218

Index   223

Acknowledgments

Throughout our personal and professional lives we have been fortunate to have attracted talented and dedicated people who were turned on by what they do. Creating this book was no exception.

A very special thank-you to Sally Fitch, free-lance editor, and Joan Wieser, Director, Human Services, University of Miami Hospitals and Clinics, for reading the entire manuscript, before it went to the publisher, and sharing their impressions.

Attorney Robert Koop Johnson shared his insights on divorce and the value of premarital contracts.

Dawn Litchfield, of Litchfield Asset Management, Inc., and Donald Hughs, of the Consumer Credit Counseling Service of SWF, Inc., shared their experience in money management.

Our thanks to Mary E. Glenn, Acquisitions Editor at AMACOM Books, for believing our book was worth publishing and for guiding us through the process.

It is impossible to imagine how many hours and stages go into writing and processing a book for publication. Most of those processing hours were contributed by Deborah Nelson and Anita Decoteau, CPS, who were dedicated to getting this book published. Deborah took us through the proposal and first draft phase and Anita read, challenged, and polished the copy to meet our publisher's deadline. Anita's husband, Charles E. Decoteau, is also to be commended for being the kind of husband every working woman needs, who by helping her, helped us. We have learned a great deal from all of them and thank them profusely.

Special thanks to Lynda E. Woodworth, Associate, Public Relations, and Marcia Brumit Kropf, Ph.D., Vice President, Research and Advisory Services for Catalyst, for sharing their research studies and guiding us toward more.

Many working couples contributed their valuable time and experience to this manuscript by completing our extensive questionnaire and then agreeing to participate in structured interviews. We have changed their names and titles, but the examples you read are from real life.

Special appreciation goes to author Wallis E. Wood, who helped us write the first proposal and came up with the title, *He Works/She Works.* Wally is a true professional and an enlightened human being.

Love and appreciation to our parents for helping us be what we are today. The best thing about them was that they were always on our side.

And . . . thank you for purchasing the book. Without a reader, a book is just a dust collector. We look forward to your feedback.

Foreword

When I was growing up, my mother woke up early each morning, put on a dress, hose, pumps, and an *apron* and got ready for the day. Her work revolved around taking care of family and home. Period. She went about her routine of cooking, shopping, cleaning, and ironing as if this were the natural order of things for a wife and mother. Very often she would wonder aloud if that was all there was to life. Eventually, when my younger brother was in high school and she thought he could fend for himself, she accepted a job in a social service agency. My mother never reached her potential and felt an emptiness because of it.

I started my married life by supporting my husband as he attended graduate school and then becoming a mother to three children. That was also the natural order of things. Although very happy with marriage and my three beautiful children, I felt that something was missing. I was sure something must be wrong with me because I was not content with my life as it was. I too felt an emptiness.

During that time of longing, Betty Friedan's *The Feminine Mystique* was published. Reading it changed my life. I realized that what I needed was a life for *me*. Being supportive to my family and keeping house was important but simply not enough. Many of my peers felt the same way I did. So, we began the struggle to enter the work world, attempting to balance work and family. We did this without any direction or guidance and with very few role models. We were trailblazers, continually faced with conflict and uncertainty. Neither husbands nor wives knew how to handle the demands created when both partners worked.

Several years later, when I was responsible for developing education programs for executives, I had the very good fortune to meet Drs. Jaine and Jim Carter. Because so many people were struggling to achieve balance in their lives and asking questions about how to manage a dual-career relationship, I asked the Carters to develop a workshop for dual-career men and women designed to teach them how to balance their personal and professional lives. The workshop was a tremendous hit, with standing-room-only audiences.

Work/family issues are at last coming out of the closet and the Carters are at the forefront of the movement. As an outgrowth of the workshop and their many other related experiences, they have written this book. Don't I wish all this had been available to my mother and to me and my husband, as young working wife and mother, husband and father? And don't my contemporaries wish the same thing? If we had had the tools available, perhaps our superwoman, superparent, stressed-out, burned-out syndromes could have been avoided.

Men and women who are trying to achieve a meaningful life while balancing work/family responsibilities are very fortunate to have available *He Works/She Works: Successful Strategies for Working Couples.*

We have come a long way but still have a long way to travel as we struggle to successfully balance individual, couple, family, and societal needs. Enjoy this book. Your life will work better because of it.

> Susan Sarfati
> Executive Vice President & CEO
> Greater Washington Society of Association Executives
> Washington, D.C.
> March 1995

Introduction

You're together. You both work. How does the relationship affect your career? How does your career affect your relationship? Ultimately, the dynamics of the workplace alter the dynamics of your relationship. There are times when you feel you could do better in the relationship if it weren't for work. Other times you feel you could do better at work if it weren't for the relationship. Your career will never be what it was before you merged with your significant other. The existence of each affects the other. They are interdependent. This fact creates challenges that need to be met in order for each of you to enjoy life while pursuing your goals. This book is about those challenges.

Whose job is the more important? Do you work too late or too much for him/her? What if she makes more money? Or if your jobs are in different cities? Are you both so exhausted by the demands of the job, children, in-laws, and all the other necessary ALDs (annoying little details) that there's no life in your life? Sometimes, there's no *feeling* for anything, no sense of fulfillment. Can you keep resentment from building to the point where it hurts you and the people you care about? Yes, you can successfully manage your dual-career relationship *and* successfully pursue your goals.

He Works/She Works shows working couples that personal partnerships do not have to be a power struggle. They don't have to be a struggle at all. There doesn't have to be a winner and a loser, a victim and a rescuer.

You will discover here down-to-earth, practical advice and step-by-step action solutions as well as examples from people on the line. We, and other working couples, have successfully mastered the challenges of modern life and share with you what worked for us and what didn't. *He Works/She Works: Successful Strategies for Working Couples* shows you how to cope successfully with the job, the relationship, and other significant partnerships to reduce anger, stress, self-sabotage, depression, and burnout at work and in your personal life. It demonstrates how you can manage your relationship as a true partnership in which you work to enhance both careers, reach your heart's desires, and enjoy life while pursuing these goals.

The book is written from the point of view of the man who is doing his best to be a promotable employee, loving partner, father, and son but who feels torn between his obligations to his family and his need to focus his energies on the job. It's a conflict of values and he doesn't always understand what his partner wants or how to resolve important issues. And it is written from the point of view of the woman who is striving to progress in *her* job, be a loving partner, caring mother and daughter but who is also struggling to help her partner, in-laws, friends, and boss, who just don't understand her fatigue.

We are management consultants, lecturers, authors, and radio and television talk show hosts who are husband and wife and co-producers of two children. Over the last twenty years we have worked with over 200,000 men and women either as a team or independently with our own clients. Each of our careers requires travel. During our time together there were periods when Jaine was heralded as more successful; at others, Jim was considered more in demand. How did we handle such ego-involving problems? Did the children survive our careers? How do our careers *and* our relationship not only survive but thrive in this rapidly changing society?

It wasn't always easy, but we were committed to our partnership. Did we fight? Did we ever disagree? Or think of getting a divorce, or having one of us retire? Sure we did. We're real and normal people, not robots. Early in our marriage, we tried to please each other, our children, in-laws, neighbors, business clients, and associates. We didn't know how to say no, nor did we set priorities.

There were simply too many demands on our time. We felt that each opportunity presented to us in our speaking careers would evaporate if we didn't "seize the moment." It never occurred to us that we could pass up an opportunity until it fit more conveniently into our lives. We often had no time for each other. We had very little quality time with the children. Oh, we took them to Disneyland, the park, and apple picking, and did all the other things that families are supposed to do. But we were always tired and stretched to the limit. We suffered, alone and together.

We fit the children in, and they felt it. They began to feel as though they were an inconvenience. If they weren't around, we could work twenty-four hours a day. If we never had to read a bedtime story or go shopping to replace lost sneakers, we could focus more on our careers. Our relatives felt the same way. We can't remember a time when one of them would call without starting the conversation with, "I'm sorry to bother you. Are you too busy to talk to me for a couple of minutes?"

We were always too busy. It *was* an inconvenience to talk to them. We would, of course, but they too felt neglected and unimportant. Our parents are gone now, but if we could do it over, we'd take quiet, unhurried walks on the beach, each with his or her own parents. Marriage sometimes destroys the intimacy that parents had with their growing children. Parents miss that. They hunger for it. They want to know how we are *really* doing. We understand how they feel, for it is now our time to hunger.

We made mistakes, but we did some things right. We want to share with you the lessons we've learned, those learned by other working couples we've interviewed, and those we have known throughout our careers. Self-help books abound. People read several, yet still find themselves trapped in old behaviors, victims of dysfunctional relationships. There is a missing link. That missing link is consistency, demonstrations, support, and *action*! If you have any influence with your significant other, use that influence to get his or her commitment to enhance your relationship together. This book can be the catalyst to opening the lines of communication and guiding you toward more fulfilling relationships.

Ten years ago, we started listing the problems participants in our management education seminars said were pertinent to their personal and professional lives. As we analyzed this collection, we discovered that over 80 percent of these problems had to do with people issues concerning bosses/subordinates, husbands/wives, co-workers/clients, and relatives.

As a result of this collection, we have focused our career efforts on the development of strategies to help people live and work cooperatively, successfully, and harmoniously. In addition, our own challenge of combining work and family has evolved into a quest for solutions that can and have helped working couples.

To add to our research, we developed and mailed five hundred separate questionnaires to both the men and the women in working-couple relationships. They were advised not to consult with one another and told that their responses would be confidential. We have used comments and observations from these questionnaires in Chapters 2 and 3.

The responses from the questionnaires, our collection of participant problems, and the research we have gathered from various sources have provided a controversial forum for why working couples may not be connecting. We are not suggesting that these opinions and observations form the majority view with regard to male/female opinions about gender differences, but they are certainly worth considering as a possible explanation for why dual-career partnerships encounter difficulty.

To add a broader perspective, we interviewed fifteen successful working couples who shared with us what did and didn't work in their partnerships. These couples come from a variety of geographic locations around the United States and Canada and combine a mixture of ethnic backgrounds, experience, and education. From a career perspective, they are involved in many different occupations, including secretarial services, nursing, physical therapy, education, law, financial services, entrepreneurial businesses, consulting, politics, construction, production, entertainment, upper and middle management, supervision, and journalism.

He Works/She Works is designed to help couples communicate with each other, as well as with colleagues at work, their own children, and other significant people in their lives. It is not a theoretical book. It goes beyond understanding by providing practical steps that couples can take to accomplish specific goals.

This is not a book about whether women *should* work. That is your business. Your values—not ours—will determine the answer to these questions. Our business is helping you to achieve your goals, whatever they are.

This is a book for people who have already chosen to join together to make a life for themselves, and in that journey have also chosen to pursue careers. We focus on the couple in this larger world rather than on the couple in its private relationship and provide practical suggestions you can implement—at home to improve your relationship with your significant other, and at work to enhance your careers.

We have written in a way that men will relate to, factually and systematically, recommending workable skills that can be implemented immediately. Women will also be able to relate to the real examples of life as it really is for working couples. The major focus is winning partnerships.

In writing this book, we encountered a functional challenge. When we wanted to relate an anecdote about Jaine from Jaine's point of view, should we use "I," "Jaine," or "she"? We settled for referring to each of us by name.

Take your time reading this book and absorbing the suggestions made. Go beyond gender differences. Discuss with your partner how you can use the suggestions to enhance your personal partnership. Then read it again, next month and the month after that. There is *nothing* more important than the significant relationships in your life. Nothing.

SECTION ONE

Working Couples: Identifying the Challenges

Chapter 1

Working Couple Challenges

Technology has transformed the world, turning it into a global society in which information is power. Every time technology changes, it affects business and ultimately the family. Work and families affect society. Our organizations compete worldwide, which creates even more competition, forcing our companies to hold prices against countries whose people work for far lower wages than do ours. Because of increased competition, organizations have had to trim costs by reassessing how they do business, restructuring, and downsizing personnel. This has resulted in fewer jobs at less pay, which means more competition among workers for fewer available jobs. This comes at a time when the 76 million baby boomers who are still alive have reached their peak earning years. The competition for jobs is fierce.

As companies stretch to produce more with fewer people, downsizing has resulted in greater volumes of work for employees who have survived the cut. This, coupled with the high cost of living, but lower wages, has made it necessary for more women to work in order to help support their families. The pressure of work/family responsibilities on dual-career couples has increased relationship tension, which results in more work tension.

It is an integrated system. What affects one affects the other. Separating work stress from relationship tension, understanding how each contributes to the other, and developing strategies to cope with these stresses may well be our major challenge in the coming decade. The paradigm shift (the way we perceive the world) is changing the way we view work and family. In our society right now, we have a double backlash—a backlash against men *and* a backlash against women. We are having to redefine relationships at work and gender roles in the home. This may be keeping men and women from facing the real issues of what partnering is all about. To gain insight into these and other challenges working couples face, we asked working couples to share with us the unique challenges they encountered when attempting to combine work and family. What do working couples perceive to be the advantages and disadvantages involved in a dual-income relationship? The following is a summary:

Advantages	Disadvantages/Challenges
• Sharing a goal. • Couples having more in common. • Both professionally challenged. • Men having more choices. • Both men and women enjoying higher self-esteem. • Opportunity for women to be all they can be. • Children involved with real role models. • Children more self-reliant. • Greater opportunities (from a financial standpoint) for children. • Opportunity to upgrade lifestyle. • Potential for retirement funds, children's education, and security. • Potential for more disposable income. • More opportunity for cultural enrichment (through travel or other work experiences). • Greater depth and breadth of life experience.	• Risk of getting caught up in financial wants versus needs. • Too much to do. • Always rushed. • Constant child care worries. • Always feeling guilty. • Dealing with fatigue. • Coping with stress. • Running out of "cope" and being short with loved ones. • Never having time to sit down and read a book or relax or be alone. • Risk of getting caught up in careers at expense of partnership. • No time for just us. • Partnership losing spontaneity. • Less sex. • Society doesn't understand. • Working mothers still treated as if they are the "bad guys." • Children feeling they are an inconvenience. • Children obliged to do more to help the family. • Women feeling resentful because of unequal distribution of personal responsibilities. • More financial stress. • Fear of everything: losing job, not being available for children, divorce, bankruptcy.

Most working couple challenges can be traced to:

- *Careers.* Whose is more important? Which one should "trail" if one partner is offered a better job that requires relocation? How can you cope with a frequent traveler or commuter relationship?
- *Money issues.* Who earns what? What if she makes more than he does? How is it spent or saved?
- *Time.* How is it spent? Who is prompt and who is late? How can you get everything done within the available time? Are you spending too much of it at work?
- *Parenting.* Child care, discipline, activities, cost.
- *Quality of lifestyle.* Where to live? Who to see? Who is responsible for what around the house?
- *Family ties.* In-laws, blended or extended family relationships. The cloak of guilt. Spending time with, taking care of, coping with disapproval and acceptance.
- *Dealing with ex-spouses.* Poor communications and emotional withdrawal.
- *Feelings and emotions.* Not sharing, feeling used, dealing with resentment, diminishing sex life.

Career Challenges for Working Couples

In order to maintain a successful, workable lifestyle, working couples must strive to develop coping strategies that deal with gender redefinition and learn to compromise and connect with one another. They must also commit themselves to the accomplishment of mutual *long-term* goals. For example, we never sat down and said, "Your job is more important than my job." It was not a competitive situation. We looked at what we were doing, whether it was good for what we wanted together, and whether it would be good for our two children.

That's a noble goal, but it's tough to stay focused. Seldom do we find that one person's career is on an equal footing with the other's. For a variety of economic and other marketing reasons, one may be growing and challenged, the other coasting or stuck. For example, one may go away to law school and become 100 percent focused on his new activity, but then find that his partner hasn't grown at the same rate he has. This frequently happens with careers. Or one partner gets a promotion to a very challenging position, which causes her to focus a great deal of her time and energy on the job to the exclusion of the family. Career growth creates a major diversion from the focus on family. When this happens, a partnership can survive if the partners discuss how this extra stress and dedicated time will affect the family, and if they plan how they are going to support each other through this period.

What happens when both of you undertake a growth activity at the same time so that both of you will be growing simultaneously? It sounds good in theory, but in practice it doesn't work. One of the partners needs to be focusing on the partnership. When all energies are directed away from the partnership, you lose connection. This usually spells trouble. When one partner is focused on a career challenge, the other needs to relate to the stress and be encouraging, supportive, and available. There should be an understanding as to a time limit for this focused support; otherwise the available partner will start to feel resentful. It's also a good idea for the supportive partner to look around for a growth (but not totally consuming) experience. Then both partners can stimulate each other and find common bonds. This may prevent one from nagging or being jealous and critical of the person who needs to focus.

When career-oriented people join together, they are making a commitment to grow old together. Along the way they will first grow up; then they will grow in their careers and finally in their ability to comprehend life. This growth will inevitably be unequal. They will not necessarily be growing in every area of their lives at the same time. He might be growing in his career this year and she might be growing in another direction next year. The key is to grow together.

When career opportunities come up for one partner, what happens to the other? Moving to a new location often creates major stress in the relationship. Rather than trailing behind a relocated partner, a growing number of working couples are choosing to commute between two locations. Sometimes it works. Some couples report that the opportunity to disconnect rejuvenates the relationship. But for couples who haven't yet had a chance to really bond, set their goals, share their stories, or dream together, it puts a heavy strain on the partnership. They begin to grow apart. Most commuters find that the road becomes very lonely and they begin to ask themselves if it is worth it. You want to hug your wife tonight, not two weeks from now. Eating out alone is about as thrilling as watching grass grow, and for all commuting marriages there is that temptation that is as old as humankind—looking around for someone else to make the loneliness go away.

Working couples had these other concerns about their career goals. Partners don't appear to understand the pressure the other confronts at work. For instance, a man reports: "She doesn't understand the specific challenges of my job. When a client calls, I have to run, even if it's on the weekend. I can't afford to say, 'This is my time with the family.' The client will go to someone more interested in his business."

A woman has a similar problem: "If the boss wants to discuss a special account or project just as I am walking out the door at 5:30, what am I supposed to say? Sorry, boss, I'm not interested enough to stay a little late?" and "I have to go to several organizational conferences and conventions. His job makes it impossible for us to go together, so we are separated for whole weeks at a time. He doesn't like these meetings because he perceives I'm being catered to at some lush resort. Actually, I'm working eighteen hours a day with top management and potential customers."

What challenges does being in business together present? Betty and Bill share: "We truly do believe the biggest challenge is how busy our work keeps us. We are traveling extensively. I guess the challenge is that it's hard for us to turn off work and that thinking process, and get focused on other things. We have a tendency to take our business setbacks out on each other. We never talk about anything else."

Monetary Gain From Two Incomes

Money is a great source of conflict for most working couples. This is what we call the "delusions of grandeur" challenge. Money does not really spell freedom, and the more you have, the more you want. Commitments seem to increase correspondingly with income levels. Often couples get caught up in upgrading their lifestyles, spending more money just because they are both working.

What is wealthy? What is middle class? It depends on where you live and what your income will provide. According to a national study of the changing U.S. work force by the Families and Work Institute, the median 1991–1992 household income was $42,500. That amounts to $425,000 over a ten-year period, yet most couples report that they never feel solvent. Couples need to develop a serious financial plan on how they can profitably manage their money. What are they doing at present?

Many working couples have three checking accounts—his, hers, and joint for the household. Women are increasingly making more than their partners, but the majority of investment decisions are still made by men. Most couples know what their fixed expenditures are but don't do budgeting beyond that point. The largest challenge for working couples is that they don't "talk real" about money issues. Too many things are left unsaid and unplanned. One man commented, "She makes more money, which is great. But then she spends it frivolously. I hesitate discussing this with her because, after all, it's her money. As a result, we are always playing catch-up and have nothing in reserve."

Then there is the cost of both partners working: "We have to look good," complained one couple. "After all, you have to compete at a younger age and look like you have been in business a hundred years and have been making a million dollars from day one. You can't go with, 'Gee, I'm kind of poor. Give me the shot.' To compete and get to the top, you have to look like a seasoned pro and that takes money."

Money is probably the number one underlying destructive element in most partnerships. From a divorce attorney: "I don't see people fighting when they are living in a mansion, not worrying about how they are going to pay their rent. I see couples fighting when he can't believe she wants to go out and spend $100 on Christmas decorations they use once a year, when they can barely pay their rent. He is yelling at her and she is mad at him because he won't let her celebrate the holidays."

In blended families, one spouse may feel that the other is too lenient about money with his children or ex-spouse. Or she makes more than he does and sees part of her income going for the support of his ex-spouse or children. She doesn't speak up about how she feels because she doesn't want to make him feel inadequate.

A divorce attorney notes that many couples never really understand their finances until they are going their separate ways. Getting a divorce is the first time both get a clear picture. Perhaps if they had just kept themselves updated along the way, they wouldn't have gotten the divorce. Too often, one partner thinks that they have more than they do, while the other partner is paying the bills. In 25 percent of divorces, one partner has no idea of their financial situation and that partner is usually the woman. The husband has not only maintained complete control but complete secrecy as well.

Often money issues are confused with lifestyle choices. This is often an ego problem exacerbated by a distorted definition of success.

Fred is a consulting engineer. He hates traveling and being away from home. Because he needs to support his family in the manner to which it is accustomed, his career decisions are based on how much money he can make. Ellen is a computer programmer, likes her work, and wouldn't be happy doing anything else. Each makes good money. They have two children. Could they adjust their income so that he could work on projects requiring only limited travel? Yes. Will he? No. Fred believes they need to have the biggest and best of everything: car, house, boat, a diamond for Ellen. They spend more than they make. Fred blames Ellen's extravagances, yet he is the culprit. Every time they fight, one or the other rushes out to buy a "let's make up" gift. They are trapped by their own spending behaviors and fail to connect with each other about what is really important.

Part of the financial challenge facing working couples is setting up a contingency fund—dollars for the unexpected. As Doug and Diane, a working couple we interviewed for this book, explained, "It's the little things that will kill you. It's not the big ones. The big ones you plan for. You plan to pay the mortgage; that's fine. You haven't planned for a car breaking down or the roof leaking. You should plan for these little things." The ideal situation is to have a contingency fund for emergencies, but with the high cost of living, most working couples don't have one.

The Use of Time

The time challenge cuts across everything we do. The general consensus is that there is never enough of it. There is simply too much to do and not enough time in which to do it all. Not having enough time results in increased stress as we rush to accomplish more than is humanly possible within any twenty-four-hour period. Accomplishing all the necessary, but annoying, little things that are required of working couples who attempt to juggle work and family results in not having enough quality time. What is quality time? It usually boils down to what is work time and what is nonwork time. Of necessity, work time is a major part of every day. What happens to nonwork time and what constitutes quality time depend on the partnership's personal circumstances. If you have children, time for self or the partnership is dramatically reduced.

Women told us that they felt a need to be in six places at the same time and that they, quite literally, never have enough time to sleep. Their biggest complaint, however, was not having enough time with their significant others or with their children. Most said that the person for whom they had *no* time was themselves. They also said that they would have more time if their partners only helped more with family obligations.

Men told us they thought women spent too much time on annoying little details, and resented the implication that they, too, should involve themselves in what they considered nonessential activities. "Women don't get it. Work is hard. I'm *on* all day, every day, and also in a physical fitness program where I have to work out. This is very important to me. Whether the bed is made every day, or the dishes washed, is not a priority with me." Most couples have dramatically different perceptions regarding what constitutes essential activities. They also differ on what constitutes quality time. One man explains his idea: "Quality time, if you don't have children, is to go somewhere and carry on an interesting conversation. What makes the conversation interesting is not having to talk lovey-dovey stuff. It's, 'So what's going on in your world?' That is possible when you are both working professionals. Having more things in common is my idea of a great relationship."

Betty and Bill, a working couple in business together, shared the fact that Bill likes to socialize. "I'm a very social person and am involved with a number of organizations. I need that time away, not so much to get out and carry on a bit, but just to be around people who do the same things as I do."

Betty, on the other hand, prefers to stay home. "I would much rather take time for myself, turn on the answering machine, and create. That's the way I get away." But one thing they both agreed on: "We really value our friendship. Normally when we are at home in the evenings, we are both content to sit in the same room and read, just chitchat, or listen to a tape. We both are really happy just being together. If we had children, our focus would have to change."

Couples with children admit that they have no time for each other. By the time they get home from work, feed everyone, take care of any items they have brought home from the job, and get ready for the next day, they are too tired to connect. Some say that they feel like ships passing in the night and that any chance they have to connect comes on the weekends. Repeatedly, we heard that working couples have to know what their priorities are. You each need to be very clear on what takes precedence. This is the only way you can have time for yourself and for each other.

The Children Challenge

The overwhelming factor when considering a couple's coping stamina is children. In our study, couples who were highly career-oriented and committed to advancement confirmed the fact that they wouldn't be as free to consider company requests if they had children. Work does affect the family through time pressures, stress, travel, and working late, and often results in latchkey kids and surrogate parents. Two major decisions that concern parenting are whether to have children at all and/or when to have them. The timing of childbirth can be critically important if partners want to advance in their respective careers. For example, having children too early may create problems for the career focus of both. Waiting too long may introduce other difficulties relating to age. Openly and honestly discussing the priorities relating to family and career is necessary to resolving work/family challenges. Once a couple has children, the major challenge is finding affordable, safe, quality child care.

Child Care

Before the decision is made to have children, working couples should explore their options. For many potential and existing parents, this is an ongoing source of stress. There are few supportive policies within companies and other institutions to help with this critical search. There is also a growing concern with the potential sexual and physical abuse of children in day care facilities. The Family Leave Act has guaranteed twelve weeks away from the job, without pay, for working parents after a child is born. Your job is guaranteed upon your return, which is a step in the right direction. The qualifier is that you must work for an organization with fifty or more employees. Few organizations at this time have on-site child care facilities. The ideal arrangement would be if one or both parents could work close enough to the child to allow for frequent visits. The primary need of working couples is flexible work options.

Until the world accommodates this vision, it is up to parents to ensure the daily well-being of their offspring. Children, of any age, should not be left alone. There is just too much going on in our society to believe that children will be safe and secure without vigilant monitoring; therefore, working couples need to seriously plan how they will deal with child care. Who is going to do what? Where will we find safe and loving child care? Who will stay home when the child is sick? As the child gets older, who will attend school meetings, schedule doctor appointments? The list is endless. Traditionally, it has been the woman's responsibility. Christy, a computer programmer, observes, "Most males are not prepared and trained to handle children. Unless they make a logical and planned move to learn to deal with kids, they are not very good at it and don't accept it."

Debbie, who has two children ages 5 and 8, agrees.

I'm tired of picking up after everyone, working and folding mountains of clothes every night. If I don't do it, it doesn't get done and the kids go to school with wrinkled or dirty clothes. Trust me. Teachers assume I am a lousy working mom and the kids are treated like underprivileged children. These teachers conveniently forget that they, too, are working moms. I get up at five o'clock every morning in order to get myself ready, prepare breakfast, get the children up and dressed for school, and go to work. He gets up at seven, dresses himself, and goes to work. He complains I am in a bad and harried mood every morning. Well, what does he expect? It's very hard to feel like a professional when the children, or the school, are calling you at work. He absolutely refuses to pick up the children if they are sick. I have the sole responsibility for them.

Multifaceted Families

The American family picture has taken on many aspects of the corporate merger mania of the seventies and eighties. As a result of changing value systems, the divorce rate is now over 50 percent. Most divorced people do eventually remarry, creating a growing trend toward second-time-around relationships, according to the National Center for Health Statistics. As a result, the American family is an unpredictable montage of mothers, fathers, children, grandparents, stepchildren, stepparents, stepgrandparents, visiting ex-partners, and whoever else may evolve.

Each family has its own way of doing things. In essence, each has its own culture and value system. This requires major adjustments. There are financial (support payments), event scheduling (visitation rights), and people coordination issues to deal with. Coping with emotions and feelings from prior relationships can and does increase tension in the whole family.

Ex-spouses can present challenges. When it comes to parenting, the primary goal should be to raise healthy children. It's difficult to provide uniformity when raising children from separate households. Major sources of irritation are when the children play parents against each other, child support isn't paid on time, the new spouse isn't appreciated, or calls from children are delayed while an ex-spouse dominates the time prior to putting the children on the line. One of the greatest sources of stress are custody battles, when the lawyers and courts decide what couples can do for themselves. Of course, ex-partners have to be on reasonable speaking terms and have the best interests of the children in mind, as opposed to being dedicated to their own egos.

As a nation, we need to realize that parenting is the most important thing we do. It is not a hobby, but we tend to worry about everything else first. When working couples decide to become parents, they need four things to help them live by this value: more time, more money, better services, and more respect.

Extended Family Ties

There is a definite link between strong family ties and working-couple happiness. Renee confides, "I think I had some problems initially when Richard and I were married. We are both close with our families, but in very different ways. The separation from my parents was a challenge. We had to discover a system that worked for us in terms of the outside (our families) and the inside (us)."

How do working couples tackle the challenge of major holidays? Deciding whose family to visit, and for which holiday, is a major dilemma, especially for those with children. With blended families, it's a mammoth dilemma because it is almost impossible to please everyone. Barbara confirms this: "If we go to his folks' house, my folks are put out and I feel guilty."

Richard feels that his and Renee's arrangement is better. "Both of us are very close to our families, but we find it a lot easier if I visit my folks and Renee visits hers. We have encouraged them to come and visit us for the holidays. We have room for everyone."

It is important to maintain close ties with the extended family, as working couples need their support. It is also necessary to develop new traditions with your own immediate family. With good planning, you can have reunions and quality time with each extended family, together. The rule is that when the pressures exceed the pleasures, it's time to find alternatives.

The Cloak of Guilt

Over and over we heard the lament about guilt.

"I feel guilty when I don't spend the holidays with my parents."

"I feel guilty that I'm not with my children while they are growing up."

"I work such long hours that I never see my wife and kids."

"I'm always so tired. I feel guilty that I keep refusing my husband's sexual overtures."

"I feel guilty if my partner is working around the house and I am trying to relax. I feel like I should be up and helping out."

Working couples are shrouded with guilt and that keeps them running. The people who suffer most from this sense of guilt are the partners themselves who spend so much of their time and energy trying to be perfect parents, career professionals, loving children to their parents, good friends to their friends, and responsible members of society that they have nothing left over for self.

We all are trying to connect in a meaningful way. Each is striving for spontaneity, self-disclosure of feelings, and acceptance. Each also wants to feel that he/she can trust the other not to discount his/her feelings. Neither would deny the importance of each of these attributes as part of building a successful partnership. What couples need are the skills.

Summary

As a society, hyped by the media, we have created such high expectations about the way couples are supposed to live that we are driving couples apart. Working couples are overextended financially, emotionally, and physically as they buy now, pay later, then suddenly awake to find they have no money. The rate of bankruptcy filings has increased dramatically, and continues to rise because people assume obligations without planning for the necessity of eventually having to pay the piper. Even if they do think through the long-term ramifications, they convince themselves that "it's not going to happen to us"; they continue to bury their heads in the sand and enable one another to seize the day.

Already stretched-to-the-limit couples want children too. Now! And because they can't afford the extra expense children eventually require or adequate day care, they expect employers to provide day care centers, allow for paternity and maternity leave, and offer a whole slew of other benefits. But when these extra (sometimes mandated) fringe benefits become too expensive for an organization, the organization downsizes. More people are then out of a job, which results in further bankruptcies. We create a worldwide double bind when we expect employers or government to accommodate our personal lifestyle preferences and needs.

Are we implying that women should not have professional careers and if they do that they should not have children? No. We simply advocate creating realistic guidelines and expectations *before* obligating yourselves. Life is no dress rehearsal. This is the real thing. Human beings, although extremely resilient, are on a crash course as they fumble through life trying to make some sense of their lives against a diagram created by past generations. These diagrams no longer work. New paradigms must be explored if we are to survive and enjoy life while pursuing our goals.

We are a quick fix-it society. Some focus on fixing self, others on their spouses, children, or anyone else who happens to enter their life circles. When we operate in a quick fix-it mode, we are quick to judge what we don't like and want to change it. Quick fixes just put Band-Aids on sores that continue to fester. In order to make meaningful changes toward solving society's work/family problems, we must first create alternative prescriptions that will help cure the festering infrastructures of our lives.

The key, regardless of style, is to understand what causes our discontent, our disagreements, and the disintegration of our relationships. To do this we must learn to be empathetic with each other's position. Focus on understanding the issue of difference versus blaming. Accept the fact that being challenged doesn't mean you always have to find a resolution. The objective is to face challenges together and to seek options cooperatively. As in the planning process, the real value in people working together toward common goals is to find workable solutions. Challenges won't go away. You have a choice between looking at them as an adventure or suffering them as a nightmare. An adventure bonds and strengthens the partnership; a nightmare pits one person against the other and destroys the relationship.

In the following two chapters we share with you some observations and perceptions gleaned from hundreds of men and women with whom we have talked. Certainly not all men and women feel this way, but it helps to explore why many of us are not connecting.

Chapter 2

She Works: Wonder Woman Is Weary (From the Woman's Perspective)

We were told, and ardently believed, that we could have it all. The full-blown career, the cleanest house in the suburbs, children and Little League—they were all part of being an eighties kind of woman. Some of us burned out sooner than others. All of us made sacrifices, through the many roles we played, and no one *liked* us. Our husbands complained that we were automatons. Our children felt as if we didn't love them, as they became couch potatoes and victims of violence on TV. It wasn't fair and it was lonely.

Then came awareness groups and psychotherapy sessions at which we plaintively asked, "What's wrong with me? I have *everything*! Why am I not happy? Why am I so tired?" The answers started coming near the end of the eighties. With a flash of insight, we began to awaken to the fact that we were being *used*. We were lawyers, doctors, judges, and CEOs, but we were still swabbing out the toilets at home! When the children were sick, we were still the psychological parent, getting up in the middle of the night to care for them. We were still the ones taking off from work because day care centers refused to accept our sick children. The tiredness led to a state of apathy, which, in time, led to burnout. "I *can't* take any more!" were cries we heard from masses of women. "Then why do you?" we asked. The "yes, but" responses included:

"We need the money."

"I don't want to fall back in my career."

"I'd waste all this experience and education."

"I keep feeling I *should* be doing it all."

What happened to all the self-fulfillment we were supposed to feel? The management positions, the promotions, and all the perks that were supposed to go with success were still elusive. "I'm still doing my own secretarial work, yet I'm called a manager," we hear. And finally, the awareness: "It's not coming. Nothing is changing. I'm hitting my head against a glass ceiling and I've got a headache. I can't do it anymore."

With awareness, we can begin to change. The paradigm can complete its shift. We can look at our choices and make decisions without feeling guilty about the roles we decide *not* to play. Freedom to choose what we really want, not what others expect us to want, is what will determine the uniqueness of the nineties kind of woman into the new millennium. What most women of this decade want is to work *with* men rather than against them.

Because of downsizing, mergers and acquisitions, and the increasingly high cost of living, women work because they have to. In most cases, a couple cannot live on his income alone. However, the attitude of many men continues to be, "I'll allow you to work, but nothing is going to change around here. If you can't take care of the needs of the home and have my dinner ready, you can't work." He won't face the fact that he can't support his family alone.

More than two out of three married women with children between ages 6 and 17 are working outside the home, up from one out of four only thirty-five years ago. Statistics show that most American mothers are full-time employees. Standards of living are higher. Modern homes are more complicated and filled with a multitude of objects demanding attention, and we tend to expect our homes to be in perfect order. Dinners must be healthy, multichoice gourmet feasts, and children given quality time. The cost of help, when we can find it, is so prohibitive that it eats up half our salaries.

Studies show that women still do the bulk of household chores. In *The Second Shift*, a study of fifty mostly middle-class, two-career couples, Arlie Hochschild, a sociologist at the University of California, Berkeley, found that wives typically come home from work to another shift, doing 75 percent of the household tasks. In another study, *Family Diversity and the Division of Domestic Labor*, David H. Demo and Alan C. Acock asked,

"How much have things really changed?" Their results indicate that the percentage of chores done by the women in the partnerships ranged from 80.2 percent to 83.5 percent. But before you take a club to your significant other, read on. You may discover that the enemy is neither man nor woman but, rather, a system that rewards our self-defeating behavior.

Identifying the Enemy

Women, by nature or by conditioning, want to establish small groups of intimate friends. While that's fine in the general scheme of things, we need to transfer our skills at bonding to a more universal goal. We need to help each other succeed. No matter what we say, we still don't do an adequate job of supporting one another. I have seen the enemy and it is us. All too often, women hurt each other, through their facades of efficiency, and do not offer true support. When we pretend to be in perfect control of our various roles, women who are struggling may feel as if they are alone in their perceived inabilities. Look at the way we treated First Lady Hillary Clinton. We called her a bitch and made jokes about her having the real power in the family. Both women and men resent, as presumptuous, any power she may have gained by association with her husband. We did the same thing to Nancy Reagan, another presidential wife, and continue to sling mud at any woman celebrity who hints at being successful, unless she is extremely overweight or "damaged" in some other publicized manner.

It's not much different for the rest of us. After talking with thousands of working women managers throughout my career, it is clear to me that the majority of women secretaries and administrative assistants still do a man manager's work first before tackling a woman manager's work. These secretaries also talk negatively about their women bosses, referring to them as nitpickers. Over 80 percent of the women attending my classes for women managers responded that they would rather work for a *man* than a *woman*. While the percentage is decreasing, it still remains distressingly high. The reasons women give for not wanting to work for another woman include a perception that women are harder to work for, less likely to support other women for promotion, and less able to move materials and budgets upward because they have less power within the organizational structure. They also claim that women are perfectionist nitpickers who are catty about and jealous of other women.

Remember, I have been asking *working women* if they would work for other working women. They are enrolled in classes I teach that are designed to improve their management skills so that they can gain more credibility and create cooperative teams. Yet they have admitted that they really don't want to work for women. Is this a dilemma? How can we expect other people to work with us and for us if we won't work for ourselves! If we are to succeed in our careers, as well as our personal lives, we must stop waiting for the "messiah" of women—big brother government, women's lib, transitional men, or benevolent organizations—to come to our rescue and begin taking personal responsibility for our lives.

> *If we are to succeed in our careers, as well as our personal lives, we must stop waiting for the "messiah" of women—big brother government, women's lib, transitional men, or benevolent organizations—to come to our rescue and begin taking personal responsibility for our lives.*

We need to learn how to enjoy being a woman, fully bonded with the man of our choice, and still climb the career ladder. The challenge, as we endeavor to fulfill our potential, is to accomplish these objectives without burning out, burning our bridges, or breaking babies. In order to successfully merge these goals, we have to find acceptance, support, and plain old physical help.

Men as Partners

Women are not the same as men. Instead of complaining about the differences or lamenting, "he just doesn't understand me," women must begin to use their knowledge of male/female differences to structure communications that appeal to men, create strategies to help each reach specific goals, and then establish personal boundaries (rules).

We can negotiate differences without discounting either sex. Unfortunately, too many of us *have* forgotten how to help men rejoice in being men. It often appears as if we are trying to turn our men into women. Why? Because we are so burned out from doing it all that we have finally realized that after putting in a full day at work, we cannot put in another full evening of work at home. Didn't we ask for equality? Well, yes, but it isn't what we expected. Women's presence in the workplace has grown and will continue to increase, but for most of us, our roles haven't changed much. What did we gain? We gained the right to do it all, to feel split in twenty different directions, and to wear the heavy "cloak of guilt." And we are still blaming our men.

Women working is not a new phenomenon. Women have always worked in one capacity or another, and the majority of women do get married. What is new is the lack of support from family living nearby. Changing jobs as the result of a partner's job relocation prevents us from forming the ties that bind and help to mend. Also keeping women from reaching their full potential are the injunctions of our dinosaur dads who taught us that we would always be taken care of, by some man. These dads did us a great disservice. While they did not mean to hurt us, many of our parents taught us to be beautiful, but asleep, as we waited for the glass slipper to be delivered by the magic rescuer who would come to save us from a dismal future. Instead of getting glass slippers, many of us have hit glass ceilings.

Getting Our Perceptions Validated

Women's challenges have an impact on working couples. According to Marcia Kropf, Vice President of Catalyst, a women's issues research organization, women still face many difficult challenges. Some of these challenges have to do with work and family issues and methods to enable women to continue working. In order to work, women must locate child care for their children, find a schedule that's flexible, strive to keep their careers on track, and morally support their partners. This would be easier if women made more money.

Fifty-nine percent of employed women work in low-paying jobs either because of lack of training or because they need to be available for their children. While the disparity between male and female salaries is narrowing, a poll conducted by *Working Woman* indicates that less than 5 percent of top executives are female. The higher that women advance, the larger the wage gap becomes. A United States Chamber of Commerce survey, taken in 1987, found that corporate women, at the vice presidential level and above, earn 42 percent less than their male peers.

It may get better. The Fair Pay Act (FPA) has been introduced by politicians who seek equal pay for equivalent work requiring equal skill and training but involving different tasks. If passed, this would boost wages for working women in female-dominated, lower-paid jobs.

Even without the bill, women are gaining ground. In the 16th Annual Salary Survey conducted by *Working Woman*, results indicated an 18.3 percent climb in pay for female executive managers over the past fifteen years. Men's pay gained only 1.7 percent. The results show that women in higher-level jobs are doing much better. However, there remains a gulf between successful women and those still climbing, because often successful women don't want to be associated with women's issues, according to Marcia Kropf. They feel it might hinder their advancement. We refer to these women as women with the "I made it" syndrome: "I made it through constant sacrifice, denial, and by scratching my way to the top, so why should I make it easy for you?" Most men take pride in mentoring other men. It's a testimonial to their power. Most women still don't know how.

Separating Work and Family

Even when all organizations realize that you cannot separate work from personal issues, and government policies that favor women's issues are implemented, there is still the issue of role definition. The paradigm pertaining to role definition continues to shift, but, even as it is shifting, history shows that the scale will always tip in favor of the old paradigm. In the 1990 Virginia Slims Opinion Poll, conducted by the Roper Organization, six out of ten women stated that more help from their husbands was the single biggest factor that would help them balance work and family responsibilities.

Vigilant standards for joint responsibility must be agreed to by both partners. Then, women must insist that these standards be maintained. Studies show a growing role for men in caring for children. In 18 percent of dual-paycheck couples who work separate shifts, the father is the primary child care provider during the wife's working hours. That is still a very small percentage, but it's a start. When the number of men who willingly assume their share of family responsibility increases, so will the perceived value of this work. Success breeds success. When the job is perceived as valuable, other men will feel more comfortable chipping in and carrying their fair share of family responsibilities.

What about men who do not want to spend more time with their families? After having talked with thousands of men and women throughout our careers as management and business consultants, we have arrived at the conclusion that many men "talk the talk" but do not "walk the walk." Intellectually, they know that women cannot continue to do it all, but their thinking hasn't really changed. We still hear statements like "help mommy out" or "just leave the dishes." This benevolent attitude does not resolve the problem of how things will get done.

> *"Help mommy out" or "just leave the dishes" does not resolve the problem of how things will get done.*

As a result, many women feel that, instead of women having it all, it is men who have it all. A growing number of men, on the other hand, feel that they are second-class citizens condemned to "glass cellars." We are not connecting.

For example, most of the couples in our survey responded that they have someone to come in to help with the housework and, if necessary, the yard work. Women complained, only partly in jest, that men have no understanding of the reality that *before* the house cleaning service arrives, women have a great many get-ready tasks that must be accomplished. These get-ready tasks range from changing the beds to washing all the clothes so that someone else might fold them, from cleaning the toilets (since most women are embarrassed to have someone else do their toilets) to picking up everything around the house (since no one can dust with a week's worth of newspapers and magazines piled on counter tops). Women do these things, not men. Also, men frequently don't understand (or choose not to understand) that most women *need* a tidy environment in order to meet the overwhelming demands on their time. She simply must stay organized. Therefore, she will ask that any contributions the man is supposed to make to the household chores be accomplished on a predictable schedule.

Most women like to have their homes clean for the weekend. In one situation, Rob agreed to take all of the throw rugs in the house outside to shake them. The cleaning woman came on Friday, picked up all the rugs so that she could mop the floors, and left them in piles around the house. On Saturday, the piles were still there. On Sunday, the piles were still there. Finally, Rob's significant other, Helen, "reminded" him, asking when he planned to shake the rugs out. He responded, "Damn it, I told you I'd do them. Get off my back!" Most women agree that "helping" with an attitude of "I'll do it when I'm damned good and ready" just causes more stress.

Just as most women would have, Helen resentfully took the rugs out herself. Rob didn't blink an eye that evening as he playfully tried to initiate sex. He couldn't understand why she refused him. She told us she would rather have had dirty rugs in place than piles of untidy rugs lying all over the house. If only he hadn't said he'd do them, she would have had the cleaning lady leave them in place.

Women just want to know what they can count on so they can make the necessary adjustments. And men will have to accept the fact that tired women won't feel very passionate.

One of the man/woman dilemmas is that men don't like to be told what to do. And women don't like to *have to* tell them what to do. Real agreement must be reached so that the woman isn't always put in the position of policing her mate and other significant others.

> *Women do not want to have to police the partnership.*

Women are more likely to think about what needs to be done at home, and to do it, than to enter into prolonged negotiations with their significant other about "fairness." Many eventually give up and just do it all. Doing it all usually leads to burnout. Of course, the relationship suffers. It may even dissolve. It is not at all unusual for ex-partners to confess that they found the same circumstances in their next relationship. And the next. You might as well try to make this one work. It's less stressful in the long run.

Many men plead incompetence and/or lack of instinct for taking care of the children or tackling other household necessities. Too often their plea of incompetence is a ploy used to avoid doing unpleasant tasks. They pitch in only when asked, and if a woman asks too often, she is accused of being a nag. Women get tired of asking and expect a commitment from their men that what needs to be done needs to be done by both of them, even it if *is* unpleasant.

The truth is that some men really don't know what is expected of them or what is necessary to keep a family going. They have never been taught and have become accustomed to someone else always taking care of all the annoying little details. Women need to take the time to tenderly train their partners in the various ways there are to save time and still maintain quality standards. Then they have to lovingly hold their partners accountable for results. If they don't, women will continue to do it all, which leads to resentment, which, in time, leads to disconnection and possibly divorce. Both partners need to examine their role expectations.

As a woman, it never occurred to me that I wouldn't work. My mother, Mary Louise, worked hard. Dad worked all the time. During the start-up years, the shop was in the basement of our city house. He would work until he was too tired to think, crawl up the stairs, spread newspapers on the carpet, and grab a few hours of sleep. Then he would crawl down the stairs and start all over again. Don't ask me about personal cleanliness. It was another generation.

The only way that Mom could take time off, without incurring Dad's wrath, was to get sick herself. She did this frequently, until just having the flu or a cold was no longer a strong enough reason for her to have the day off. That was when she started having surgery. In those days they kept you in the hospital for several days after surgery, which gave Mom an opportunity to be pampered and have a little time to herself. She had many surgeries. Eventually, when Mom was tired of looking for excuses not to work so hard, she left the relationship to try life on her own. But there were few jobs then that paid enough for a woman with children to support, so Mom would end up in another relationship in another city and the cycle would begin again. Since she moved so often, she was never able to develop long-term friendships. My mother told me that she had never been a happy woman.

The reason for her sad life, as I see it, is that she never took responsibility for her own happiness. She looked to the men in her life to approve or disapprove of her actions, her very being. She then blamed all her problems on the men in her life and was waiting for the magic rescuer until the day she died. She died lonely and alone.

Vivian, my mother-in-law, lived all of her life in Toledo, Ohio. She also worked, but she had a regular nine to five job as a secretary and was able to get home to take care of family responsibilities. Grateful for her contribution to the family, Jim's father helped out with household chores. He hung out the weekly wash, did the dinner dishes, and performed a variety of other small jobs to keep the Carters well and healthy. They worked as a team. The Carter marriage lasted thirty-six years, until Jim's father died.

Did Vivian ever wish for more? A high powered career, perhaps, or a bigger house? She probably did. Was she happy in her simple, uncomplicated existence as a pink-collar worker, caring wife, and mother? She told me once that she had a happy and fulfilled life, that she was proud of her son—who could do no wrong, and that she had loved Jim's father very much. Vivian had an aneurysm that erupted while she was finishing lunch with a group of women friends with whom she had had lunch every Friday since she was in high school. She died surrounded by those friends. She was never lonely.

What is the difference between these two women? They both worked because they had to. It was necessary to help support the family. But one had a truly supportive husband and a network of friends and relatives who lived in the same area. The other had a boss, her family lived in another state, and she was never able to develop any long-term friends. One was always tired, while the other took care of herself. One looked for the magic rescuer, while the other took personal responsibility for the outcomes in her life. Vivian could ventilate her concerns and problems with friends and family. Mary Louise had no one who was "on her side."

Why do many women get "sick" more often than men? One answer may be that it's the only time they get sympathy, can escape unpleasant tasks like working twenty-four hours a day, or have an excuse for avoiding sex. Even when the man does things around the house, the woman has to be there to find things for him and to clean up the mess he makes while doing it. The following is a typical scenario when a man washes the windows:

> She: Harry, it's been a year! The windows are filthy. You've been promising me for six months [*she feels the need to convince him of the necessity of the task*].
>
> He: Okay, already. I'll do them! Get me the bucket with some water and vinegar. Where is the three-foot ladder? Where is that squeegee we bought? Can you find it for me?

When these facts are brought to his attention, he asks, "Who changes the oil?" The reality is that he usually takes the car to an auto mechanic for service. Even if he does change the oil, the process is not tiring or even hard labor and it is not boringly repetitive! How often does the oil need to be changed? By contrast, washing dishes is a *daily* chore. So is making beds.

So, in order to get a half day off, she gets sick or has a friend or relative fall ill. Sometimes this works, sometimes it doesn't. When it doesn't work, she gets up and struggles through resentfully. Since she is resentful, she won't talk as she mopes around the house. He calls her a martyr. She is. She should have enough self-esteem to say, "I'm burned out. I'm not going to do anything today but rest." That takes assertiveness and a healthy dose of self-interest. Often, exercising self-interest is interpreted by others as being selfish. So, many women avoid it like the plague. This is a mistake. When we don't pay attention to self-interest, it leads to co-dependency.

Co-Dependency Is Big Business

Co-dependency is today's term to describe women with low self-esteem. According to this concept, people who are co-dependent have an exaggerated sense of responsibility to other people. Most of the men and women we know fit this definition. A co-dependent person is one who has let another person's behavior affect him or her and who is obsessed with controlling that person's behavior. Most people are affected by their partner's behavior, but people-pleasing still appears to be more frequent with women than with men.

The old system of expectations for women continues to defeat women. According to Gloria Steinem, in *Revolution From Within,* even for those of us who were brought up with a healthy sense of self-worth, it is difficult to maintain high self-esteem. Pretty young women deny this, claiming that they are aware of their beauty and great bodies. The truth is that, too often, they don't really believe that they are attractive and look to others to affirm their value as human beings. Intelligent and educated women claim they don't need beauty to feel good about themselves. One woman, who has her law degree, said she was planning to go back to school for her Ph.D. When asked why, she responded, "I want to be so overqualified that no one will ever be able to reject me again." Perhaps that is women's basic, underlying goal.

Many women want to please all of the people all of the time. They start by being as beautiful as they can, without coming across as conceited. They want to be smart, without coming across as smarter than the other person. They want to have an attractive husband who is intelligent and a good provider, but they don't want to cause jealousy in other women. The results? They frequently downplay their own capabilities and attributes. One woman said of another, "I love her. She has everything going for her. She's intelligent, beautiful, and fun-loving, yet she's just self-effacing enough to make her seem real." "Just self-effacing enough." Women love other women who are self-effacing, and men like women who don't act "uppity." Society likes women who can handle it all. For many women, their greatest sense of self-worth comes when another person comments about them, "I don't know how she manages it all so well." It is this self-effacing, overcompensating behavior that keeps us down professionally and personally. It is difficult to feel good about yourself when you are always putting yourself down.

Attitudes That Keep Us Down

What *do* we think of ourselves? We think that if we can't be perfect we must be worthless. To perpetuate the myth that we are powerless, we are encouraged to abdicate fiscal responsibility. Money in our society is enabling. It confers power to get what you want. Actually, women hold the majority of wealth in this country, but men still control it. You may be thinking, "No! I'm a professional, I control my own money." Okay. But who is your stockbroker, your banker, your CPA, and your attorney? Mine are all women chosen for their competency and compatibility, but I had to make a conscious choice to look for and develop these female professional relationships.

Unfortunately, many women merely *read* books on how to improve their lives but never really *do* anything about them. The results? Women won't deal with their real difficulties. Would anybody clean toilets if they didn't have to? As long as women allows men to avoid the johnny mop, they will remain in the stereotypes they have accepted for themselves and continue doing it all.

Setting Boundaries and Defending Them

What happens when a woman retreats and does the household work the man has agreed to do? She rationalizes that she is doing it in order to keep peace. However, as resentment builds, the love dies. When she does *his* work, her behavior is self-defeating, and their arrangement to share responsibilities is sabotaged. If he has agreed to participate in various tasks that need to be done in order to keep the couple's life moving smoothly, he must be held accountable for results.

> *Hold partners accountable for results.*

Nagging doesn't make it. Tears and recriminations don't make it. The only way to bring about positive redirection in another person's behavior is to structure consequences that are either negative or positive. Reward the behavior that is positive and acceptable. Punish the behavior that is unacceptable. Keep in mind that if you do nothing it will be perceived as acceptance of the behavior and have the same effect as positive reinforcement.

By taking the rugs out herself, Helen implied that Rob's behavior was acceptable. He interpreted her reaction as positive reinforcement. Not only did he get out of doing a chore; his significant other didn't say a thing. After three or four such instances occur, and she has collected enough negative feelings, she will probably erupt. At that time, he will be sincerely confused by her seemingly irrational and unpredictable behavior. Her emotional behavior will reinforce his belief that women are temperamental and unpredictable, and he will start building resentment.

They are not understanding one another, not communicating and clearly not handling the underlying problems in their partnership.

To prevent misunderstandings leading to resentment, the next time your significant other forgets to complete a chore, don't do it yourself. Instead, arrange for a discussion, sit down calmly, and explain what needs to be accomplished, and why.

> For years I complained that Jim never dried off the faucets on the kitchen sink when he did the dishes. He would put the last dish in the dishwasher and then just leave the kitchen. I would go into the kitchen, wash and dry the counter top, then dry off the sink and faucets. Of course, the whole time I would be grumbling and mumbling about the lack of "completed staff work." One day, as I was relating this annoyance to a male friend, he asked, "Why is it so important?" I explained that the faucets would rust out if they weren't dried. Jim, overhearing, looked shocked, "Why didn't you ever explain that to me before?" "I thought you knew!" I replied incredulously. He *should* have known.

Feeling that our partners should know better is one of the major obstacles we need to overcome as women. Somehow we think that men *should know* what to us seems obvious. They don't. In reality, no one *wants* to do household chores. Just as with any job, there are volumes of annoying little details that must be attended to but that no one *wants* to take care of. All members of a partnership should contribute toward their accomplishment.

Other obstacles that need to be discussed were volunteered by working wives:

- "Men's sense of timing."
- "He offers to 'help me out' when I am folding *his* underwear and socks."
- "When he 'helps' with the cooking, he barbecues hamburgers or chicken on Saturday evening. I still buy the food, make the potato salad, and clean up the mess."
- "He says 'You go shopping and I'll *baby sit*.' They are *his* children, too. He is not baby sitting, he is taking the opportunity to interact with his offspring."
- "He puts on a clean shirt and his good pants to go to church and doesn't change out of them to sit around the house. When he is asked to change his clothes to prevent extra laundry, he responds 'I'm not doing anything.' If he valued me, and the demands on my

time, he would realize *somebody* has to wash and iron that extra shirt. It could have been worn again!"

- "Before I can consider a job change or a career move/advance, I have to factor in whether I will be able to pick up the children from day care, who will take his widowed mother shopping, and whether I will be home in enough time to cook dinner. All he has to consider is whether he will like the job and if it will give him an opportunity for advancement."

- "He constantly misplaces things. After I find them, he accuses me of having moved them."

- "Everyone else in the family gets coveted birthday presents and holiday gifts, which I buy and wrap. I get labor-saving devices for the house or another Frederick's nightie. What I need is a massage and a full-time housekeeper."

- "He has never ironed a blouse for me or folded my clothes."

- "Since I've been working, he spends more money on nonessential items like CDs and video games, but we still never have enough for a cleaning service or a baby sitter. Sometimes I feel like I'm keeping *him*."

- "Who picks up the cleaning? In fact, who remembered to gather the cleaning and take time off from a lunch hour to drop it off? Who picks up the children, drops them at piano lessons, and picks them up again? Who has to remember that we're out of milk? If he does run out to get milk, he's gone for two hours and we've gone ahead and substituted something else."

- "He comes to me and asks, in his little boy manner, for me to help him out with his professional work, doing some typing or other projects that should have been done by him or someone else at work. Yet I can leave a clean basket of laundry by his chair to be folded as he watches television. He'll say, 'I'm watching television!' Does *watching* television take both hands? Why can't men do more than one thing at a time?"

Sound familiar? What are the prescriptions?

Summary

Women must learn to change their thinking and their expectations. Every one of the complaints just mentioned could be resolved through assertive confrontation and by holding partners accountable for results.

We must also strive to change our terminology. When our choice is to spend more time with our children, let's consider using "taking a sabbatical" rather than "hopping on the mommy track." A sabbatical is time off to do research and grow. The term *glass ceilings* leaves a "poor me" impression that someone or something outside of ourselves is holding us back, that we have no control or power. This presents a negative image and we need all the positives we can muster.

Women must learn to set limits. In order to do this, we need to have a realistic understanding of our limits. This can be done only when we are ready to turn our backs on the expectations of others and begin to pursue our own real goals.

Pollyanna predictions proclaim the coming of the paradigm shift, women piercing the glass ceiling, and a changing definition of gender roles. Perhaps, but we are only at the beginning of that shift. New guidelines need to be developed that will serve to enhance the growth of both men and women. Until the shift is complete, the struggle will intensify. In the interim, both men and women are the losers. We must develop proactive strategies to bridge the gap between what is and what we hope to be. Until we do, too many couples will fall into that gap and lose their partners, their children, their self-respect, and their love.

We are not the same as men. Instead of just complaining about the differences or lamenting that "he doesn't understand me," we must begin to use our knowledge of these differences to structure communications from the man's point of view, and then adopt strategies to reach specific goals and establish boundaries (rules) toward developing the team framework men prefer.

Let's begin to rejoice in our differences, to value them, even to reward them. We are different pieces of the same whole. Putting those pieces together is our number one challenge in the coming decade.

Chapter 3

He Works:
The Discounted Gender
(From the Man's
Perspective)

As the number of women in management grows, so too does the perceived threat to many men. As women's jobs become more demanding, it is even more difficult to balance work and family. While corporate help may be a growing trend, there is not much change for workers on the line. Male managers aren't pushing flexible work hours. This may be attributable to a growing resentment among some men of what they believe to be the special treatment accorded women. There is an all-too-common attitude, consistent with the old complaint, "Women are always whining and asking for special privileges." Of course, we men can't actually say this out loud, even to close friends. We never know, for sure, who may be a "spy" for the other sex, screaming discrimination or sexual harassment, so we stifle the anger and resentment.

A growing number of men are feeling emotionally and financially trapped and, as a result, are operating from the emotions of anger, passivity, and resignation. According to 1990 IRS data, women already have greater control of the wealth in the United States. The wealthiest women average $1.17 million net worth, while men average $1.11 million net worth. Further, feminists stir the financial pot to the boiling point when they ignore why women earn less. Statistics reveal that full-time working men work an average of nine hours more per week at their jobs than full-time working women do; and, in order to make more money to help support their families, men are more willing to work at two jobs and to take less desirable jobs than women are. Warren Farrell, in *The Myth of Male Power*, refers to these less desirable jobs, which include garbage collection, high-rise building construction work, and working in mines, as "glass cellar" occupations.

There is also the perception of a severe erosion of available positions for white men owing to civil rights legislation which, in many cases, has led to preferential treatment for women and minorities through affirmative action mandates. Other factors are the women's movement and the increased global competition that has led to corporate downsizing. Further, a side effect of women working in previously male-dominated positions is that they are often willing to work harder than men and for less compensation. Several corporate executives have admitted, off the record, that they prefer hiring women "because of their inexperience, insecurity, and the fact that these women just want a chance to prove themselves." They say women will work harder for less money. Now enters the sexual harassment hullabaloo. Men find that they can no longer interact the way they used to without fear of reprisal. This fear is a result of the federal government expanding the definition of harassment to include anything a woman designates as a "hostile work environment."

Off-the-record conversations with men from a variety of organizations show that men feel that women change all the rules when they get into a man's world, expecting things to change according to their value systems. For example, Margaret Kent and Robert Feinschreiber, in *Love at Work*, encouraged women to use the workplace to find mates. There are no chapters, however, that encourage men to use their jobs to meet women. If this were reversed, women would call it a double standard. Men are expected to readily acquiesce to equality at work, while at the same time they are still expected to offer to carry women's briefcases and get heavy boxes down from top shelves.

Men, convinced that women should have their chance, accepted these workplace changes, but a deeper resentment has evolved as women invade male-dominated clubs and locker rooms. These areas, at least, offered men the opportunity to talk their kind of talk, use language as they chose, and tell whatever jokes they wished. Women now demand access to these last bastions of male bonding. Men want no part of women's clubs or locker rooms. Any man who was foolish enough to think equality meant that he could enter women's locker rooms to interview female athletes would find himself barraged by cries of sexual harassment. Is it any wonder that we have a new category of men called "angry males"?

Of course, we also have the issue of equality in the home. Men are now expected to be more nurturing, happily changing baby diapers without making a face. Here, too, they are not allowed to show anger for fear that they may be accused of emotional or physical spouse abuse. Male bashing has become a favorite female pastime. Men who feel guilty for the sins of their fathers have no defense against women's accusations of past unfairness, so they go underground with their anger. This is turning into a seething frustration (according to the U.S. Bureau of Health and Human Services), fired by mounting resentment. Some have turned this resentment inward, as the increase in the male suicide rate attests. Others have begun to scream "Uncle! Enough already! Give me some space to be me." In counterpoint to the song for women, "I am woman. I am invincible," we hear the song from men, "I've gotta be me!"

Men and Women Are Different

Men and women may be equal under the law, but they are physically, mentally, and emotionally different. Men and women even define the word *career* differently. In one study, when asked to define job satisfaction, women who responded defined it as personal growth and self-fulfillment, making a contribution to others, and doing what they wanted to do. Men have been programmed differently into game-playing behavior patterns that promote learning and accepting specific rules, adopting strategies to meet goals, obeying signals, and operating in an overall framework of teamwork, risk taking, and competition.

Most men measure success through high achievement and how well they provide for their families. They don't usually ask, "Is this the job I want to do?" Instead they consider, "How much does it pay?" When a couple decides to have children, they discuss the options the woman will have after the child is born, such as returning to work full-time, working part-time in order to spend more time with the child, or quitting working entirely. A man has two options: continuing to work at just one full-time job or looking for a second job to replace the income the partnership will lose if she decides to stay home.

Too often, money issues are reduced to emotions, and many men still don't do well with emotions. Men look at money as a power tool. How much a man earns equates with his sense of self-worth. After all, he is raised to be a provider. Also, money is a way to display how successful a man is through his house, car, boat, and other material things. Many men like to control the money in a partnership. It is a power issue. Women are now beginning to see money as a form of independence. Money represents security. Women are gaining confidence with money.

Like other couples, working couples fight over money. Men focus on what comes in, women on what goes out. These are gender differences. The major battles are fought over spending, saving, investing, and borrowing.

Women are caught in a double bind. They do most of the family shopping and are often stereotyped as shopping until they drop. Men accuse them of being spendaholics. The reality is that men and women both spend, but for different reasons. Men tend to make the big showy purchases (cars, boats, golf club memberships) without giving them a great deal of thought. Some are obsessed with electronic toys (computers, stereos, video cameras). Women spend more on their physical appearance (clothes, cosmetics, plastic surgery) and they also make the major buying decisions on household furniture and appliances. Men have more confidence about making money than women do. The more men make, the more impulsive they are in spending, their attitude being, "I've got it, why not show what I can do with it?" However, women control consumer spending by a wide margin in most consumer categories. According to Farrell, because men earn more, women expect them to spend more of it on them. But the same analogy does not apply to women when they earn more. They are not expected to spend more of their money on men.

Peter Brown has come up with some rough gender differences as they relate to politics. In an attempt to reduce taxes so that there will be more individual disposable income, men envision a smaller role for government and social welfare programs. Women, by contrast, tend to see big government as their magic rescuer, providing legislative benefits such as equal pay, family leave, on-site child care, and other mandated fringe benefits. Men see government as encouraging dependency, as saying in effect: "You can't do it yourselves. We'll do it for you." Most men know that there is no such thing as a free lunch and that more government means less money in the family coffers. They perceive government programs as a form of socialism and fear the loss of democracy.

A loss of democracy is exactly what some men feel they are experiencing at the governmental level, at work, and in their homes. In a continuing effort to please the women they love, men are stretching to change even more than they have already. Because women work to help support the family, more men are having to adjust to the fact that women simply can't handle it all. Women complain that they do two full-time jobs, the one they do for someone else for pay and the one they do caring for a home and family for free. Even though men work longer hours at their jobs, small percentages of them are beginning to help with home responsibilities like grocery shopping or picking up the children from their day care centers. A few help with cooking and house cleaning. These increased pressures for sharing family responsibilities are creating significant conflicts at home for working couples.

> *A loss of democracy is exactly what some men feel they are experiencing at the governmental level, at work, and in their homes.*

The Transitional Male May Be Replacing the Traditional Male

Many men are rethinking their careers and family goals. Although some men still operate from the position that working wives are only a temporary phenomenon, others are aware that it is a growing national trend that may be here to stay. As a result, men of all ages are challenging their values, including career decisions. In one study, 60 percent of fathers under the age of 35 said they were shaping their career plans around family concerns. These men are in transition as they evaluate their traditional value systems in view of changing family needs. Experts have spotted this trend. In a survey conducted by *Fortune* magazine in 1992, men were asked which was more important to them, their personal lives or their careers. Sixty-four percent responded that their personal lives were more important. At least, that's what they said.

Transitional men are more likely than traditional men to work at bonding with their children. If this trend continues and men are able to create greater connections with their children, without traditional males putting them down, working wives may gain real help with caring for and raising their children. Some men actually take pride in homemaking chores. It isn't as easy as it looks. It takes talent to prepare a visually appealing menu day after day and skill to arrange for everything to come out at the same time. We know a physician who vacuums and dusts the house in order to relax, a truck driver who washes and dries the laundry (his wife won't let him do the folding because she says he doesn't do it the "right" way), and a salesman who prides himself on his floor-cleaning skills. Unfortunately, there are still many macho men who consider males who help out with household chores as being henpecked and castrated.

While Jim was in middle school, one of his dad's friends telephoned from work. When he asked what Jim's dad was doing, Jim said, "He's doing the laundry." This guy laughed at and teased Jim's dad from then on. At work they called him "the laundry man." He took it in stride but let Jim know that he had let him down by telling. It was a mixed signal for Jim. Today Jim does most of the cooking in our house, and has received a fair amount of kidding from a number of his male friends about it, but he enjoys cooking and has never felt less of a man for doing it. This focused activity actually relaxes him, but he still never does the laundry. Funny how those childhood experiences stay with you.

Role requirements for men are changing, both at home and at work, but many men aren't buying into these new requirements. There is a dichotomy between traditional and transitional men. Traditional men look at the way they have always functioned, as males, in the role of hunter and provider. They are accused of being workaholics and look to their wives to manage the home and children. These men feel that if they put in the time at their jobs and make a greater effort to produce, they should get more rewards. For them, being a good provider *is* doing their jobs and they resent being made to feel like failures if they are not changing diapers or becoming their children's best friend. These traditional men look at transitional men as shirkers who are not going all out for their jobs and who are therefore not as deserving as the men who give the job their all. The decision to spend more time with the family and less time on the job is now being referred to as the "Daddy track."

Today, many organizations are hostile places for involved fathers. As a result, men have to be devious in order to beat the system. These men take sick days, carefully arrange their appointment schedules, and create out-of-office meetings in order to permit them to deal with family issues. Changing corporate structures and refinements are bringing about the emergence of managers who are moving toward the transitional male role. When that happens, there will be greater sympathy in the workplace for those who are involved fathers.

Men's Movement Goes Deeper Than Housework

The mythopoetic movement, led by Robert Bly, has helped men to explore their vulnerabilities, intimacies, and degree of self-determination. Men are beginning to question the socialization that requires them to give their lives to protect others, as well as to develop the courage to ask the women they love to accept them as feeling human beings and to stop blaming them for everything that happens to the family. Men, like women, are asking for equal rights.

Men are not big on reading relationship books. It is a problem of identification. They do feel a sense of obligation, responsibility, desire, jealousy, loneliness, pride, and the whole range of human emotions that women are always talking about. But they experience their emotions in a way that they have been taught is acceptable. They let off steam by getting angry, kicking butt, raising their voices, swearing, pounding their fists into walls, and working out. They are trained to bear pain, to reach gain, and not to show hurt. For example, when she touches his hand on a moonlit walk and says, "What are you feeling?" she wants to get closer by sharing her feelings. He thinks, "Oh my God! What is the right answer?" as his stomach tightens. He figures he is in trouble. Touching feels good to her and she wants more. For him, touching hands *is* connecting. It's enough. Questioning the connection is usually not comfortable for men. They don't have experience in sharing feelings. As a result, men spend a great deal of time trying to come up with the *right* answer about how they *should* feel. This difference in processing presents a major challenge for men in relationships.

> *Men are not big on reading relationship books. It is a problem of identification.*

Women, by contrast, openly process, saying what they feel at the moment without qualifying it. Women do give mixed messages, however. They often *say* they want one thing but reward the opposite. "I want a warm, loving, open man," she may say, when in reality she is looking for the best provider to ensure the well-being of her offspring. The best provider is the man who works long hours to get ahead. This kind of man may be short on sensitivity. Women also give lip service to their husbands' taking an active role in raising the children. Children are the traditional source of identity for most women and she and her mother let you know that she knows what is best for the children. Because of their insecurity in these areas, men further compound the problem by letting women pull rank in important areas of child rearing, such as applying discipline, finding child care, and dealing with illness.

Men, too, give mixed messages to their partners. They see the total commitment necessary to maintain a successful partnership as giving up their individuality. They equate commitment with ownership. Not wanting to be owned, they have never fully clarified what a good relationship means. They *say* that the family is the most important thing in their lives but then focus exclusively on their work. When a man says to a woman, "You are important to me. I want to give you the best," it means he is committing himself to work hard to protect and care for her and their children. This is the way men show their love. The reality is that his work is his life. He wants to be the best because being the best is how he measures his success. The classic male workaholic feels that there is nothing outside the job. His personal relationships are downsized. His significant other goes on hold, waiting for the relationship to improve. When it doesn't, he loses her and then *his* life goes on hold until the next relationship, and the cycle repeats itself.

To break the mixed-message cycle, we need to capitalize on the fact that women are better at building relationships and close friendships than men are. They can maintain both a personal partnership and work partnerships. Women need to encourage men to develop and keep male friends, as men's relationships are ordinarily more business-oriented than personal. The reason for this is that when a man loves a woman he puts all his emotional energy into that relationship. Unfortunately, men often give up their male friends to have more time to spend with the family. They also feel that their partners expect this. She may say, " I don't care if you go to the football game with Joe," but he knows she would really prefer that they all go as a foursome. A man who is trying to please a woman usually gives in to his partner's desires so that he and Joe never really get to be alone, together, to just be men.

Working couples say that the longer they are together, the better they are able to work out these double-bind messages. Each finds time to spend with friends, of the same sex, outside of business. Young working couples in their twenties struggle with this issue most. It takes candor to create alternatives that work for both partners. Each needs to realize that a partnership that is smothered in oneness will eventually find it difficult to breathe. Each needs to discover activities that can be enjoyed without the other, and men should not be required to give up their fishing trips or enthusiasm for sports. They, like women, need to get away from responsibility once in a while. Allowing private time sometimes brings couples closer together.

What Men Say About Women

In addition to a need for more private time, just to be themselves, men in our survey shared what they perceive to be additional barriers to connectedness in a relationship.

- "Women need to lighten up. They take everything too seriously."
- "They are negative and have a lack of vision."

- "They are workaholics. They work constantly, as they can't stand to leave something unfinished."
- "It is difficult to please women. They ask you to do one thing and then pile on fifteen other things, 'while you are at it.' It's as if they hate to see a man relax."
- "They don't give themselves enough credit for their abilities."
- "They have an unrelenting sense of guilt—about everything."
- "They are always playing the martyr, trying to make men feel guilty."
- "They have no concept of financial matters. Making sure all the bills are paid, on time, is not financial management. They need to learn cash flow management and truly understand that it takes money to make money, and that takes risk."
- "Women like to remind you about what you are supposed to do, in all situations, not just around the house. Even if you are in a business situation with them. For example, I attended a meeting and picked up a book at a table. This woman said, 'Someone is sitting there.' I put the book down and moved elsewhere but thought, 'Who appointed you the queen of the table to say who can pick up what, or sit where?' They take it upon themselves to be the social conscience of the world, for everybody and everything."
- "Women pick and pick and won't let an issue rest. They want to process everything. It gets oppressive. They just won't drop an issue until they have hashed it to death."
- "Women feel they have to be with their significant others every second of every waking hour. They allow no room to breathe."
- "They are unable to live in the moment. They are either worrying about the future or feeling guilty about the past."

The good news is that a growing number of men are no longer retreating into silence to avoid relationship issues. What is taking place is an examination of traditional male/female roles. Men and women are equal partners in the relationship, discussing careers, money, lifestyles, and family and trying to reach mutual agreement on their expectations concerning the relationship and their careers. They are developing plans with a vision of the future that includes having a purpose for being together, along with goals, strategies, and action steps designed to make the partnership a success.

As a result of this evolving change, men have now been given permission to be in touch with their feelings. This process takes time. We need to guard against the dangers of becoming a unisexed world in which all of us dream the same dreams, create the same art, and feel the same emotions. It is precisely our differences that add excitement, a sense of discovery, and challenge to our lives. Without differences, we have no variation and become a single theme of the same old song. We must preserve the positive male attributes that have led us this far in our evolution. The challenge is in determining which gender is to be the arbiter of what is positive.

Summary

All the forces in our culture demand that a little boy disconnect from his relationship with his mother in order to become a man. Why is this important? Because we men learn, at a very young age, that healthy growth demands a disconnection in order to build a strong self. That is why men are usually more interested in helping themselves to grow than in helping others or in nurturing relationships with others. So there is a relational paradox in normal male development in this culture. On the one hand, men yearn for the experience of growth and connection just as women do. On the other hand, the demands of personal growth discourage connection, and that has profound implications for gender differences.

This is a hazardous time for men as they negotiate the mine fields of professional and personal relationships. They are tired of having people tell them what to do, what they are allowed to say, and how they are supposed to feel. Men wonder if women really want male partners or a variation of themselves with male parts. As a society, we had better be very careful in designing the new male. When we lose our individual differences, we may lose the very balance that joining together is supposed to create, men augmenting female strengths and women augmenting male strengths. Together, men and women form a dynamic team.

> *Male bashing may be an interesting pastime for women, but it can be a destructive psychological game.*

All of us need to come to terms with the fact that in male/female relationships, when either sex wins, they both lose. If we are to preserve what is positive and effective in men, we have many challenges before us. We have to believe that a man is more than just a paycheck, a porter, and a protector. Men need to speak up and let people know that a family isn't supposed to be a pressure or an obligation. It is a joint responsibility in which both partners can gain mutual satisfaction. Working men and women are equally important partners, joined together to support each other, both emotionally and financially. A healthy relationship is built on openness and honesty. As a man, I have been impressed with the distance men will travel, in quite a short period of time, to learn how to have healthy, connected relationships with women, when they are given a chance and when they are valued for it.

Working couples must stay aware of and discuss the major changes that are taking place among men and women. They also need to understand that power, wealth, and influence do not necessarily lead to happiness. Stepping out and speaking up will continue to be difficult for men until the paradigm makes its complete shift. In the meantime, couples have to create their own realities based on true equality and mutual acceptance.

Chapter 4

You Work: Self-Worth for Value Added

In Chapter 1, we discussed the challenges working couples face. Chapter 2 presented the issues from her point of view, and Chapter 3 from his perspective. Now, we want to discuss how the way you feel about yourself affects your partnership.

Barbara is one of the hardest workers we know. Some would even call her a workaholic, for she never appears to stop working. If she is not working at work-work, she is working on her next creative idea. When she is not involved in an income-producing project, she is washing the floor, throwing in a load of wash, dusting everything in sight, or doing one of dozens of other activities.

Barbara is the unofficial counselor and confidante of all her acquaintances. Her usual expression is, "How can I help you?" She feels best about herself when someone says, "Gee, Barbara, I don't know how you manage it all!" And she *can* do more things—faster—than anyone with whom we have worked.

Barbara is devastated when she makes a mistake, is late for an appointment, or forgets something. Her dread is that her spinning world will start to splinter and she will lose one of the pieces. She knows that then her reputation will be ruined and no one will ever trust her again.

Sammy also is a hard worker. He is slower at getting things done than Barbara is so he works all the time and feels guilty when he is not working. His efforts are scattered. He attempts to divide his time among the many responsibilities to which he has committed himself, switching from one project to another without ever having brought closure to a single one of them. He complains that he never seems able to "kick over the edge" to success. The brass ring is always "just around the corner" with the next project, event, or product. He is always looking for that magic idea, that "hook" that will make him a real success.

What makes these two run? Why do they always focus on *doing* something or helping someone? We think it's because they fear intimacy—being close to themselves or to others. When you stay busy with work and other activities, you can avoid getting involved with people and, therefore, avoid the risk of disapproval or rejection. After all, if no one really knows you, how can they criticize or reject you?

Why are some people so afraid of criticism? Criticism implies that you may not be perfect, and if you can't be perfect you must be worthless. We refer to this as the Perfect/Worthless Syndrome. Too often we look for validation of our worth from outside ourselves. That doesn't work because self-esteem comes when you begin to appreciate your own inner worth and value as a human being, independently of your accomplishments or possessions. It's an *inside* job and hard to come to terms with.

It's easier to blame our insecurity, anxiety, boredom, self-doubt, frustration, procrastination, failures, and everything else on other people— parents who were too strict or too lenient, an unaccepting significant other, a demanding boss, uncooperative friends, or difficult children. We blame others because of our fear of taking personal responsibility for what happens to us: "My teachers didn't like me. That's why I got bad grades in school." Or, "I was raised in a dysfunctional family, so I am dysfunctional and no one can blame *me*." Or, "My boss has favorites. He only promotes the ones who butter him up."

We are not discounting any of these perceptions. Your boss *may* have favorites. Your original family *may* have been dysfunctional. We are merely saying that the situations in which you were involved in the past are not what continue to keep you down. Any current limitations you perceive are not caused by outside influences or past circumstances. They are the result of fear, a negative self-image, and the choices you continue to make. Negative self-images usually operate on such a subtle level that we are unaware of them. Awareness is the key to freedom from our own self-limiting and self-sabotaging behavior.

In order to be successful and to enjoy life, you need to understand the role self-esteem plays in your life. An understanding of self-esteem and its role in helping you to achieve balance in your life is critical because the most important relationship you will ever have is the one you have with yourself. Wherever you go, you are there. You can change jobs, significant others, and your geographic location. But you are still there. Self-esteem is the foundation on which you operate from day to day, year to year, and over a lifetime.

> *The most important relationship you will ever have is the one you have with yourself.*

What Is Self-Esteem?

Self-esteem can be defined as the value you give yourself on a scale from 0 to 100. This value fluctuates continually and is very subjective, representing everything you know or believe to be true about yourself. The information feeding into your self-evaluation includes the way you looked and behaved when you were an adolescent. If you were overweight then, you will most likely continue to perceive yourself as fat. It may also include what you did five minutes ago. When things are going well for you, you feel better about yourself. When something lousy happens, you feel bad about yourself.

Remember that day, not long ago, when you focused on one particular negative about yourself and the whole video of your imperfections played itself out in your head? When it was over, your overall self-esteem was at the bottom of the bucket. Nothing else went right the rest of the day. This negative video you produced is actually an edited version of the negative images you have preserved about yourself—clips of all your failures, the perceived put-downs by others, and the challenges you never got around to tackling. Self-esteem is also influenced by the comparisons we make with other people. We like to look for flaws in others, to watch them fail, and then to gossip about how stupid they are. That way, we look great by comparison.

How highly you value yourself—in other words, your positive self-esteem—depends on how consistent your actions *are* with what you believe your actions *should* be. For example, if you believe that "to err is wrong," your self-esteem will plummet every time you make a mistake. Eventually you will reach a point where your fear of being wrong or making a mistake will weigh more heavily with you than your desire to please other people. At that time, you might withdraw from the arena of active participation in decision making or conflict resolution.

There are two self-esteem values with which we all function. One is our private evaluation of ourselves, what we really feel we are worth at any given moment. The other is the mask or facade we present to other people, especially outsiders. There is nothing wrong with wearing a facade, so long as you know you're wearing one. The danger of vertical illness (walking around pretending that everything is great and that the world is your oyster) increases when you wear a mask for so long that you buy into your own propaganda. Your partner sees this before you do. Role-playing increases the possibility that you will feel phony and begin to devalue yourself. This could happen if one of your values is to be "true to yourself at all costs." Deciphering the difference is more difficult for men than it is for women, because men tend to operate in a hierarchial illusion. They often appear to be role-playing even in their private lives.

Women unconsciously encourage the "strong male" facade. They want to feel that a strong person will take care of them in the event something goes wrong. A friend of ours once observed, "I was *born* to be taken care of! Daddy always told me not to worry. He would always protect me." Daddy is dead and she is in a perpetual rage. After a divorce, she has no one to pay her bills and make her happy.

Double-bind expectations (unconsciously expecting someone to take care of you while consciously asking your partner to be more honest, open, and feeling) send mixed messages. If a man tells his significant other that he is worried about losing his job, she feels threatened. He senses this and puts on a facade, choosing not to burden her with his fears or any other reality that might make her unhappy. But masking doesn't eliminate his fear.

We have found that you can have two different levels of self-esteem operating at the same time: One level is how you evaluate yourself at work; the other, an entirely different value you place on yourself at home. When this value difference is significant, you most likely feel split or torn and in internal conflict. Your behavior will probably come across as hostile, withdrawn, and inconsistent. It has been our experience that women tend to feel higher self-esteem at home than they do at work, while men tend to feel higher self-esteem at work. This may be because men still feel uncomfortable with intimate relationships.

People with low self-esteem attempt to escape their reality. They don't like who they are and fear they can never be who they think they should be. So they blame others for their failures and merge into roles and expectations that leave them feeling empty and afraid. Role-playing can be a dangerous defense. If you don't know who you are, neither will anyone else.

Who Pulls Your Strings?

A major barrier to achievement and success in all areas of your life is the belief that you cannot, or do not deserve to, succeed and/or be happy.

When you don't feel you deserve to be happy or successful, you will adjust events in order to make that belief come true. It's the self-fulfilling prophecy. You expect certain things to be or to happen and you somehow make them happen. Where did your expectations come from?

> *A major barrier to achievement and success in all areas of your life is the belief that you cannot, or do not deserve to, succeed and/or be happy.*

Your major values concerning right and wrong, good and bad were formed by the time you were about eight years old. These values were assimilated from statements and suggestions made to you or demands made upon you by the people who had the greatest influence on you when you were growing up. These influential people included your parents, siblings, clergyman, grandparents, other people's parents, and close friends. If approval was hard to come by in your particular environment, you learned to accept yourself as less than perfect and therefore unworthy of happiness. You may have accepted the injunction, "Work hard, your reward will be in heaven." Or, "If it's worth doing at all, it's worth doing right." Or, "Don't just sit there, *do* something." You began to believe, even if on an unconscious level, that nothing you *did* was ever quite good enough to please these important people. You probably still feel that way and are engaged in an endless and unfulfilling quest to please everyone. Being a people-pleaser, and trying to please all of the people all of the time, is a losing game. It just can't be done. The one who suffers the most is *you* and, ultimately, the partnership you're in.

Many of the messages that you received early in life from those influential people can continue to keep you down or, at the very least, in a constant state of conflict within yourself.

"As a little girl," Barbara explains, "one of my earliest memories was coming home from school delighted with having received all A's, but one. My mother was flowery in her praise and pride, but my father, whom I loved dearly and was always trying to please, looked at the report card and said, 'The A's are nice, but what's that B doing there?'

"I was crushed! My dad had just affirmed that I was not acceptable until and unless I brought home all A's. That feeling of not being quite good enough became a major issue in the development of my self-esteem and feelings of self-worth. I was not acceptable unless I was perfect and I have never quite been able to be perfect. Since I am not perfect, I must be worthless."

Our strongest need in life is for approval. As with Barbara, some of the values formed in your early childhood remain with you forever. When you return to the people from whom you need approval, your conditioned early values come up against new free-choice values. For example, your parents may have believed that if they "spared the rod" they would spoil the child. Your education and experience reinforce your belief that physical abuse has negative consequences. Besides, it's illegal to hit children! However, when you visit Mom and Dad, or they visit you, they criticize you for not punishing the children strongly enough. You are in conflict. Whenever you go against an early value, you feel guilty.

The degree of your conflict may be major or minor. Your ability to cope with it will depend upon your awareness that a values conflict exists. When you are unaware, you will experience a feeling of disharmony or anxiety. Accept your right and their right to be different, think differently, and act differently. You will then be able to accept conflict as rational and normal. You may have a brief moment of anxiety, caused by guilt or fear, but you will be able to come to terms with these feelings based upon your new system of values. Consider it a learning experience.

It used to happen to us. When we went back to our respective parents' homes, we felt and acted like little children trying to please our parents. As a result, we tended to go on the defensive. Of course we were not aware, at the time, that we were on the defensive, but it was there. We became irritable and snippy. Again, self-awareness is the key. Now that we are aware of this tendency, we commit ourselves to avoiding the defensive mode and operate from the assumption that others are not really trying to put us down. They are just locked into old patterns of behavior and interaction. We take personal responsibility for our reactions and choose to change old patterns. It isn't always easy. But if our parents could have done better, they would have. Just as if we could do better, we would. It was very rewarding actually to love them instead of being on guard and closed off. Now that they are all gone, we wish we had been a little nicer, called a whole lot more, and understood that they were young, vigorous, frightened people being held captive in aging bodies. They probably were wishing that they had enjoyed life more while pursuing *their* goals.

Values and Conflict

Believe it or not, everyone has values. Even that unethical boob who stole your client away has values. You may think someone's values are stupid or even distorted. But each individual values different things. Some values are more important to you than others. In order to determine the relative importance to you of all the values you hold, you must first develop a list of what they are. Look over the Values Hierarchy form and then fill it out. You may be quite amazed at what you discover about yourself. By ranking the values on this list, you will begin to get some idea of what you really think is important. Your partner should also make a separate list.

Values Hierarchy

INSTRUCTIONS: After filling in the Values Hierarchy form, rank-order each item you have listed in each section on a scale of 1 to 5, with 1 being the most important and 5 the least important. The results will be your own personal hierarchy of values.

A	The three most important things in my life (people, places, or things):
B	The three least important things in my life:
C	The things I wish to accomplish with my life:
D	The things I most fear that people might think of me:
E	What I would like people to say about me when I'm gone:

Now go back over the values you have just ranked in order of importance to you, and allocate to each the approximate percentage of time you actually spend on each. It can be quite shattering to discover that while you have ranked family as your number one priority, you actually devote only a very small percentage of your time to family activities and needs. Throughout your life, your values change regularly, depending upon the people and circumstances you encounter. It is not unusual to experience conflicting values. When this happens, you experience distress. You also feel guilty. That very feeling of guilt can best be exemplified in the statement, "Damned if I do and damned if I don't." You need to decide what is truly a priority for you.

Since the process of questioning your values continues throughout your entire life, you must be prepared for change. This is one area where working couples have great difficulty. For example, your partner may say to you, "When we got married you said you wanted four children!" Well perhaps you did at the time. But needs, wants, and circumstances change. Talk about it. What worked for you yesterday may not be working for you today. Level with each other and make adjustments.

The Imposter Syndrome

The primary sources of your self-esteem are your perception of your ability to master your environment and your feelings of being positively valued by yourself and others. The sense of mastery comes from achievement, control over one's environment, and a sense of power. For many of us this happens with our work. Even at work our self-esteem may suffer, no matter how successful we are by others' standards, if we feel like an imposter. The Imposter Syndrome is a feeling that your success has been undeserved and that at any moment "they will find you out." If "they" do find you out, you fear you will be unmasked as a fraud. As a result of the Imposter Syndrome, you and your partner may not be able to enjoy your very real accomplishments.

The feeling of being positively valued by others comes from relationships with loved ones, friends, and associates. If you feel that you have control over your environment but are not positively valued by others, you'll feel off balance. Self-esteem will drop. It also drops when the people you value do not appear to value you. We spend a great deal of our lives trying to get people to approve of us.

What Is Your Banana?

We like this illustration. It may or may not be true, but it makes our point. The way they catch monkeys in Fictionland is to construct a small box in which they anchor a banana. There is no way into the box except through a small hole at the top of the box just large enough for a monkey to put its hand into. The monkey reaches into the box and grabs the banana. But there is no way to get its hand out unless it drops the banana. The monkey won't drop the banana. As a result, the monkey's captors can move the box wherever they choose and the monkey will follow. The monkey is a captive because it chooses to be held captive rather than lose the banana.

Many of us are like these monkeys. We allow ourselves to be held captive by our own self-defeating beliefs and behavior. We all sabotage ourselves at times, but some of us make a habit of self-sabotage. How do we do this? The primary way we sabotage ourselves is by blaming others for our failures and unhappiness. While this allows us to play the victim, it also keeps us captive. Victims can't help what happens to them, can they?

> George explained that he wanted to be a consultant to management but that his wife wouldn't let him. We envisioned a huge, menacing woman with a chain whip. "What do you mean, your wife won't let you?" we asked. "Well," he said, "she has a great need for security. She is afraid that if I left my present secure job I might not be able to support our lifestyle."
>
> "Do *you* think you could make sufficient income to maintain your present lifestyle? And are you happy with your lifestyle?" we asked. "That's not the point," he said, "She is happy with it and I don't want to make her unhappy."

She is happy with it and he doesn't want to make her unhappy. That may appear to be a noble attitude—giving up one's dreams and desires for someone else. In fact, George is playing the victim and blaming his wife for the outcomes in his life. He was hoping we would play the magic rescuer by either telling him that he was an honorable man or agreeing with his underlying message that his wife was a bad, demanding person. He was looking for a way to remain personally perfect without taking any risks.

The truth is that others don't do anything to you that you don't allow them to do. George is afraid of starting his own business, but he doesn't want to admit this to himself. If he stays in his old job, he doesn't have to risk failure and possible ridicule, so he blames his inactivity on his wife. Of course he should consider his wife's fears, and they should negotiate a compromise, but the final decision has to be George's. He has to live with the outcomes he creates for the rest of his life and answer to himself at the end of it. So do you.

In order to truly enjoy your life you have to pursue your goals. Take personal responsibility for what happens to you. If you don't like what's going on in your life, take the necessary steps to change it. When you blame others for your life, you give them control over you. This is a major burden for them, and they will eventually resent you for it. It is also difficult to restrict the idea of powerlessness to a single area of your life. If you feel powerless at home, you will probably also feel powerless at work and with your parents, friends, and even your children. Powerlessness is a habit.

> *Powerlessness is a habit.*

A sense of powerlessness and victimization pervades our society. Powerless people are burdens on the rest of us, especially their co-workers and significant others. Because of the socialization of women, the concept of powerlessness in women is accepted to a greater degree by society. Women especially need to make a conscious effort to decide, and then believe, that they are *not* powerless and to embark on a continuing campaign to improve their self-image. When your self-image improves, you will act in a more powerful way and others will begin to treat you as if you have value. Women must begin to help validate *every* woman's right to feel, to have opinions, to disagree, to be unique individuals, and to pursue their own goals.

One way to begin to validate your existence is to take time each day to fantasize how you want your life to be. How would you handle your life if you had unlimited money and influence? Write these fantasies down on a piece of paper. Think about them. Imagine that your dreams are already realized and that you deserve them. Then focus on self-empowerment. Give yourself permission to go out and make a conscious, assertive effort to get what you want and *deserve*. Get in touch with your own inner wisdom. You already know what is good for you. When you begin doing what you *know* to be in your own best interest you will begin to feel powerful. Your self-esteem will increase and people will approve of you more. But you must take action. You must begin to change your behavior, make your own choices, and be responsible for those choices, because to know and not to act is not to know at all.

> *To know and not to act is not to know at all.*

Stop Sabotaging Yourself

Learn to ask yourself, "What is my contribution to the present circumstances of my life?" "What am I afraid of?" "How can I take personal responsibility for the outcomes in my life?" "What do I need to do to keep myself from becoming a victim again?" Self-saboteurs tend to look for and surround themselves with people who are *less* than they are—less successful, less happy in their personal lives, less good in school, less attractive. That way, they can feel superior to these people and rationalize that they are at least better off than most of their associates. This is a form of co-dependent behavior. Some of us even choose our partners on the basis of their *deficiencies* rather than for attributes that will enhance their individual uniqueness. In that way, self-saboteurs don't have to worry about not being good enough to be loved. There will always be someone to tell them: "That inferior jerk you chose should be happy to get you." Instead, make a conscious effort to surround yourself with superior, intelligent, and fun-loving people. Search out and spend your time with winners. Friend-test. Try out possible friendships with people who will challenge you. If one doesn't work, try another. Reach out and expand yourself. When you are accepted by winners, you feel better about yourself and your self-esteem goes up.

Stop expecting negative things to happen to you. Negativity is a habit. We *learn* negativity; it's not a natural state. Remember the self-fulfilling prophecy? You expect certain things to be or to happen and you *make* them happen. Some people work very hard at snatching defeat out of the jaws of success. Expect great things to happen and then get out of your own way. If you always do what you've always done, you'll always get what you've always got. If you don't like what's happening to you, do something different. Trust your ability to master your environment and know that you deserve to be positively valued by others. Endure when faced with difficult or complex challenges. In this state of mind, you are likely to succeed more often than fail, and this serves to confirm and reinforce your sense of power.

> *Don't snatch defeat out of the jaws of success.*

What Does High Self-Esteem Look Like?

It isn't always easy to spot someone with high self-esteem or to detect when yours is up or down, because self-esteem fluctuates with circumstances, moods, and interactions. When you have a successful day and everything is going nicely with your significant other, you may feel that you are a 95 (on a scale of 1 to 100, 100 being the highest).

On another day, you may receive a phone call from the school criticizing you for sending the children to school with colds. Boom! There goes the old self-esteem. You tried to slip something over on the school and they are on to you. In with the guilt, that worthless feeling, and down with the self-esteem. "I just can't handle it all," you think (negative self-talk). "Why is it that other women are able to keep all the balls in the air? There must be something lacking in me!" Wrong. No one can keep all the balls in the air all the time. It's a game. It's an illusion. You are comparing your inside with someone else's outside. This is what we referred to in Chapter 2. When people play perfect, the illusion hurts others by comparison. Those seemingly perfect people are probably trying to hold it all together, just as you are. If we could share these little fumbles with one another, we would all feel better.

It doesn't have to be a big fumble. It could just be your *hair*! We love that expression, "I'm having a bad hair day." It means "I'm not feeling good about myself today." It's making fun of the whole idea. If we could only have more fun trying to be Superman and Wonder Woman, we would see the humor in all this seriousness and look upon ourselves as just a bunch of human beings trying to outdo each other, in order to collect a lot of "stuff," so we can impress each other because we don't feel good about ourselves without it. People with good self-esteem can laugh at themselves and at the crazy situations they get themselves into. They care, but not *that* much. They also feel comfortable giving themselves a pat on the back: "I really handled that assignment quite well."

High self-esteemers are able to handle their accomplishments and their shortcomings with assertive honesty. They can also decide which shortcomings are limiting their ability to enjoy life, then work on modifying them. They are open to criticism and to suggestions for positive redirection. They can acknowledge their mistakes and are adaptable and flexible enough to look for new and exciting ways to accomplish better results. They are consistent. You can count on them. There is balance between what they say and do. People with high self-esteem take personal responsibility for their own behavior and feel confident that they can handle the challenges life has to offer. They do not need to blame others.

What Can You Do If Your Self-Esteem Is Low or Faltering?

If you have a tendency to low self-esteem, you need to go into production and create a new video of yourself. This new edited version should contain the good news about you. Begin by agreeing that a mistake is just a mistake, nothing more. This truly should be a learning experience about something to avoid doing in the future. Some "mistakes" actually result in winning discoveries. Whenever you perceive you have made a mistake, ask yourself, "What are the good things that actually happened to me as a result of this mistake? What, if anything, would I do differently now?" Then take action and let it go. You are okay. You may not be okay at everything, but that's okay, too.

Discipline yourself to collect the good news about yourself. Keep an accomplishment journal or file or box.

Several years ago Jaine was worrying about a major keynote address she had coming up before two thousand people. She had worked big audiences before, but this was the largest she had ever faced. She designed the program, rewrote it, prepared the visuals, and rehearsed, rehearsed, rehearsed.

The night before the presentation, as she agitatedly stood pressing her outfit for the next day, she asked our son Todd, "What is it I tell you to do when you are feeling nervous?" He said, "Go look through your letters from satisfied customers." He was only ten! Good parenting pays off. She went to the file, pulled out the satisfied customer folder, and started reading. She was very impressed! It proved to her that she had successfully spoken before very prestigious groups for years. She could certainly do it again. She slept well and did an excellent job the next day, confident in her ability to get her message across.

Begin to collect positive comments you have received in letters from friends, relatives, and even past significant others, along with the rewards or awards that have come your way from bosses, clients, and fellow workers. There will always be times when that old devil doubt presents itself to you. When it does, pull out the good stuff and start reading. Analyze your role in creating positive outcomes, then duplicate that behavior in other circumstances.

Watch what you say to yourself! Every time you enter a negative thought in your conscious or subconscious mind you are reinforcing your low self-esteem. Stop! Think about what you just said to yourself. If you were someone else's child, how would that message be perceived? "You are so stupid! Can't you do anything right?" Sure you can. Think of that time you did everything wonderfully, then tell yourself about it. Get up every morning, look in the mirror, and give yourself a compliment: "You have great eyes. I wish I had noticed them sooner." Or, "What a nice and caring person you are. No wonder your partner loves you."

Evaluate your assumptions, your alternatives, your present lifestyle, your job, and your relationships. Look for what is *right* in them. If you can't find enough rights, perhaps you are in the wrong relationship or the wrong job. Before you make any irreversible decisions, however, be sure you are not in a state of burnout right now that is causing *everything* to look rotten. Let go of perfection. Stop comparing yourself unfavorably with others. They are probably wearing a mask too.

Develop and maintain many options, friends, career alternatives, and opportunities for winning. The winner is the person with the most options.

> *Develop and maintain many options, friends, career alternatives, and opportunities for winning. The winner is the person with the most options.*

Summary

Self-esteem is part of your value system. When you do what you feel you "should" do, you feel good about yourself. These "shoulds" come from other people, but they quickly become your expectations for yourself. Your self-esteem is influenced by your perception of your ability to master the circumstances in your life and by your feelings of being positively valued by others. Your perceptions may be inaccurate. You may be more capable and more valued than you currently believe. Search for objectivity in evaluating your self-worth, and then reward yourself when you have accomplished a desired a goal.

Stop sabotaging yourself by blaming others for your failures and unhappiness. Conquer the Perfect/Worthless syndrome: the belief that you don't deserve to be happy. Believe that you are not an imposter and that you do deserve success and acceptance. We all have to fake confidence at times, when we get hit with self-doubt. But you will have higher self-esteem once you successfully let go of destructive behaviors that keep you from taking responsibility for your own actions.

Chapter 5

Why Partnerships Fail

All partnerships are made up of three elements: the He, the She, and the We. The We is the partnership system that develops from the interaction between the He and the She. A change in one part of the system has a definite impact on the other parts. Events take place in a circular movement in which the behavior of one person influences that of a second person, which influences a third, which may then go back to the first, triggering a new cycle. It's a system that causes a domino effect. Push one over and they all fall down. The connection is broken.

What causes the breakdown? We have different values, expectations, and perceptions. We want different things out of life and we interpret data according to our own filters. These filters are developed by experiences, education, and the "shoulds" and "should nots" that were programmed into us by people who were influential with us as we were growing up. Even if we were raised in the same family, the same town, during the same decade, it is still a challenge for us to connect. When individuals, each with their private agendas, form a partnership, it is a miracle that connections survive at all.

The fact that each of us is different is not the problem. Differences can add variety and spice to our lives. The problem lies in not understanding and valuing individual differences in people, both at work and in our personal lives. This is what leads to partnership failure. Making partnerships work requires a continuing effort to understand what each partner is seeking in the relationship and to explore why some partnerships are a source of growth and fulfillment while others are destructive and defeating. People often speak of the search for connection as the primary goal in their lives.

What does it mean to understand connection and mutuality in a relationship? In a connected exchange, you are affected by the other person and the other person is affected by you. You have impact. When we connect, we feel empathy for each other. We each take an active interest in the well-being of the other as a totally different, but whole, human being who is okay just as he or she is. This is what we mean when we talk about unconditional love. Too often, however, we confuse the concept of unconditional *love* with unconditional *acceptance* of behavior. Unconditional acceptance of behavior can lead to enabling unacceptable *actions*, which turns the enabler into a martyr and keeps the person who is using ineffective behavior from growing. Each of us has a perfect right to judge our own behavior, without stepping on the rights of others, and to be responsible for the consequences. To do that, we must risk holding others accountable for their actions.

A Double Take on the Relationship

Men and women often have different perceptions on everything, including what constitutes fun and relaxation, a clean home, quality time, conversation, and role expectations. These differences require constant negotiation. Just as in any negotiation, each has both mutual and conflicting interests. To add to the dilemma, men and women are often involved in an avoidance/resentment impasse. Women usually strive for connection and move in closer to make that happen. Men have been conditioned to function on their own and to avoid attempts at intimacy. When she moves in, he moves away. This pattern only makes matters worse and leaves her with the difficult choice between continuing her efforts to care for the relationship and saying, "To hell with it!" and allowing resentment to build. He avoids, she resents. They are at an impasse. The problem is in the movement of the relationship, not with either the man or the woman. Both need to understand the other, to be flexible, and to be willing to change and adapt, depending on the needs of the situation.

Both men and women strive to have their feelings and perceptions validated. We refer to this as "honoring." Men's perceptions are validated simply because they are men. When a man says, "I don't feel good about this guy, let's not hire him," that's enough. Rarely is he questioned, except perhaps by his significant other. When a woman makes the same kind of observation, she is asked, "Why?" and forced to defend her perceptions. That's why many women, instead of making definitive statements, ask questions, like "What do you think about this guy? I have a feeling he is unethical because. . . ." The simplest and easiest way to validate another is to look interested and respond, "I understand where you're coming from. That's a valid point (observation, action, or feeling)."

Recognizing and Avoiding Actions That Cause Disconnection

Role conflicts may arise within a partnership because of how each partner was taught that men and women should behave. A redefinition of what it means to be a wife and mother, as well as a husband and father, is currently taking shape for working couples, and this will help to reduce these conflicts. The resolution itself is actually less important than the process we go through of exploring our feelings of intimacy and satisfaction even before a resolution emerges. However, this processing of personal relationships is what men don't like to do. It is not something in which they have been conditioned to excel. Therefore, in order to begin the process, both partners need to commit themselves to staying within established boundaries and to avoid what we call the "IDs" (pronounced eye-dees). These IDs are imbalance, indifference, dominance, devaluing, discounting, disapproval, disrespect, and disconnection.

Imbalance

We are in a state of imbalance when one partner gives more to the partnership than the other does. This may be a fact or only a perception. It isn't necessary to have equal power over everything. Each partner has different strengths. The important thing is for both people to feel that the balance is equitable and comfortable. When one partner begins to feel that something is skewed, it is best to work at evening things up. Women say they feel that they are continually giving more to the relationship than do their partners. Men and women differ as to what it means to show attention and about what nurturing consists of.

> Anna explains that she is always "waiting" for Alan: "For example, he promises we will go out to dinner this Friday after work. When Friday comes, I rush home to change, and wait. He never gets there until after seven. I *know* this, yet I still rush home, just in case. Because I also know he will be upset if *he* has to wait.
>
> "I always make sure all of his clothes are clean and put in the proper drawers and I go out of my way to cook meals he says he likes. I am always *caring* for him, but he doesn't seem to acknowledge these activities. In fact, he takes them for granted."

Men, on the other hand, will say that their way of *caring* for their partners is to work extra hard so that they can advance in their jobs, be more successful, and therefore provide better for the women they love.

During a role-processing session, perceptions of imbalance need to be addressed.

Indifference

Perhaps the most hurtful thing you can do to another human being is to be indifferent. We witness this during divorce. Often, one partner has been so totally disconnected for so long that s/he simply doesn't feel anything for the other. There is neither hate nor love; there is only indifference. This drives the still involved partner up the wall. When you are treated with indifference, you will do *anything* to get the disconnecting partner involved again—even if involvement means to provoke anger or engage in a prolonged child custody or property settlement battle or threaten harm to yourself or the other person. Sympathy and fear are at least emotions, and some emotion is better than none at all. Often, women feel that men are indifferent to their feelings and needs. They sometimes fail to realize that men just have a different way of addressing women's needs. Men don't see themselves as "emotional catering services." Share your perceptions about indifference with your partner. Give specific examples whenever possible. But remember to stay out of the blame game.

Dominance

Dominance is manifested when one vies for control over the other through manipulation (see Chapter 9), competition, withdrawal, withholding of rewards, or disruption of the flow in the relationship.

> Kathy was an expert in this area. Whenever she was unable to get Kevin to show her attention or give her what she felt she wanted at the moment, she would withdraw to her room and refuse to talk to him. If Kevin did not capitulate, she would continue the silent treatment and add refusal to have sex with him. If all this did not work, she would implement the final withdrawal and go back home to her parents, where she would gather support. The only way Kevin was ever able to get her to return, with their child, was finally to give her what she had wanted in the first place, but by this time there was always a little extra penalty thrown in to ensure that he had shaped up.

Devaluing

Perhaps the single most destructive action in any partnership is the process of devaluing the other. Sadly, most of us are not aware of the ways in which we devalue another. Not looking at people while they are talking, failure to make eye contact, or tossing their opinions aside as naive, uninformed, childish, or emotional are all devaluing actions. We all do these things to children on a regular basis, whenever we watch television while we pretend to listen, or by talking to each other while *they* are trying to talk.

> We learned the true impact of devaluing from our son Todd. Everyone in our family is high-energy, Type A, polyphasic, and fast-paced. When we all get together, it is almost impossible to get a word in edgewise. Often we notice that we are literally talking on top of one another. When we recognize this, we each try to slow down and *listen* to what is being said. We became aware of this process only after Todd called it to our attention.
>
> One evening he had been relating an exciting event that had happened to him on the football field at school. While he was talking, Jaine looked over and noticed that Jim had not closed a cabinet door, so she said, "Jim, please close the cabinet door." Todd was still talking. Jim walked over and closed the cabinet door, remarking, "The dishes won't fall out of the cabinet, Jaine, if the doors are not closed." Todd continued to relate his story. Jaine responded, "I know, but you might hit your head as you pass by." Todd stopped talking to us and started conversing with the cabinets. "You see, cabinets, my folks are not interested in listening to my story, so I might as well be talking to you." He did this in such a humorous and spontaneous way that we all laughed, but we got the message. He was feeling devalued. We were not connecting with him.

Discounting

Women feel discounted when men attempt to solve their problems for them before fully hearing them out. Men feel discounted when women put down their tendency to want to protect women. There are times, however, when men *do* feel that the people, problems, and misunderstandings women worry about are trivial.

> Mavis was telling Marvin that she was upset because one of her clients had not returned her phone call for over a week: "I know he must be dissatisfied with the project, because he is just ignoring me. It's really not fair. I worked my head off on that deal. If he's unhappy, the least he could do is call me to discuss it. I can always modify the plans."
>
> Marvin could not understand why she didn't just call the client

back: "Just call him again and ask him what the problem is," he advised. Mavis was frustrated because Marvin didn't understand her feelings. She knew she would have to call the client again to address the conflict. What she was upset about was that she wasn't appreciated and didn't feel the client's actions were fair. Marvin was not understanding how hurt she was. Even when men understand this concept, they find it almost impossible not to expect women to forget about their feelings and just take action. It's their nature.

Disapproval

> *Often, people don't hear what we say because what we do speaks so loudly.*

Often, people don't hear what we say because what we *do* speaks so loudly. When a man disapproves of what a woman has done, or plans to do, he will frequently:

- Ignore the request for action.
- Frown, smack his teeth and mouth, and nod his head from side to side, indicating, "I can't believe it!"
- Actually say, "That's the most illogical thing I ever heard," or "you must be kidding!"

When a woman disapproves of what a man has done, she has a variety of facial expressions that scream, "I really can't believe you said (did) that! You hurt me so!" She might also:

- Cry
- Get sick
- Criticize by bringing up every other time in the last forty years her partner has performed similar acts. (We refer to this as "emptying the dirty clothes hamper.")
- Tell him what he should do, for example, "You're not going to wear those pants to the party, are you?"

When a woman complains about the clothes a man wears or the kind of entertainment he enjoys, she is disapproving of his preferences and also attempting to control his taste. Since one of man's primary needs is for respect and acceptance, when he doesn't get it, he disconnects.

Disrespect

We feel disrespected when we are not acknowledged as a person in our own right. Often friends and family will act this way, even when they love us.

> During the early days of Jaine's career, when she was required to travel, her mother or a long-time friend who lived in the neighborhood would take care of our small children. Whenever we had to rely on the neighbor, we would have to get ourselves up, get dressed, wake the children, get them dressed, get breakfast, get the children into their snowsuits (it was always snowing when we had to do this), get them over to the neighbor, and then get to work. Since Jim was on the road all the time, this was Jaine's responsibility.
>
> Jaine would go to the university or organization, conduct her conference or seminar, then rush back to the neighborhood, pick up the children, rush home, take off their snowsuits, rush to get dinner ready, interact with them in some way, give them their baths, read them a story, and encourage them to go to sleep. Once they were asleep, she would take her bath, do her hair, prepare her clothes, throw in a load of wash, do the dishes, straighten up the house, lay out the children's clothes for the next day, pack any necessary lunches, then rush to get some sleep. Most seminars were three or four days, so this went on for several days in a row. No one ever acknowledged that this was a difficult routine for Jaine.
>
> On one occasion, Jaine had to travel out of town to conduct a three-day conference and Jim had to assume the routine. Since this was a role reversal, Jaine spent days planning, preparing, and freezing meals the family could eat while she was out of town. When she came back, our neighbor took her aside and said, "Jaine, I felt so sorry for Jim. He looked exhausted, the poor thing. You just can't expect him to take care of the kids and go to work, too."

Believe it. It happened. Jaine's job was considered unimportant and less valuable than Jim's. It was also assumed that getting children into snowsuits was easier for her than it was for him. People still do not respect the multiple roles women have to play. Partners can help, tremendously, by simply acknowledging how valuable each partner is to the harmonious functioning of all family members. Do this acknowledging in the presence of other people on a regular basis. Let people know how much you respect and value your partner. Make a habit, too, of saying to your partner, "I can't tell you how much I respect and value you."

Disconnection

We all want intimacy, and yet we also want freedom and individuality—to connect and to be able to disconnect, to have a shared existence and yet a separate existence as well. Most partners feel very uncomfortable during the disconnection. They are fearful that their partner will never want to reconnect. When misunderstandings occur, you may feel it would be easier and less time-consuming just to forget the whole thing. And maybe that's just what you need to do, for a time—to disconnect and take a temporary breather. Always assure your partner that you will be back: "I love and value you, but I need to get away from this *issue*—not you—for awhile. I'll be back . . . and then we can continue." It is up to the disconnecting partner to return and reestablish the connection *within* twenty-four hours.

Women dislike these disconnections, as they prefer to stay connected at all times. But they feel more comfortable if their partners assure them that they will be back. Keep these "time off" periods to a minimum. Unresolved conflict has a habit of escalating and then couple sabotage begins. Women comment that they feel that their partners disconnect too often and are emotionally unavailable to them, that their partner will not risk vulnerability by sharing his true feelings and fears. When people have had their vulnerability used against them during an argument, or as a manipulative tool, they become reluctant to share again. The critical teasing men are forced to endure with good humor while they are young contributes greatly to their fear of showing non-strengths. Claude M. Steiner refers to this as the Gallows Transaction.

> Ed told Ellen that he was afraid he might lose his job. He explained that many of the signals were there: His company was downsizing, he was being left out of important meetings, he was now cut off from decision making. He worried that they would not be able to pay the household expenses or keep their little girl in private school. Ellen started crying. "What will we do if you lose your job?" she sobbed. "We can't live on just my salary. We'll lose everything."
>
> Ed took her in his arms and tried to get her to stop crying. "Don't worry, honey," he said, "I'll figure out something. I'll always take care of my family. Maybe I'm just being paranoid. Try to forget I said anything." He was upset with himself for bringing it up and causing Ellen to feel such fear. He promised himself he would never make that mistake again in the future.

And so, we wear our masks and wonder why we are not connecting. Here is a cardinal rule for successful connections: Never, ever, bring up a shared weakness in fear or in anger.

> *Here is a cardinal rule for successful connections: Never, ever, bring up a shared weakness in fear or in anger.*

When the Relationship Isn't a Priority

What, or who, is the number one priority in your life? You identified that in Chapter 4, when you completed your Values Hierarchy. Remember, however, that when individuals focus on their own needs and ignore preserving the partnership, it usually spells trouble. Ignoring partnership issues can mean that you are being insensitive and often inconsiderate. Treat the relationship with tender loving care because preserving the relationship is what makes attainment of mutual goals possible. If you are committed to the relationship, you will focus on the relationship. It will be your number one priority. Each of you needs to feel secure, important, challenged, and in control of your destiny, confident that you are being responsive to common goals. You also need to believe that you are being treated with honesty and integrity.

Keep the lines of communication open at all times. In order for each of you to commit yourself to a quality relationship, there should be a blend of your shared existence (cooperation) and separateness (individualism). The key lies in balancing the two. Each of you needs to relate to the other so that the outcome of your mutual goals is satisfaction.

How do you do this? Start by examining your attitudes. Does your attitude contribute to building a winning dual-career relationship? If not, work on changing your attitude. You do this by changing your thinking.

- *Believe what you used to do isn't acceptable.* Modify your self-talk from "I *should* do this to improve the relationship" to "I *must* do this."
- *Believe change is possible.* Make a commitment. Don't pacify your partner with words. Anybody can talk the talk. Your partner has learned to see through your words. You must walk the walk by *doing* things differently.
- *Rethink how you are going to reach your mutual goals.* If you are tired

of traveling in your job, don't apply for the national accounts manager position.

Healthy people don't make excuses and they don't blame others. They take full responsibility for their actions. Working couples who follow this principle find taking personal responsibility results in more freedom to choose among many alternatives. Each of you can shape your own destiny with help from your partner. This attitude will strengthen your partnership.

If you feel insecure about your ability to do what is expected of you because your track record includes a series of failures, consider that great career couples have all experienced setbacks, either individually or together.

When Helga fell ill with the flu, she asked Hugo to come and cuddle with her in bed. He didn't feel like it and found other things to do. Helga was hurt and angry. She felt that if he loved her he would have attempted to make her feel better.

After Hugo failed the sickbed test, Helga made up her mind that she would never again ask him for attention. She threw herself into her job, left early, and arrived home late. At first, Hugo paid no attention to her new behavior. However, after two weeks of stifled communication and no sex, he realized something was wrong.

He bought some flowers and invited Helga to dinner. She refused, saying she was too busy at work. So Hugo asked a male friend to join him for dinner and a night baseball game, arriving home after eleven in the evening. He hadn't called to tell Helga where he was going or that he would be home late. His attitude was, "Two can play at this silence game."

When he got home, Helga and most of her clothes were gone. He was stunned. What, after all, had he done to cause this to happen? He loved Helga, but he would be damned if he was going to beg her to return.

Who is to blame? Both partners had single-focus attitudes, and each was playing a "lose/lose" game. That is why 50 percent of us end up in divorce. What starts as a single event, with one person having hurt feelings owing to to one of the IDs, escalates into playing the game Eric Berne calls "Now I'm going to get you, you S.O.B."

A better way to handle this kind of impasse would be to let go and admit that your partner does not mean to hurt you. Anticipate reasonable behavior. When you anticipate reasonable behavior from your partner, s/he can feel it, even if you don't. In our example, Hugo could have made the call to Helga. All she was waiting for was for him to reach out and connect. During the call he could have reassured her by saying: "I value you and want you with me. Please let's iron this thing out." Once they are together again—in this revised scenario—boundaries would have to be set and guidelines developed for how they are going to constructively deal with hurt feelings in the future.

Consequences affect behavior. If either of you knows that you can get away with pushing partnership boundaries or that you can manipulate your partner and still survive in the relationship, you'll continue to do it. If there are no negative consequences for breaking a commitment, there won't be much motivation for continuing to honor agreements. Unpleasant consequences discourage the behavior that caused them. Ignoring your partner's actions may have a result similar to reinforcing them. So, if you don't like what is happening in your partnership, do something about it. You have to *do* something.

Working-couple relationships fail because of broken promises and failed goals. Can this be changed? Yes. It all comes back to keeping your commitments. You can't do this if you are so stretched to the limit by other commitments that you have no time for partnership renewal. Overpromising and underdelivering usually results from not thinking through what you are committing yourself to. Every time you don't keep a promise, it's a reflection on your honor and integrity. It hurts you, your partner, and the whole family. People feel they can't trust you. Don't promise what you can't deliver.

Setting overly ambitious goals is self-defeating. Set realistic goals and begin to achieve mutual success. The process builds inner strength as you discover you are in charge of you. Each success makes you more comfortable, more in control, more effective, and more responsible to yourself and others. Recognition of the real burden of having too much to do and not enough time to do it in has proved to be a harsh reality for many working couples. But there is power in partnerships. Two can accomplish more than one. But it has to be the *right* two, with mutual goals, or you will find yourself climbing an endless flight of stairs . . . in reverse.

A process we have found most beneficial is to schedule a meeting to identify the actions, people, places, or things that are helpful and those that are hindering to the partnership. Whenever you attempt to accomplish anything, there are forces that work *for* you (helping) and forces that pull *against* you (hindering). Unless you are aware of, and understand, which are for and which are against, you will feel torn, off-balance, and unhappy. For example, he *says*, "I'm really proud of you and your career," but he *acts* as if taking care of the home and children is her job. He helps a little, but she will be criticized as a bad wife and/or bad mother if the home and children are less than perfect. She *says*, "I want to support you in your career, but why do you have to work late again?" It's the damned if you do/damned if you don't dilemma.

Below is a form that both of you should complete for each important goal in your life. What is *helping* you to be successful in your career (such as education, experience, relationships, mentors)? What is *hindering* your success (for instance, a long commute, not enough time, little cooperation from your partner's children, co-workers, boss)? Identify your helping/ hindering forces individually. Then schedule an appointment with your partner to discuss your perceptions, allowing for open dialogue to determine how each of you perceives the challenges you face.

Goals	Helping	Hindering

Avoid turning this into a blaming session. Its purpose is not to rehash old gripes (you can do that at another meeting), but to mutually commit yourselves to a plan of action that will enable you both to get what you want. Both careers are important. The highest salary earned has no relevance in this discussion. Combine your helping and hindering forces into one list on a flip chart. Put the chart on a stand so that each can see it as you talk. The aim of brainstorming is not to judge ideas but to come up with a better understanding of what is keeping you from achieving your goals and to develop alternative solutions to each problem.

Next, look at the factors helping the partnership and discuss ways of developing or augmenting these factors to build additional strength and support. Brainstorm during this family meeting so that each of you can describe your most important wants from your lists. Spontaneously contribute ideas to help each other achieve desired goals. Encourage free thinking and creativity. Wild ideas are acceptable. Don't try to pick one best solution during a brainstorming session. There will be time to evaluate the options later. Finally, make sure that your "wants" list contains what the two of you desire and not what other people expect of you.

> *A flip chart is a worthwhile investment for a family. It's always helpful during a brainstorming session, and is a great place to leave notes or instructions, to wish someone "Happy Birthday," or to say "I love you."*

It is not surprising that so many of us are unhappy. We keep trying to gain approval by attempting to be what we think other people want us to be. Too often, we don't know what they want us to be because *they* themselves don't know. Somewhere along the line the critical balance has become skewed. You can love your job and everything you're doing, but when you take on that one extra responsibility, you throw yourself out of balance. You can handle extra work and other responsibilities for a while. It's when you begin doing too much for too long that you burn out. When this happens, you simply don't like any of it anymore, because it is physically and mentally impossible to operate at high speed forever.

Our son Todd described this phenomenon in an aptly visual way: "I feel like I'm a spinning ball going at top speed. Little pieces of me start splitting off and as I reach up to grab one of them, to put it back in place, another piece breaks off. I'm literally splintering apart. I feel like I have to perform, to the max, in each area of my life and I'm operating in fear all of the time!"

When your universe starts to splinter, there is usually overwhelming fear. The fear is that if you don't keep performing, you'll lose your job, your family, your partner. You are convinced that if you don't put in that extra effort, the extra day, the extra overtime, you're going to lose it all. This same pressure exists in many of today's businesses. Many are forced to operate with a minimal number of people. They are downsizing, reorganizing, and outsourcing to save money. Unfortunately, couples also downsize on necessary stress-reducing help. The reason? As with organizations, they are trying to save money, and therefore live like a single paycheck family. It doesn't work.

The annoying little details, which we all need to handle in order to survive in this society, are a mammoth contributor to the pressures encountered by dual-career households, Jaine explains.

I love every single work project in which I am currently involved. Each of them turns me on. But, taken together and along with all the other annoying little details I have to tend to, they are taking their toll. As a result, I can't enjoy the things I love because I'm worrying about all the details that aren't done. I'm not alone. Many working women feel the same way. They might enjoy being the CEO or the top administrative assistant in the company, but it's hard to feel successful while you are swabbing out the toilets at home. Jim loves to cook, but making dinner every night is an annoying little detail when it becomes a habitual responsibility.

Couples need help. There was a time when you could buy the help you needed at an affordable cost. This is no longer the case. You can get day care, but at what cost? How far will you have to drive? How long is the waiting list? Once you find it, you're lucky if you can truly afford anything else. What would it cost to have someone in to clean once a week? They often make more per hour than you do. You soon find that you are working to pay for the support services you need in order to work. You are not ahead of the game. You feel guilty because you don't have any more disposable income than when you started, and you are both so tired. Both of you feel that you are neglecting many of the people and goals you said were true priorities and you feel personally as if you are doing something very wrong.

Many men feel that if they could be better providers, their significant others wouldn't have to work so hard and they would have more disposable income. This dilemma is defeating. Somehow you have to break the cycle and say, "Wait a minute! Time out. This is all we can do. This is all we need to do. If we're going to live together, pursue a career, and raise children, then our focus needs to be on our *priorities.*" Then sit down and agree again on what those priorities are.

The Value of a System

The surprising thing is that meaningful relationships are closer than we realize. Tragically, we don't know how to recognize them until it's too late. When we do recognize a good relationship, we don't have a predictable system for nurturing it. The value of a system is that it's predictable. Predictability gives us a sense of power and personal control and it doesn't have to be boring. Knowing how to please other people is a comforting, freeing, and valuable challenge.

One very simple principle has the power to instantly transform your partnership. Go into every relationship as a giver, not a taker. Most people are looking for someone to make them feel good. They walk in with demands, and if the other person has different demands, they reluctantly negotiate. The more you focus on giving to others, the more they'll want to give back to you. You'll end up getting more than you give.

This attitude will improve not only your personal life but your business life as well. Business is about relationships. Every successful professional knows this. Success is the result of good judgment about people. Good judgment is the result of experience, but experience is often a result of bad judgment. You can be sure that people who are more successful than others got that way because they failed more than other people did. Failing and learning from such failures and from those of others teach us what works and what doesn't. If one action doesn't work, try another. If that one doesn't work, try a third. It's the people with the most options who end up enjoying life while pursuing their goals.

Summary

Partnerships fail because the people involved fail to understand and value the unique contributions that each has to bring to the partnership. Often, we judge others based on our own strengths and by how we would handle a situation if we had the power to control everything and everyone. However, greater power comes from connecting. When you connect with someone, each of you is empowered. Each has more energy.

To enhance connection, learn to validate your partner's perceptions and feelings. This can be accomplished by avoiding the IDs: imbalance, indifference, dominance, devaluing, discounting, disapproval, disrespect, and disconnection.

To avoid disconnection, make the partnership a priority. Then analyze what is helping the team and what is hindering it. Develop strategies, together, for eliminating or minimizing the hindering factors.

Any attempt to reconcile differences or problems will fail until you realize that problems within a relationship are symptoms of your fear of revealing yourself and then being rejected or devalued. Only when you risk disclosure are you able to open yourself to learning about yourself and others.

Start your discovery by working at setting realistic goals to achieve mutual success. The process of setting goals helps you to build inner strength as you discover you are in charge of you and the circumstances in your life. Chapter 6 will help you to do that.

SECTION TWO
The Power of Partnerships

Chapter 6

We Work: Making Partnerships Work

We all go through life touched in some way by relationships. If we are lucky, at some point along the journey at least one relationship will reach out and change us for the better. Or at least change the way we look at things. Maybe it will motivate us or challenge us, or maybe it will move us in such a way that we will wonder, "Isn't this the way it's supposed to be?" With a bit of work—and luck—that question will change to revelation and we'll stand up and shout, "This *is* the way it's supposed to be!" But that doesn't happen by accident.

Too often, people just let events push them around, reacting instead of taking control of them. One day you wake up and wonder why you're doing it all. It seems meaningless and too much trouble. It isn't. You just need a plan. You need to make conscious decisions that will help you to take personal responsibility for outcomes. No self-respecting business would consider operating without a plan. Well, your life is at least as important as any business.

Once you have a plan, stop enabling each other to deviate from the plan. To be successful, you both need to learn the principle of delayed gratification, which is putting off rewards until you have earned them.

> *Learn the principle of delayed gratification, which is putting off rewards until you have earned them.*

Kathy was married to an enlisted man stationed on Okinawa in Japan. One evening, as she and Ken were sitting around with another couple, the woman said, "I want to have children while I'm young so I can grow up with them." It sounded like a good idea, and Kathy decided that she too wanted to have a baby, now. Her in-laws advised waiting until Ken got out of the navy so that there would be more money coming into the partnership. If she didn't wait, she would probably have to find a job to help ends meet. "Oh no!" was Kathy's reaction, "I'm going to stay home with my children." They had the child. Kathy felt tied down and missed her parents in the States, so she left Ken in Okinawa and went home. They are now divorced and she is working. Someone else is minding her child. Her husband is saddled with monthly child support payments until the child is eighteen. This obligation will be carried forward into his next relationship.

No single activity helps working couples more than preparing a partnership plan, yet it is an activity that most of us avoid as too overwhelming. If you could calculate how much heartache, stress, and expense it would save you and your partner in the long run, you would gleefully undertake the challenge. Clearly, Kathy and Ken had no plan.

The Working Couple's Planning Process

Research undertaken by the National Center for Health Statistics shows that divorce is highly concentrated in the first year of marriage and that one third of failed marriages occur within the first four years. Amazingly, almost 40 percent of those surveyed said that major problems were already present when they married or had developed early in the marriage. Those in their late twenties and early thirties are especially prone to divorce. Perhaps this is because these couples don't have enough experience to know that problems can be resolved if only they committed themselves to putting their individual egos aside for the good of the partnership. Couples also have to agree to stay off the defensive and to strive to approach partnership challenges with an intent to learn about each other.

We strongly believe that couples should discuss what each wants and expects out of the partnership *before* they get married. You might even formally schedule a meeting in which you set couple goals for yourself, your work, and your partnership. If everyone did this, it would reduce the divorce rate significantly. Sadly, most of us don't. The following steps illustrate key areas on which to focus in order to make your career and personal lives merge successfully. Even if you are already married, these strategies will work.

Premarital and Postmarital Agreements

The planning process, ideally, should have begun with a premarital agreement. But if you don't have one, it's a good idea to establish guidelines now in a postmarital agreement. In this era of redefinition of spousal rights, blended marriages, merged families from previous marriages, and inheritance issues from several sources, it's best to have a formal agreement in writing. It is an important part of your financial plan. These agreements are not about love or trust. They are about compassion, understanding, commitment, and just good old common sense, and they will help you to successfully manage your dual-career relationship.

Just as many couples do not wish to address the issue of drawing up wills, because of the implication of death, they are loath to consider the concept of premarital counseling or even the concept of premarital contracts. To them it seems that having a contract would be entering the marriage with the idea that perhaps it won't succeed. With the divorce rate at over 50 percent, divorce is not only a possibility but a probability. Preparing in advance forces both of you to discuss your needs and wants with regard to lifestyle preferences, whether or not to have children, whose job will be more important, how you will handle dual-income finances, and any other of the host of challenges that can and will affect your marriage.

Planning does not imply a lack of love or romance but rather, a caring concern by and for each of you. Once a contract is in place, it releases both of you to focus on your true goals of succeeding in your careers while enjoying a positive personal partnership.

The philosophy behind a postmarital agreement is that the couple acknowledges that the agreement is conducive to the partnership's welfare and to the highest purposes of the marriage relationship. It is entered into to prevent strife, to settle questions about marital and property rights and thus remove a frequent cause of family disputes, while enhancing the prospects of partnership harmony. For example, whose money is it? When we discuss money, we need to understand two terms, *equal* and *equitable. Equal* means 50/50, whereas *equitable* is determined by what you contribute. Through the pre- or postmarital agreement, working couples can establish a distribution of wealth clause in case the partnership fails. The question is how long will one partner finance another before assessing the return on investment.

Christine and George are both lawyers. She is established in her firm as a partner, making $150,000 a year. He moved from firm to firm until he opened his own practice, which is only marginally successful. Nothing is ever right for him, but he still earns between $50,000 and $60,000 a year. After eight years, they have two children, and she does 80 percent of all child care, cooks for the family, and pays for home care. Christine finally decides that their relationship is not equal and so she files for divorce in California, where they live. California is a community property state, so he gets 50 percent of all the assets through state equal distribution laws.

Laws and the courts make decisions on the basis of equality, not on what is equitable. Women, in general, who have looked to the government and the law as a viable partner on equality issues, are finding that this partner is in the Dark Ages when it comes to equity issues. Working couples must establish their own guidelines regarding equality and equity issues for the sake of greater stability, harmony, and, ultimately, success.

A pre- or postmarital agreement is a contract. It is an agreement as to how you are going to do certain things within the partnership, and it's a great way to start your relationship. Spell out in advance what each of you expects and wants out of the partnership, in both the short and the long terms. The key to a good premarital agreement is that it be enforceable. The primary basis for enforcement of a premarital agreement is its fairness or, in the absence of fairness, complete disclosure. Fairness may be open to interpretation, but the critical issue in a marriage is openness and honesty. When you go into it, you must disclose all the material and emotional things that affect you, including your finances, state of health, or the fact that you have a crazy uncle whom you are obliged to visit every Tuesday. Whatever is going to affect the partnership should be disclosed. Get everything out up front. That's one of the benefits of a premarital agreement.

Realistically, all couples should look to formulating a premarital agreement as they go into the marriage, but even if they are already in the marriage, a contract can help with the planning process. If you have a valid, enforceable pre- or postmarital monetary agreement that prescribes what is going to happen if the partnership breaks up or if one of you dies, you will both be freer to concentrate on making the partnership work. You will give time a chance when you know that there is no *rush* to get your fair share. You already know what to expect. This removes most of the issues concerning property from that cauldron that seethes when people are getting divorced, so you won't have lawyer A arguing with lawyer B about who is going to get the sofa. It has already been decided.

Drawing up an agreement like this gives people boundaries or guidelines as to what to expect of each other and what is going to happen in the event of tragedy, divorce, or death. Some of the negotiations can get unpleasant, but how they are resolved often determines the quality of the partnership. Pre- or postmarital agreements are not designed to make it easier to walk out of a partnership. There are good times and there are bad times in any partnership. Hanging in there until you have developed a history together will be easier if you know what the other person wants.

What about working couples who *are* trying to plan for a divorce? Do everything you can to avoid it because if you do finally go through with it, you will then always know that you have done everything you could to prevent the divorce. You are not going to have those doubts and fears that "maybe I should have tried a little harder. Maybe I shouldn't have walked out that night."

Building a Working Couple Plan

Marital contracts are part of a working couple's planning process and need to be reassessed or updated regularly. You both change. A good plan should reflect these changes. The same principles apply to the Working Couple Plan as to an organizational business plan. Planning is putting together your best efforts and pulling in a common direction. Planning is actually a decision-making process by which you develop your objectives, strategies to reach these objectives, and then the action steps necessary to achieve them. A plan emphasizes present decisions that affect the future. Most people would not think of building a house from scratch without a plan, yet they attempt to build a life together based only on love. Planning forms the foundation of your life together and can improve the depth of your love.

Why plan? If you don't have plans, how will you know when you have reached your goals? How much money will spell success to you? How many possessions will you need in order to convince yourselves that you have arrived? What guidelines do you have for determining if your children are functional members of society? Your plan will put some direction and focus in your life.

Where do you start? You start with a vision. What does each of you want to be? Where do you want to be? How do you define happiness and success?

Two years ago, we had the opportunity of taking our television program to a major network, but it would have required moving to New York. The opportunity was tempting. Who wouldn't want to take a chance on the big time? How do you make a life-changing decision like that? We looked at our joint vision, consulted our plan, and made the decision based on our mutual goals. The timing wasn't right and it would have required us to leave Heaven. Our goal, with regard to our quality of life, had already been achieved, so we turned down that golden opportunity, for now. Will we revisit that decision? Not until other primary goals have been achieved.

Both of you need to participate in the planning process. Plans should focus on key result areas (KRAs), and in a Working Couple Plan we suggest that you include these areas:

- Careers of each—now and in the future
- Finances—his and hers
- Growing the relationship
- His time/her time/our time
- Family issues—his/hers/ours
- Children—present and future
- Other

Key questions to be discussed are:

1. Where are we now? Planning to live together, get married, are married, etc.?
2. Are we committed to living for work or working to live?
3. How did we get where we are today in our careers and in our lives? What brought us together?
4. What is working well (helping) in the partnership? What needs improvement?
5. What is working against (hindering) us?
6. Where does each of us want to be in terms of career, geographic location, finances?
7. How and when can we realistically expect to get there? What is our timetable?

To answer these questions, analyze your history together. Look back over the past five years and share your successes and failures. If you have children, get them involved. This process helps remind you of your successes and of what you did to make them happen. It also reminds you of missteps that you want to avoid in the future. Since many families today involve mergers, there may be new players who know nothing of your past. This process helps fill in the gaps. One ten-year-old told us, "I have a new mom. The other one got outplaced." Sad, but true.

Situational Analysis

One of the most revealing aspects of the planning process is the Situational Analysis, which involves identifying your Strengths, Weaknesses, Opportunities, and Threats (SWOT).

Situational Analysis

	Strengths		Weaknesses		Opportunities		Threats	
	Work	Family	Work	Family	Work	Family	Work	Family
CAREER -Hers								
CAREER -His								
Expectations/ Values								
Quality of Life								
Stakeholder Expectations— Other Family Members								
Geographic Location								
Other								

The SWOT chart presents for your consideration major areas that affect your partnership. It addresses the question, "What if we don't do anything differently?" Perform your Situational Analysis by identifying external threats and opportunities and then internal strengths and weaknesses. What opportunities exist for you in the marketplace? What threats to your success do you envision? Schedule a formal sit-down together, using your flip chart. Actually, this is an interesting activity you may enjoy.

Once your SWOT process is completed, you will have quality information to assist you in putting your plan together. While the planning process is not difficult, it does take discipline, because until it is done, you can't see any immediate gratification. Be patient. As a result of your patience, you will have a vision, a Situation Analysis (SWOT), and be ready to prepare your mission statement.

Your mission statement is a form of commitment. It attests why you are together and what you hope to accomplish in the partnership. Try putting your joint mission together in one paragraph. Once you have it, print it up and hang it on the wall or refrigerator. This tells the world what you are all about and serves to remind each family member of why your family is special. When times are tough, or a member is really upset, look at the family mission, its unity and purpose. It helps tie you together. Have fun developing your own. Our mission statement helps us to decide which opportunities are really golden and which may take us away from our goals.

The Carter Family Mission: To promote a quality of life that provides love, respect, encouragement, and support for each member's uniqueness.

- To recognize and encourage the development of each member's uniqueness.
- To help each member achieve physical, spiritual, emotional, and financial growth and security.
- To continually strengthen family ties, which are the roots of our heritage.
- To be short on criticism and long on praise.
- To support each other through life's challenges and rejoice in our own and each other's successes.
- To hold each member accountable for his or her own happiness and to require each to take personal responsibility for his or her own life crises.
- To encourage laughter but to respect pain.

Your plans can be for as long or short a period as you want them to be. Most business plans project out three to five years, with an annual operations plan. Remember, a plan is only a process; it's not set in concrete. It provides you with a track to run on and helps keep you focused. Most important, it provides you with the basis for making decisions, changes, or switches in direction.

Setting Partnership Objectives

The purpose of setting partnership objectives is to turn your mission into a reality. An objective defines something you want or need to do. You are now looking for clear, defined outcomes. Some couples like to set objectives for each key result area (KRA), that is, work, family, financial resources, leisure, self. If that seems overwhelming, look at your KRAs and set priorities. If both of your careers are important (as opposed to one's being merely to supplement the family income for a vacation), then put the letter *A* next to both careers. If you have children, determine the A priorities relative to their needs and activities.

Some KRAs may not be important at this time and you can defer setting objectives on these until you need them. Focus on the 20 to 30 percent that will give you 70 to 80 percent of your results. Sound familiar? It's the Preateau Principle: "If you spend eighty percent of your time planning, it will only take you twenty percent of your time implementing."

Once you have prioritized your KRAs, it's time to set objectives. Here are the guidelines:

- As a couple, ask yourselves whether it is worth expending your time, energy, and financial resources to attain any particular objective.
- Use your mission statement and SWOT analysis as a basis for developing your objectives.
- Use the SMART formula for writing the objective. Each objective should be:
  S —Specific
  M—Measurable
  A —Aggressive
  R —Realistic
  T —Time-related

Tom wants to obtain his MBA. He plans to go to school in the evening, all year, and to carry two subjects per term. If he does this, he will complete his graduate work within four years of starting. Is his goal **S**pecific? Yes. Is it **M**easurable? Yes. Is it **A**ggressive? Yes. This is a value judgment. Is it **R**ealistic? Yes, it is calculated on what is known today. Is it **T**ime related? Yes.

A major part of every Working Couple Plan involves money. Regardless of who brings in the most money, you probably have limited experience in joint money management. If this is a new marriage, what worked in the past is not guaranteed to work in the new partnership. Educate everyone in the family as to what comes in and how it is spent. When any one person overspends, everybody in the family loses. Family members should be held accountable for how we spend "our money." It's a state of mind. The partnership and/or children need to develop shared money goals.

A family objective could be to reduce household expenses by 10 percent during this calendar year. It meets all the criteria of a SMART objective. Your next step is to develop a strategy to achieve this objective. This is critical to making your dreams come true. You can't gloss over the development of strategies to accomplish your objectives.

> *Setting strategies to achieve goals is critical to making your dreams come true.*

This is the "how" of the plan. You need a realistic outline detailing how you propose to achieve your mutual objectives. If you don't do this, you have only ended your efforts with a dream but with no *plan* for how to make your dream come true. A strategy for reducing the household expenses might be to utilize coupons and to take advantage of sales and retail specials when making any purchases.

Together, analyze the best use of your resources, strengths, and opportunities. During this process,

- *Look for trade-offs between short- and long-term needs.* You may have to give up something today for a better life tomorrow. Examine the degrees of risk you are each willing to take and develop an understanding of how these risks affect the future. Answer the question, "Is it worth it?"
- *Develop alternatives between existing career opportunities and new career opportunities.* Consider your present location as well as other parts of the country and consider your current separate careers as well as the possibility of becoming co-preneurs in a new business. It may also involve the need to acquire new assets and divesting your financial portfolio.
- *Be realistic when considering your resources, capabilities, and potential.* Be the same with family needs and quality of life issues. Refer to the key result areas suggested on page 78. You may wish to add others.

Taking Action

The last phase of the planning process is to develop action steps. Action steps are activities necessary to implementing your strategies in order to get the results you want. Action steps help you decide what you are going to do and when. These steps result in a specific, mutually agreed to time schedule for achieving your goals. Each family member can play an important role by making sure each specific action step is taken. An action step for meeting your strategy to reduce household expenses would be to clip food coupons from the Sunday paper or home mailers each week.

If you have children, assign this action step to them. It will make them part of the plan. We refer to this as "seeing yourself in the plan." It is the planning process in action. For working couples, action planning identifies the work each must do. When you learn to shop with coupons and make it a game of how much you can save, you will be surprised at how these savings begin to add up. Tally these savings over a year and then involve the entire family when deciding how to use the savings. Deciding how to spend the savings is an *action step*. Step by step, the process involves:

- Identifying the tasks that must be done to accomplish a particular strategy
- Deciding who will do what
- Determining when it will be done
- Calculating whether you can afford it
- Analyzing whether it is working

Your *objective* is to improve the quality of your life outside of work. A *strategy* for improving the quality of family life is to *reassess* how you are currently spending your time when you are off the job. A *second strategy* would be to compare your quality of life with that of other couples in the same socioeconomic bracket. An *action step* is to do an analysis of how you spend your time and on what. Activities can include:

- Housecleaning
- Driving children to day care
- Driving children to various activities (such as Little League, ballet, YMCA)
- Preparing meals
- Grocery shopping
- Laundry
- Entertaining
- Taking cars in for service
- Yard maintenance

Make an exhaustive list. Brainstorm ways in which your extended families, friends, and employers can help you achieve your action steps.

Are these same people a hindrance to the accomplishment of your action steps? Look at all activities in which you are involved and then set priorities. Redefine the activities. Do you want and need to continue each? If so, who should be doing what?

> In their partnership, Mary interviews all care givers and does the preselection. She and Ed jointly meet with the final candidates. Ed looks at the best ways to feed the family and determines how much money they have for eating out or picking up prepared meals and looks for easy ways to cook at home. They work as a team.

If you have children, household chores should be part of your program. Chores help them feel connected to family success and harmony. Other options for completing household chores could be finding an outside cleaning service to come in twice a month or dividing the house down the middle. He does the left side of the house and she does the right side. Next week, they switch. The idea is to prioritize your activities and develop action steps that use all of your available resources to their best advantage.

Investigate who and what are out there to help you. Here are some services you might want to use:

- *Personal service companies.* They do everything from running errands to planning dinner parties.
- *Handy-person services.* They can fix or find almost anything.
- *Employer's EAPs (Employee Assistance Programs).* These are no longer just for substance abuse. They now include assistance from elder care to day care.
- *Sick call.* This is for parents with children too sick for school or day care. Offered by the Voucher Corporation (1-800-531-2828).
- *Major retailers.* They will set appointment schedules for their customers, and some of them have shop-at-home services.
- *Your own telephone.* You can shop, bank, and schedule via this handy instrument.

Planning puts your partnership in a new perspective. Throw out all the old rules that dictate how you *should* live. Make a fresh start.

Watch Out for the Crabs!

If you've ever spent time on the southeastern seaboard, you know that crab fishing is a favorite pastime. Observing the behavior of the crabs caught and put in an old washtub is a real lesson for working couples. The crabs don't like the washtub environment. In their stress, they ooze a purple slime that makes them even more uncomfortable. Sooner or later, one of the crabs works very hard to pull itself out of the tub. What do you think the other crabs do? No, they don't cheer on the struggler. Their attitude is, "If we can't get out, you can't get out." They try to pull it back into the slimy tub. Don't become victims of the "crab" syndrome. When we try to improve our relationships, there are negative forces at play, both outside and within the partnership. The key is to be aware of these negative factors and to help each other cope with them.

> *Watch out for the crabs!*

Here's an example that puts the whole planning process together.

Sample Planning Process

Key result area:	Quality of life
Objective:	To own your own home within one year, with a price not to exceed $200,000.
Strategy:	1. Develop specifications for your dream house.
	2. Research the most cost-effective way to achieve your objective.
	3. Investigate areas that will best suit your needs, vision, and family mission that are also within your price range.
	4. Choose between buying an existing home or building your own.
Action steps (for Strategy #4):	1. Determine the cost of new construction in various areas that meet your needs within thirty days.
	2. Visit open houses in desired areas to search for homes in your price range.
	3. Prepare a cost/benefit analysis on buying an existing property versus building a new home.
	4. Decide between buying or building by [*fill in date*].

Go through each strategy and prepare a list of action steps. Then take action, review outcomes, and make adjustments. Remember, action steps aren't taken in isolation. Discuss them until you reach agreement.

Summary

From the planning process, you discover that these discussions result in new opportunities. You are able to prevent surprises, stop making "seat-of-the-pants" decisions (which are often time-consuming as well as emotionally draining and costly), correct problems before they become crises, strengthen the partnership by reinforcing mutual values, and focus corrective action on unwanted situations instead of on each other or other family members. No other process delivers such positive results.

You will need to review your plan on a quarterly basis. Of course, certain opportunities may arise that will force you to rethink the plan. Great! At least you'll have a blueprint for making decisions. Update the plan every year. Make this an involved learning experience. Celebrate your successes and learn from your failures. Questions you should answer during your plan update session include:

- Has anything in the Situational Analysis changed?
- Have your priorities changed?
- If your priorities have changed, what do you need to do to modify your plan?
- Are your objectives and strategies still in line with your expectations for yourself, your partner, and your family?
- Should you change how you are using your resources (people, places, things)?

Planning has helped us to stop feeding on each other's adrenaline while dispersing our energies. Opportunities are thought through and put in the perspective of our total career and life plan.

One day, one of you might suddenly say, "Let's go to Paris for our vacation." The other might respond, "It's not in the plan. We can't afford it." Still enthusiastic, the would-be traveler argues, "We can take out a loan to finance it. Wouldn't it be nice to do it while we're still young?" "No, not if we have to suffer for two years to pay for it," answers Feet-on-the-Ground. "We will always be young enough to enjoy Paris." You have both agreed to the plan, and you don't do something if it is not in the plan. Instead, find an alternative you can afford. There are many terrific places to go and things to do. Plan for them. Once you have learned to make decisions based on your mutually agreed-upon plan, your life will truly be more hassle-free.

Summary of Key Points

- List wants, individually.
- Have a formal family meeting.
- Set priorities.
- Eliminate, consolidate, and postpone.
- Downsize.
- Take care of self.
- Review regularly.

Chapter 7

Making Workable Decisions

Successful working couples, whatever their individual motivations, need to conduct a systematic analysis of their problems, opportunities, and challenges in order to strengthen and enrich their relationship. Working couples do reasonably well at meeting the expected obligations, such as regular monthly payments for the home or car and paying for clothes and other budgeted items like work, travel, and vacation. It's the unexpected that causes increased financial burdens, stress, and arguments. These unexpected situations aren't always negatives, but they do require readjustments. Unfortunately, much of what happens in the world—unexpected market and industry changes, new technology, population increases or decreases, crime, changing trends, and changing values—is outside your control. That makes it even more critical for you to have a system for making decisions and solving problems.

There is a difference between problem solving or decision making and resolving disagreements and arguments. The need to make a decision does not necessarily mean that you disagree that a problem exists, or disagree about who caused the problem, or that you are blaming each other for the condition. The car breaks down, whether you disagree about it or not. Where to take the car, how you will pay for it, or whether to purchase a new one are decisions that have to be made. These decisions must be made in keeping with your lifestyle preferences. Even though all problems are not the same, making a decision is usually required when you have a problem. The two go hand in hand.

It is true that you can also disagree about how the problem should be solved and about who is to make the actual decision. We share some helpful suggestions on how to manage disagreement in Chapter 9. In this chapter, we discuss a process that will actually help you to make decisions that will enhance your life together.

We have found that it really helps to stop thinking of problems as *problems* by learning to reframe them so that it is possible to look at them in a different way. They are just choices you need to make, situations you have to handle. Many of these situations and choices involve boring, day-to-day matters like what to have for dinner. Others will change your lives in some meaningful way. These decisions deserve your concentrated time because you will live with the results over a lifetime. These include, but are not limited to, where to send your children to school, whether you should buy a vacation home, where or how to invest your retirement fund, or whether a job relocation will help the partnership. These questions present challenges the partnership needs to consider carefully. Overcoming challenges can be more *challenging* than just solving problems.

How Not to Make Decisions

Over the years, we have purchased a vacation home or two. Each of these was purchased spontaneously because we loved it at the time and convinced ourselves it was a good investment. One of these vacation purchases was on Marco Island, Florida. The Forging Industry of America had engaged Jaine to be the keynote speaker at its annual conference to be held on Marco Island. Neither of us had ever been there, but a friend swore that it was one of the most beautiful places in the world. "You must go together," he counseled. "Book Jim off the platform, rent one of those condominiums on the beach, and relax after the conference." Always tired from our heavy travel schedules, we grabbed at the chance.

We met in Miami and drove to Marco Island. As we drove over the bridge from the mainland, we were hooked. Instant peace descended upon us and we were in heaven. We found the condo, on the most beautiful beach in the world, and let ourselves in. It was one o'clock in the morning and the moon was shining over the Gulf of Mexico, palm trees were swaying in the gulf breezes, and a welcoming bottle of wine awaited. Who wouldn't be impressed? We certainly were.

We mutually decided that we had to have *that* condo. We didn't look at other properties. We hadn't even driven around the city, and we hadn't considered that it was a one-bedroom condo and we had two children! We bought that condo on emotion. That is *not* the way to make rational decisions.

Recently, we were on a vacation in Carmel, California. We *love* Carmel. Usually, we rent a cottage on the beach and spend our time browsing through the hundreds of quaint boutiques. A friend told us that if we were going to buy property in or around Carmel, now was the time to do it. We called a realtor and went out to look at properties. Most of them were easy to like. We found the most beautiful home ever created high on a hill overlooking the Pacific Ocean where sea gulls and sea lions spring into view. The big problem was that the owner of the property had not realized that property values had plummeted and was asking a pretty hefty price for his gem.

We went back to our little cottage and sat by the fireplace trying to convince each other that we could manage this property if we sold our beautiful home in Naples, went back on the lecture trail, and cashed in our IRAs. We dreamed and lied to ourselves through most of the evening. Then, just before we went to bed, Jim suggested that we work through the decision analysis process. Having all the real estate figures pertaining to that property, we went over the interest rates for the mortgage we would have to carry, the property maintenance costs, the federal and state taxes, and how much it would cost us to fly coast to coast to visit our property.

Our analysis determined that for what it would cost us each month to maintain the property we could rent beautiful properties anywhere in the world, whenever we want, and won't be tied down to one property. The box on page 91 has some questions to ask yourselves before you make any purchases. Information is power and power makes you free.

A Working Couple Plan (see Chapter 6) gives you the framework for dealing with unexpected changes and opportunities. This keeps challenges within your control. With this tool you can deal with opportunities as they arise in the context of a total plan versus grappling with isolated instances on the basis of a momentary whim.

Too often we let "seizing the moment" put undue pressure on us, which keeps us from making workable decisions. Let's look at how a problem analysis system can help your partnership stay focused and make effective decisions. This system utilizes seven steps to analyze a problem. At the conclusion of these seven steps, you will be able to make an informed decision based on your knowledge, experience, and research.

The Problem Analysis Process

1. *Identify the real opportunity or challenge.* This appears easy on the surface, but working couples can role-play issues and yet never get to the real issue or problem. Recently, we were talking with a couple after one

---

Is This a Smart Purchase?

To buy or not to buy is a question couples face every day as they navigate through the maze of advertising. Before you buy, determine if your impulse to buy is really worth the money you'll spend.—*Consumer Credit Counseling Service of Los Angeles*

1. Do you really need this item?   Yes   No
2. Have you researched the item?   Yes   No
3. Is the price reasonable?   Yes   No
4. Can you wait to purchase?   Yes   No
5. Is it truly an opportunity, or hype?   Yes   No
6. If the item is on sale, is it a true sale price?   Yes   No
7. Will it truly satisfy an inner need?   Yes   No
8. Is it in the plan?   Yes   No

> **Keeping Score:**
>
> If you have answered yes to:
> | | |
> |---|---|
> | 7–8 | Buy it! |
> | 4–6 | Think Again. |
> | Fewer than 4 | Forget It! |

---

of our sessions. She was very outgoing (extroverted) and he was quiet (introverted). *She* lamented, "I wish he would talk more." *He* told us he keeps his thoughts to himself even when he is upset. For example, he manages the family finances but doesn't communicate what has to be paid or when the money is due. She may spontaneously purchase something that he hasn't factored into the budget. Although this irks him, he never says anything about it. Is his not talking about it the problem? It may be. However, during further discussion, we discovered that the actual problem may be that she makes more money than he does. Even though they have agreed that her money is *their* money, he is not comfortable about telling her not to spend *her* money. They have agreed to place both their salaries in a joint account. She says she doesn't care what is in the account and leaves all family finances up to him. When they are short of funds to pay a bill for which he hasn't budgeted, *he* worries. *She* is allowed to remain blissfully ignorant of their financial reality. Defining the real problem is actually the hardest part of this process. In such a case, incidental buying is only a symptom of the real problem.

    2. *Gather related data.* Get the facts. Once you have focused on and defined the real problem, the next step is to gather related and pertinent

data. Don't stop with logical, objective information. Feelings are facts, too. Data alone are often meaningless; they have to be processed into information you can use. If you are contemplating a move from Toledo to Chicago, all the data about transportation, schools, crime rates, and shopping facilities won't mean much until you decide where you are going to live in relation to where you work and how everyone involved in the projected move *feels* about it. How will each be affected? Are their fears real or imagined? Who is to make the final decision?

3. *Look for alternative solutions.* There are always options. Think through your options—together. Let's use our Chicago situation. You have two middle school children. Both of you work in the Loop in downtown Chicago. Lifestyle choices could be between living in the near north area close to the city or living northwest of the city. The near north area means an easy commute to work, access to shopping, and the availability of first-rate cultural activities. Your concerns include the public school system and high city crime rates. Living northwest of the city may mean a better school system, country living with a small-town atmosphere, but a longer commute that translates into having less time with the children. Taking a city person to the country may not be the best solution.

Part of your precouple planning should have included discussing and coming to some agreement as to lifestyle preferences. Going to the suburbs may seem like the best solution for the children, but is it? How will the children get to school-related or other social events? Who will drive them? Who will watch them after school? How much time will you be able to spend with them after two or more hours commuting every day? What are the alternatives?

- Live in the near north area and send the children to a private school.
- Plan weekend getaways to the country.
- Live in the northwest area and hire live-in help because of the longer commuting schedule.

4. *Keep brainstorming.* Really listen to each other and don't be stubborn or passive. Give and get input and then test your alternatives. You don't have to make the final decision yet. You will find that nothing will seem that overwhelming or life-threatening if you feel you don't have to commit yourself to an actual decision for the next hundred years. In problem analysis, it is desirable to test alternatives. In our Chicago example, renting for a year to try out one of the areas is a possibility. Putting your stuff in storage for a year is cheaper than trying to sell a house you no longer want.

5. *Select the best alternative and test your decision.* Give it your best shot. It's still only a test, so enjoy the good aspects of the trial period and keep analyzing, modifying, and researching.

6. *Follow up and evaluate.* Set a date to review the alternative test. How are things working? Get feedback from all concerned. If anyone is seriously unhappy with the test solution, it isn't working. Go back to the flip chart. Use each test as a learning experience. The trick is not to have so much invested in the test that you feel you *can't* back out.

7. *Make a decision.* No matter what system you use, resolving problems comes down to making the final decision and then committing yourselves to live with it. The need to make decisions is one of the biggest stressors we face. Some people are so fearful of making the wrong decision, and of having to live with the negative repercussions of that wrong decision, that they drag out the process. Others continually reverse their decisions, which we call the Buyer's Remorse Syndrome. They make a decision, change their minds, then have to make another decision. They exhaust themselves and their significant others in a continual cycle of reversed decision making. Each time you reverse a decision, you've doubled your work, your stress, and the other negatives that go along with indecision.

Use the form on page 94, or something similar, to capitalize on your knowledge, experience, and the feeling aspects of your challenges and opportunities.

Ultimately, what affects decision making are each partner's values and behavioral style. That's why it's so critical to the process for each of you to know the other's values, beliefs, and behavior styles and how these differences affect the decision-making process.

What About Values?

As discussed in Chapter 4, values are defined as the principles we use to make choices that lead to action. Most arguments or disagreements between partners are caused by a clash in the way each perceives a particular issue and the possible choices available within their individual value systems of right/wrong, good/bad, more important/less important, and more acceptable/less acceptable. Perception is based on our values. Everyone believes that his or her values are the correct values. Therefore, value issues often revolve around power, affection, honesty/conscience, laws/rules, authority, fairness/justice, the value of life, personal rules,

---

Problem Analysis and Decision-Making Process

1. Decision:

   We need to decide whether to _____

   _____

2. Possible negative consequences   Possible positive consequences

   _____   _____

   _____   _____

3. Alternative solutions: _____

   _____

4. Two best alternatives: _____

   _____

5. Alternatives we have decided to test: _____

   _____

6. Follow-up date to discuss results: _____

7. Final decision: _____

   _____

---

and time. These are the factors that motivate each of you when you are trying to reach decisions and take committed action on the implementation of the selected alternatives.

Questions you need to ask yourselves are:

1. What is right?
2. What is most reasonable?
3. What is most meaningful?
4. What do you expect of me?
5. What do I expect of myself?

Most of us don't consciously consider how deeply our values affect all phases, actions, choices, and decisions in life. Sometimes they are incidental. At other times they have major ramifications. Work, home, the family, and social life are all areas in which values are displayed. Each of you struggles with how life *should* be versus how it *really* is. The key is to take a proactive approach by focusing on your freedom of choice, which gets you back to your values. There isn't anything you can't do if you take charge of the situation.

> George and Alice have two children, ages 1 and 3. George is offered a new job with a good salary and a bonus incentive, but it means relocation. Alice has tenure in a school system. For her, this would mean starting all over in a new school system. The questions she is struggling with are: "Do I really want to stay in education, start a new career, or stay at home with the children and explore part-time opportunities?" The major question Alice should be asking herself is, "Am I working for extra money or for my fulfillment?" She admits that she is not working for fulfillment and that she would rather stay at home with their children. What about the extra money?
>
> Using a cost/benefit analysis, which is a simple process of putting the benefits on one side of a piece of paper and the costs (including feelings and preferences) on the other, she and George determined that it would not be cost-effective for her to start over in another school system. The extra expenses incurred for day care, home cleaning services, laundry, and all the other things required by working professionals do not warrant her staying in the same profession. After careful analysis, Alice and George decided that they could manage on one income until the children were in school full-time. While it required each giving up a few nice-to-have items, they concluded that this decision would be in everyone's best interests in the long run. Alice would take her time reentering the job market. "For the first time," she confessed, "I feel free to enjoy our children and look at our options."

While implementing the decision-making process, Alice discovered that she had stayed in her teaching career because:

- Teaching was comfortable and offered security.
- It was the line of least resistance and a relatively easy job.
- Teaching had always provided additional family income (belonging and acceptance).
- It was natural for her to continue with what she had always done in the past (security/ego).

All of these reasons concern "need" issues. We often confuse our needs with our values. Needs are more a reflection of what we think we should have or should do than of what we really want to do. Alice had continued teaching because people kept telling her it would be a waste of her valuable education to stay at home with the children. That made her feel guilty even to think of it. By using the problem analysis process, she was able to take off the cloak of guilt and do what *she* wanted to do.

The Role of Behavior in Problem Analysis and Decision Making

John Gottman and his research team at the Department of Psychology, University of Washington, have studied how hundreds of married couples handle conflict or disagreement. He classifies stable marriages into three categories: validating, volatile, and avoidant. All three patterns demonstrate their value systems and bring problem issues to closure in an acceptable format for the couples without destroying the relationship. Each style uses a different approach to solving problems and reaching decisions.

Validators let their partners know that they consider each other's opinions and emotions valid, even if they don't agree with them. They are good friends and value the partnership's goals more than their individual goals. They hear each other out, paraphrase what was said, and validate each other's perfect right to have feelings of their own.

Volatile couples do not validate. They exhibit great passion. Each attempts to persuade the other to his or her point of view, energetically claiming who is right and who is wrong. Winning the argument is everything. These "uproars" are actually a dance they do as part of a warm and loving relationship. While they appear to be expressing a great deal of anger, they also laugh a lot and don't hold grudges. Validating couples finish each other's statements. Volatile couples interrupt each other.

Avoidant couples usually reach some understanding about their disagreements without ever bringing them into the open. What they don't do is find out what was at the root of the disagreement. Problem solving, for avoidant couples, usually means ignoring the fact that they have differences, or results in one partner agreeing to act more like the other. These couples value separateness more than they do a shared existence. Being calm, individualistic, and having their own space are very important. As a result, they never really address conflict. This can result in their never really knowing each other.

Each type of couple has predictable behavior patterns. Validating and volatile couples resolve issues. Avoidants don't. In order to be successful at problem solving and decision making, you need to study and assess how you each approach problems and then develop strategies enabling you to be more open and participative with one another. Researchers have concluded that marital meltdown occurs when the partnership turns hostile because issues have been allowed to fester and resentments remain unaddressed. After a while, the negatives in the partnership far outweigh the positives. When this happens, working couples throw problem solving and decision making out the window. Their attitude becomes, "Let's argue, insult, and verbally abuse each other to see who can inflict the most damage." Hurt people hurt other people and they never find a way to use their skills to find a balance between the positives and the negatives. These are lose/lose situations where no one wins.

Following are some key points to remember while you are working through the problem analysis and decision-making process:

Helping	*Hindering*
• Understand each other's temperament, e.g., whether it is fast paced/slow-paced.	• Failure to define the real problem.
• Determine if you are task-oriented or people-oriented.	• Discounting your partner's thoughts, ideas, or perceptions.
• Know your partner's number one priority when making a decision. Get to the bottom line. Share your feelings.	• Jumping to conclusions.
	• Being defensive.
	• Using outdated information or misinformation.
• Appreciate each other's strengths, e.g., "You're analytical, I'm decisive."	• Failure to observe and listen, *really* listen, to his/her point of view.
• Help each other by thinking through your ideas before sharing them, asking for both points of view, and not changing directions too quickly.	• Lacking confidence to solve the real problem.
	• Engaging in fire fighting actions and looking at only short-term quick fixes.
• Help each other weigh the pros and cons of risk, be more open and flexible, and never clam up.	• Showing decision remorse, frequently reversing or rethinking the same decision.

Consider your individual differences when attempting to make partnership decisions. Some people are very fast-paced. They desire many choices and welcome alternatives, but they don't want to have to gather them. They are often impulsive and make quick decisions. They will decide on a solution but not follow through with it, which means that they have never truly committed themselves to it. They are not interested in details and prefer to scan data rather than read for substance. They are risk takers, very polyphasic, and always doing more than one thing. This type will read the paper, watch TV, and carry on a phone conversation at the same time. They like to talk and tell! They are *racehorses*.

Other people are slow-paced. They prefer limited choices or, better yet, having to decide between only two alternatives. They may find decision making difficult because they are not risk takers and are usually very careful to analyze before making a commitment of any kind. These types are patient and need uninterrupted thinking time. With this type of person, it is best to have a discussion about an issue, complete the decision making work sheet, and then let the information germinate overnight, or longer, to enable him or her to think it through thoroughly. They are cooperative in creating alternatives but need specific focus. They listen and ask questions. These people are the *turtles* in life, slow-paced, methodical, and perfectionistic.

Both racehorses and turtles are important to the harmonious flow of human interaction. Turtles need time to make decisions and feel very dysfunctional if they are not allowed adequate time. Racehorses want to avoid getting bogged down in analysis paralysis. They feel impatient and irritable if reaching a decision takes longer than two minutes. To be successful, partnerships need to develop behavioral adapt/ability, which is the ability to adapt or modify their behavioral style to meet the needs of the situation and the people involved in that situation.

Is your partner task-oriented or people-oriented? Are you task-oriented or people-oriented? Task-oriented people are usually very independent. They like to control. There is a high probability that the task-oriented person manages the finances. They are also guarded in relationships. It takes them a long time to develop trust. They don't usually share their feelings easily and may seem cool, distant, and personally perfect. In order to be perfect, they are fact-oriented, calculating, time-conscious, and impatient. They fear being taken advantage of.

People-oriented types care more about the relationship than about solving the problem. This is not a gender issue. Such individuals just want the problem to go away and for everyone to be happy. Whenever a problem crops up, they get the "gabbies" and talk things to death. They look for ways to express feelings and to smooth irritations, are supportive of their partners, and very flexible about time, showing a high degree of patience. They are either opinionated or speak softly and go underground with their true feelings.

Summary

In reality, many of the challenges working couples face are with each other. Therefore, in order to do a rational problem analysis, it is critical to approach the process by remembering to separate the person from the situation or problem. Keep focused on the challenge and the subsequent decision to be made.

Managing a working couple relationship *and* children is more challenging than anyone who has not experienced it can comprehend. When your values change, and with them your needs, you owe it to your partner to discuss these changes with him/her. Going underground and working with a hidden agenda hurts everyone.

Most working couples fail to use a problem-solving process or any other formal system in making decisions. Instead, they fall into a benefits grab to see who can take the most *things* out of the relationship. When this happens, the relationship ends up in intensive care therapy or dies. Hello, lawyers!

Making workable decisions isn't just a high-theory, low-application process. It's about understanding your values and behavioral differences, and how to systematically work through differences in order to turn problems into solutions. Many working couples keep revisiting decisions they have made in the past, which results from not having done an effective and formal analysis of the issues to begin with. Each keeps forgetting what they decided and why, which leads to anger and frustration. When this happens, each retreats to a stereotyped gender role, Mr. Logic versus Ms. Emotional, throwing around epithets and blaming or accusing the other of not understanding.

Learn to use the strengths of each partner to build a high-quality relationship. That way, everyone will win. The power of partnerships is in focusing, together, on common and complementary individual goals.

Chapter 8

Making Stress Work for You

As veterans of American business who have been on the fast track of corporations as well as our own companies, and as people who know the rigors of traveling as much as 150 days of the year, we're well attuned to stressful situations. We fully understand the pressures of the real world and have been teaching stress management for professionals for twenty years.

Over these years, we have discovered that most working couples are weary and stretched to the limit. The same technology that turned us into a global society has increased the competition in our business organizations and the pace of our lives. Faxes, e-mail, overnight deliveries, twenty-four-hour customer service, banking by phone, satellite conferences, and the threat of 500 television channels vie for our constant attention. We feel as if we are drowning in a sea of junk mail. The rapid pace of changing technology will continue. The pressure never lets up to keep up, and some of us are simply giving up.

Working couples have too much to do and not enough time to do it all in. That won't change. Therefore, the single most valuable commodity for working couples is time. We all recognize this, and yet people's schedules are still too ambitious. This frantic pace affects everyone with whom we interact—parents, friends, co-workers, employers, neighbors, school system personnel, and each other. Even our children are under pressure to achieve and excel. It's a question of values.

When asked, professionals state that they are looking for self-fulfillment, but today that inner feeling of satisfaction is becoming ever more elusive. As a result, many of us feel overwhelmed and full of anxiety. Anxiety causes physical and psychological challenges that can be as disabling as a handicap and bring about a decrease in harmony and happiness. Continuous, unrelenting anxiety (too often discounted as "just stress") is what can lead to burnout.

I Work Better Under Pressure

No, you don't work better under pressure. That's a myth perpetuated by procrastinators. Simply put, stress is energy. You need some stress to keep you breathing and moving, but *pressure* is negative stress and that consumes energy. Stress can be stimulating, or it can be a killer. A stressor (force causing stress) may have a positive or negative impact on you. Whether or not your optimal level of stress will turn into dis-stress depends on the rate of wear and tear on your body. Doing too much for too long quite literally wears you out.

Stress is energy.

Since stress is really energy, it will help if you visualize yourself as an inflated balloon full of energy. Every time you solve a problem, handle a frustration, talk to a colleague, interact with your partner, go on a vacation, or make a significant purchase, you are letting air out of your balloon. When the balloon is empty, it is empty. You can try to infuse it with someone else's energy, stretch it, punch it, and generally abuse it in a variety of ways, but it will remain flat, empty, and useless. The only way to pump up the balloon is to refill it with positive energy. It is considerably more effective, and rewarding, if you keep your balloon from deflating in the first place. The way we refill it is different for each of us.

Determining the impact particular stressors or stressful situations have on you depends on three factors:

1. How long the stress lasts
2. The intensity of the stress
3. How you are able to deal with the stress

Each of us has a unique ability to handle stress. The objective in managing stress is to stay within your capacity to cope—to have neither too much nor too little for you. Few people actually understand this concept. The misconception is that when people are "stressed out" they need to "stress under." Structuring your life in such a way that there is too little stress (need for energy) will be boring. Bored people also burn out. That's why we advise that if you have a monotonous, uneventful, routine job, you structure into your personal life more variety, excitement, and challenge. On the other hand, if you have a fast-paced, active job, attempt to plan your personal life so that it contains more structure and quiet time.

Today, most of our stressors are emotional. Unlike our ancestors, we don't have to worry about a carnivorous dinosaur craving our body. But we *do* have to consider gun-toting kids and crack-crazy criminals. A negative stressor is a negative stressor. When we allow negative stress to accumulate, we are piling on extra loads for which many of us were not designed. Visualize the balancing of stress as a weight-lifting bar onto which you add weights. Each of us is physically, emotionally, and psychologically equipped to handle our own weight limits. It is when we start piling on more weight that the bar becomes too heavy to handle and we can no longer lift the load. As mentioned in Chapter 7, there are racehorses and there are turtles. In our rapidly changing environment, we are all expected to be racehorses so we try to adapt to extra weight and we *can* for a while. It's carrying too much for too long that leads to burnout.

Burnout is characterized by frustration at having to solve the same problems day by day, make the same decisions year after year, or resolve the same conflicts again and again. It happens to people who view their efforts as running on a treadmill; they are spinning nowhere but around in a continuous circle that sets them once again to spinning. They see that they can give a project their all, or nothing at all, and it won't make any difference, so long as it just gets done. They feel no one will notice or care. They no longer perceive their lives or their jobs as meaningful or challenging. Judith M. Bardwick, author of *The Plateauing Trap*, refers to this as life plateauing. One man put it this way: "The hunt is over, the mountain climbed, and the mate captured. So what now? Is this it? Is this what life is all about? Just more of the same?"

Burnout victims aren't merely talking about the details of the home or job, but about the boredom inherent in the ongoing problem-solving process, "Should we buy a foreign car or an American? A blue couch or a beige? Should I accept the relocation with more money, same responsibilities, or stay where I am and still do the same thing?" They just give up internally, becoming disillusioned over their careers and their relationships. Frequently, their expectations have been too high. Too often, people spend enormous amounts of time and energy in achieving their career goals while neglecting their family and friends. When success isn't as meaningful as they had expected it to be, they are left with a feeling of emptiness and burnout. We hear, "I got what I wanted, but it wasn't what I expected!"

If your life is full of annoying little details, missed deadlines, interruptions, sleepless nights, incomplete projects, neglected family and friends, broken promises, and unfulfilled dreams, you are not enjoying your life. It doesn't have to be that way. By identifying the causes of your stress, getting organized, learning to make effective decisions, and prioritizing your work load, you can run your life instead of letting your life run you.

Identifying the Stressors in Your Life

It's a smart idea to conserve your available energy for the truly important things in your life. Unfortunately, the hectic pace of modern business requires a continual use of your energy. Therefore, any stress management campaign needs to begin by identifying the stressors in your life.

Using the following form, identify and write down the names of people, places or situations, and events or things that cause you stress at work and in your personal life. Your purpose is not to cast blame but to determine where your energy actually goes. Particularly, consider changes in which you have been involved over the past year. Psychologists have determined that excessive change in a concentrated period of time is one of the most critical factors leading to stress overload.

Identifying Your Stressors

Stress-Inducing Agents

Personal Life	At Work

Last year was a big one for the Carters. We moved out of a beachfront condominium into a house. This required us to purchase additional furniture as well as landscaping supplies. During that time, we were in production for our new television series as well as our two radio programs. Add to all that a near deadline on a manuscript we were preparing and you have a perfect breeding ground for stress overload and eventual burnout. That's not all. Our personal life also contained a series of challenges. Our son Todd started his first career-type job right after graduation from university. This required some loving support and professional guidance, which we were delighted to provide. But, it *was* another call on our available stress-coping energy.

Also during that time Jaine's sister was rushed to the intensive care unit of a hospital in California. We hopped on a plane to fly clear across the United States, rough drafts of manuscript in hand, to provide support, arrange for long-term health care, and give financial assistance. In the middle of all this was the wonderful opportunity to visit with son Paul Stewart, who had just gotten back from a four-year stint on Okinawa, Japan. We were delighted to visit with him, but would rather have been able to give him 100 percent of our attention.

By Christmas, we knew we were both bordering on burnout. We simply had no energy left. We still had a publishing deadline to meet but wisely decided that without energy we would never succeed. We rearranged our travel schedules, turned off the phones, and told friends, relatives, and associates that we would be unavailable during the week between Christmas and New Year's Day. We actually stayed in beautiful Naples, Florida, where hundreds of thousands of people visit each year to relax. We like it here. It's our favorite place and it's home. Our balloons are now full again and we are ready to press on with excitement and enthusiasm.

Distinguishing Internal Stressors From External Stressors

After you have identified the stressors in your life, both at home and at work, go through them to determine those over which you have control. These are referred to as internal stressors. Too often, we think we have less control than we do. The things over which we have no control are referred to as external stressors. For example, you *can't* control increased traffic in your area. You *can* control what time you leave in the morning. Leave a little earlier to allow yourself more time to get to work and eliminate the stress of rushing and the anxiety of possibly annoying your boss by being late. You *can't* control the fact that you have significant others who need attention. You *can* control when and how you give that attention.

Now, go back over the stressors you have identified as within your power. How many of these can you actually eliminate or postpone? Do you really need to have a bigger house or a newer car right now? Can you put off major purchases, moves, and other events until you have more time and energy? Don't let other people pull your strings and get you involved in projects that drain you rather than fulfill you.

> *Go back over the stressors you have identified as within your power. How many of these can you actually eliminate or postpone?*

Getting Rid of the Dog and Eliminating Annoying Stressors

The Carters had always had a dog. Doesn't everyone? Aren't dogs a good way to teach children responsibility? It sounds good. In reality, it's the grownups who take care of the dog. You can nag the children just so long before Spot piddles on the living room carpet. After a few piddles by Spot, and tears from Mom, Dad finally agrees to walk the dog. But who feeds it and bathes it and takes it to the veterinarian? How does the time you actually spend on the animals in your life compare with the joy they give you?

Of course, you can't actually get rid of the dog because it's a living thing and everyone loves it. Or can you? The last Carter dog had a habit of running away every chance he got. The last time he ran away, Jaine was up for two nights straight. Of course, she still had to go to work and manage all the other necessary activities. After two days, the animal shelter called to report that it had a little black poodle with a broken hip. We went running down to the shelter to discover that our beloved dog had been hit by a car. One thousand dollars later, our little black poodle was patched up, but he was never the same again and neither were we. We finally faced the reality that the Carters could not manage the additional responsibilities of another living thing. We put an ad in the paper for a loving family to adopt our dog. Jaine interviewed thirteen couples, checked references, and finally allowed our dog to be adopted.

It changed our lives. We are now free to stay out after work without worrying about running home to the dog. We can go a whole week with nothing in the refrigerator but milk and cereal without having to go out for dog food. We don't have to worry about fleas on the dog or on us. And we are still free to enjoy all the dogs in the neighborhood. Every so often one of us will decide that it is time for us to get a new dog. When that happens, we *help* each other by reminding ourselves that our lifestyle is not conducive to a dog.

Of course, the dog is only a symbol for this concept, which is to let go. Truly let go of any person, place, thing, or activity that is not allowing you to enjoy life while pursuing your goals, this year. Nothing is forever. If you change your mind when you are under less stress, you can always resume the activity or the relationship.

> *Truly let go of any person, place, thing, or activity that is not allowing you to enjoy life while pursuing your goals, this year.*

Preventing Brownout, Meltdown, and Burnout

Unless there is some physiological reason, people don't suddenly wake up one day to find themselves in a state of burnout. There are stages of which you need to be aware. It is highly unusual for isolated instances of heavy stress load to cause you long-term trouble. You can gear up for an annual inventory, which takes additional time and effort, with the knowledge that you will be able to rest up and get back in shape at the end of the increased load. Burnout is a gradual process and there are warning signs. At first, there is increased fatigue. After a physical checkup that indicates nothing is physically wrong with you, recognize that you may be in the first stages of stress overload, or brownout. If you do nothing about the situation, you will eventually begin to melt down and burn out. There is a life after burnout, but it is never the same life. Most of us who have experienced burnout find that we can still produce at optimum levels and be as creative as we ever were, if we are intelligently aware of our limitations. Awareness is the key.

How do you know when you are under or over your optimum level of stress? Here are some red flags to watch for. Check the ones that apply to you.

- You feel pushed all the time. There is never enough time and always too much to do.
- You feel overwhelmed, as if you'll never catch up. Every paper, person, or assignment seems to be screaming, "Handle me first!"
- You feel you are losing control. (Remember Todd's spinning ball analogy in Chapter 5.)
- You have a vague or pronounced sense of boredom, hopelessness, and loss of purpose.
- You notice you are more critical of others. You keep thinking, "If

only other people would do what *they're* supposed to do, *I'd* be okay."
- You have frequent headaches, backaches, colds or allergies, and/ or intestinal disorders.
- You have trouble sleeping. Either you can't fall asleep or you keep waking up and cannot fall back to sleep.
- You have an uneasy sense of free-floating anxiety, increased anger, and/or depression.
- You are beginning to isolate yourself more and have a real desire to run away.
- You are avoiding other people and withdrawing from peers, family, or friends.
- You have increased your consumption of mood-altering drugs, including alcohol, nicotine, caffeine, sweets, or other foods.
- Your personal habits have begun to change. You skip brushing your teeth or neglect other hygienic routines, or let the house and yard degenerate.
- Your clothes feel tight even though you have not gained weight.

Stress Signs at Work

- You experience increased conflicts with co-workers or supervisors.
- You feel overwhelmed and underappreciated.
- You make more mistakes.
- You are absent more often owing to increased illness.
- You feel more hostility and frustration and have that feeling of impending doom.

If three or more of the warning signs listed here pertain to you, it's time for you to take constructive action to get control of the stress in your life. You and your partner can help each other assess your situation and then strategize ways to reduce the stress in your lives.

Managing stress has a great deal to do with your attitude toward life changes. Research shows that people with Type A behavioral patterns tend to be in a chronic struggle with their environment. They are hard-driving overachievers obsessed with a sense of the urgency of time. They are generally poliphasic and have many balls in the air at the same time, all the time. They have a general feeling of free-floating hostility toward other people and sincerely believe that if other people would stop screwing up, their lives would be easier. They are workaholics in the true sense of the word because they are always working.

Type B people, by contrast, strive for a balanced interplay with their environment. They have a rational approach to achievement, meaning that they get done what they can get done. They tend to be more relaxed than Type A people and work hard to develop positive interpersonal relationships. They have a general attitude of acceptance about things that they can't change and strive for a balance between work and other life events.

Some feel that perfect people would exhibit Type A behavior in their work and Type B behavior in their personal lives and with significant others. Unfortunately, this is a difficult objective, but progress can be made toward modifying one's battle with life's events. Getting organized and learning how to manage your time is the greatest gift you can give to the partnership.

One of These Days We Are Going to Get Organized!

Where does all your time go? You probably have only a vague idea. All you know is that today it's Friday and yesterday was Monday. It's impossible to manage your time until you make an accurate assessment of exactly where all your precious hours go now. We have a personal philosophy toward managing time. We are thoroughly convinced that the greatest time waster of all is not having what you need, when you need it, where you need it. The equipment or appliances don't function properly, you can't find the service contract, the phone number has been lost, the boss mislaid the report, the file is not in the right place, the check was lost in the mail, and heaven only knows where the car keys went. The list is endless. If you are organized, you won't have to look for everything, which saves time and reduces stress.

Therefore, the single most important key to managing your time is getting, and staying, organized. The single most important thing you can do for your partner is getting and helping him/her to stay organized. Yes, getting organized itself takes time. Trust us, that time spent will pay for itself every day of your life. It will also save you frustration, stress, criticism for being late all the time, and complaints from clients, co-workers, and significant others. The following are some practical techniques for organizing your life and work.

Organizing Strategies

Some people have a negative attitude toward getting organized. They hate the concept. The word *organization* seems to imply that they will turn into robots, moving from activity to activity in a preplanned manner, carrying out tasks and obligations with no feeling or emotion. Nothing is further from the truth. The people who seem to fear organization the most are those with right brain dominance. These fast-paced, creative types tend to believe that if they were to take the time to get organized, they would thereby limit their creativity. Organization does not limit creativity; it frees you to *be* creative. Everyone benefits from a more structured and organized environment that leaves them free to do the unstructured and creative activities they prefer. This is as valuable in the working environment as it is in your personal life.

There are certain styles of disorganization, and disorganized people are always apologizing for being disorganized. One of the reasons people continue to be disorganized is to avoid confronting the issue of whether they can actually get and stay organized. "I can't organize myself because he controls me and leaves our room a mess" is one excuse. Or, "They make my schedule at work and won't keep the place organized; so what can I do?"

You do have control over your life and your space, and you are probably already organized in some areas of your life. Analyze those areas and look for your organizing strengths. List the areas in your life in which you are organized. What we are after is a model of organization in your life from which you can build. For example, some people are organized at work, but their home life is a mess. Other times, people have a very organized home, but their car is a disaster area. If you are still balking at the idea of getting organized, you need to determine what the payoff is for you to stay disorganized.

The job of getting organized can be made more fun if you partner this project. Working together can help you create a system that is beneficial to both of you. This does not necessarily mean that you will be holding hands while organizing a particular desk, kitchen, or closet. It does mean that you jointly decide upon an intersection point for each necessary activity for which you develop a system. In other words, if getting dressed in the morning always creates a crisis, determine together which is the best possible place to put toiletries, underwear, towels, and the like. If you are fortunate enough to have two bathrooms, organize your bathrooms as each of you sees fit. This is your private territory and you should be allowed to do things your way. Then think about where the closet or clothes storage area is located. It is inefficient, for example, if his clothes are in the master bedroom when his bathroom is clear across the apartment or house. That will mean that each day he has to hop in the shower, shave, then run across the house to get his clothes, put them on, then run back to the bathroom to comb his hair, and so on.

The opportunity to get disorganized is even greater when he doesn't remember where he left his spare change or car keys. Are they in the master bedroom in his closet or in the bathroom where he gets ready in the morning? We have found that keys present a very special problem of organization, and a very special system of intersection should be designed—for example, a hook by the front door.

Keep it simple and don't be afraid to reorganize something that you have previously organized in the past.

> When we moved into our new house, we quickly put away the dishes and silverware. After all, we had to eat. However, within a few days we realized that the cabinet we had chosen for the dishes was inconveniently distant from the place where we had put the table. It necessitated walking clear across the kitchen to get a plate, then walking around the counter to put the plate on the table. This took time and energy. At the end of the day, all we wanted to do was eat and get the task over with. So we changed the system. We took the time to trace our traffic pattern. For us, it was more convenient to store cookware under the stove, next to the oven. We placed the dishes next to an eating counter, but close to the dishwasher. This made it easier to set the table and to load the dishwasher. Now it takes only a few steps to accomplish the whole procedure of cooking, eating, and cleaning up.

All our systems are organized against one command station. This station, or reference point, is a single notebook. We each have our own and can be creative about the way we put it together. It goes everywhere with us. Family members or friends could call us when we are 3,000 miles away and we would be able to explain where they could find a particular item. Perhaps not the actual item itself, but where they could go, in what area, and even in what drawer, they could begin their search. Here's how it works.

Use a single notebook for everything—notes to yourself, receipts, phone numbers, mission statement, goal lists, to-do lists, spare key, everything! We don't care what kind of notebook you use. It can be one of the fancy Daytimers you can purchase at any office supply store, a student composition notebook, a secretarial steno pad, or any number of creative one-book systems. The important thing is that you write everything down in this book. It helps if this book also has a flap or two so that you can stuff in receipts and other necessary data such as business cards, laundry checks, coupons, and every other darn thing that you may need while away from home or office. But it doesn't matter so long as this notebook works for you. Jaine tried six different sizes of Daytimers until she found the one she would actually use, instead of leaving it in her office desk drawer.

Start your organizing activities according to their aggravation value. Divide up any complex problems into manageable segments. Then alone, and together, analyze the existing systems in your life and agree on what works and what doesn't.

> Keys were always a problem in our life. Children lost them, as children will. We will never forget the time we groveled around in the Chicago snow trying to find the one car key we had taken off its regular key chain so that our son Paul could deliver it to a neighbor. He dropped it, and was devastated as we all nearly froze to death trying to locate the lost key. We probably contributed to his feeling bad, for we had not yet learned to communicate the concept of divorcing the situation from the person. Of course, we were not angry with *him;* we were angry with ourselves for being so stupid as to take the key off the ring in the first place.
>
> We wish we could say that we never again took keys off rings, but we can't. We still do it for such reasons as not wanting to carry the whole clump stuffed into a small evening bag or tux pocket. And, of course, we continue to forget to put the key back on the ring until we find ourselves outside the house with a bunch of keys but no house key. However, there is a difference now. We have planted keys in various locations so that we are never locked out. There is always a spare key. We have a system.

Analyze your systems. Then carry out actions in a location that intersects with the system designed to deal with those actions. Bring instinctive preference and practicality together. Work out your territory before instituting a personal organizing system. Then organize one thing at a time. Create one system at a time and teach everyone the system. Postpone organizing further trouble spots until after you have established a system for the most frustrating organizing activity in your life. If invention runs dry, execute the less than perfect solution. A more satisfactory answer will generally come to you in time.

Another good organizing idea is to set up a paperwork system so that you'll know where to find things. Establish a desk or work area and purchase basic supplies. Get what you really need; don't try to make do. When things begin to look neat and organized, you will feel more motivated to continue the process. Gather all papers from all over your living space, depending on which area you are involved in, and bring them to

the desk or work area. Put all these papers in one carton. Use more car-
tons if you need them.

Schedule regular appointments with yourself to go through the papers and allocate the boxes to the following purposes: (1) trash; (2) financial materials; (3) things to do; (4) to be filed; (5) co-workers; and (6)
significant others. Schedule a sorting procedure appointment for yourself
and don't break the appointment or the task will never get done. Don't
work too long at this sorting process at any one time or you will become
demotivated and feel that you are losing ground. Use the following sorting, things-to-do, and filing procedures to empty boxes 2 through 5.
Throw out box 1.

Start with the most important box. Divide this box into two piles: (1)
"of interest" and (2) "not of interest." Throw away the "not of interest"
pile. Don't leave it lying around. It will only come back to haunt you and
end up in another box. Divide the remaining "of interest" pile into (1) a
reference pile, (2) a "to-do" file folder, and (3) an "action pile." Then
divide the "action pile" into (1) co-workers or significant others, and (2)
things you must do.

Now it's time to start your filing procedure:

1. Gather all materials to be filed in one location.
2. Have supplies ready: a wastepaper basket, file folders, labels,
   pens.
3. Now begin the decision-making process. Decide whether the
   item on the top of the pile has value. If it doesn't, throw it away.
   If it does, go on to the next step.
4. Decide what it is about and choose a folder heading. Caution!
   Decide. Don't put it aside until you come up with a creative title.
   Piles always indicate delayed decisions. You'll have to make that
   decision some time. Make it now.
5. Label the folder and put the paper in it.
6. Repeat steps 3, 4, and 5 with the next item. Consolidate under
   existing headings whenever possible.
7. Stop filing for the day when your mind begins to blur.
8. When you are ready to put the files away, put folders into the file
   drawer in *strict* alphabetical order.
9. Put the remaining material to be filed into a box or boxes and
   store them near the filing cabinet until your next filing appointment with yourself.
10. To maintain order once a file is started, each time you consult it,
    quickly go through it and remove any obsolete material like let-
    ters that have been answered, reference material that is outdated,
    and so on.

Being a polyphasic, Type A, results-oriented individual, Jaine finds it hard to stop working at a project when she is tired. In the past, her way of organizing was to gather in one giant heap everything from every shelf, every drawer, and every suitcase and cranny. Then she would discipline herself to plow through the whole mess at one time. Of course she would get tired and frustrated halfway through the task and find herself putting the same old stuff back in the same old places. This is self-defeating behavior. It is far more efficient to set aside a specific time every day and do the job in manageable segments. For example, for a half hour every day, get as much done as you can creatively accomplish and then stop. The job will get done, but at far less cost.

How did you come by all that paper you just sorted? Our research indicates that paper clutter is one of the major problems facing us in this age of technology, as most people still save all the hard copies. We are smothered in paper. One participant told us, "I have nightmares about all the paper I have to wade through!" What can you do? Put your creative juices to work, for starters. Once you have organized your existing paper, watch for and study what kind of paper creates your clutter. Is it daily junk mail? Is it the fact that you are on every routing list and feel obliged to read the "for your information" stacks that accumulate on your desk? What about magazines? How many do you get?

Once you get an accurate picture of where all your paper is coming from, look for ways to eliminate it. Deal with it immediately, as soon as it enters the house. Get off mailing lists, cancel subscriptions, and subscribe to only one newspaper or weekly news magazine. Here are two things you can do to get off mailing lists:

1. Call or write the sender directly and request that your name and address be removed from future mailings.
2. Call the Direct Marketing Association in New York City and request that your name be removed from all undesired lists. Call (212) 768-7277. It's best to follow up your request in writing.

Now you are organized.

Preventing Burnout

Here are more suggestions on how to keep from burning out:

- *Avoid setting up win/lose situations with others.* Deal with tangible facts. Go directly to the problem and avoid being drawn into personal arguments having to do with values or value systems. You can't change the way a person feels about something.

One of the best stress stories we ever heard concerned the wise old American Indian. It is said that a young newspaper reporter went to interview a 100-year-old American Indian. The news reporter asked him: "To what do you attribute your longevity?" The wise old Indian responded, "I never argue with anyone." The young reporter excitedly retorted, "Surely, that is not the only reason! There must be some other reason why you have lived a hundred years!" The Indian paused, thought a moment and then responded, "Perhaps you're right. Perhaps you're right." If you have a choice between being kind or being right, choose to be kind. Once you give up trying to change other people and accept them as they are, you will find less conflict in your life, and that's worth everything.

If you have a choice between being kind or being right, choose to be kind.

- *Carefully study the informal systems of behavior within your business organization.* Know the hierarchy and the unwritten rules and games that affect personal relationships and influence promotions and decision making. Follow these unwritten rules and games or look for another job. You cannot change the organization.
- *Keep your relationships at work on a professional level.* Avoid falling into the trap of becoming overly intimate or familiar with either male or female co-workers. Emphasize your competence rather than your personality.
- *Stop trying to remember everything.* It is said that Einstein never tried to remember anything he could find somewhere else, including his own phone number. Write things down and make notes to yourself. Of course, keep these notes in your organizing book.
- *Get the facts, then be objective.* Don't take things personally. People are more concerned with the outcome than with the people involved in the outcome. Help people get what they really want and they will be happy. Schedule time for the people and activities that are most important to you.
- *Allow more time than you think you'll need to get anywhere.* It always takes longer than you think it will.

- *Be prepared to wait for everything.*
- *Break up routines occasionally.* Really do this. It makes the day fly.
- *Get a telephone answering machine and don't answer the phone at home unless you must.* The phone company has a ring-through system that will provide you with a special number to give to your partner and children in case of an emergency. Don't start giving it out to everyone.
- *Develop and utilize assertive communication techniques.* Ask for what you want and need. You have a perfect right.
- *Practice saying no.* A great way to say no is just to say it. "No. I wish I could help you out, but I can't." Don't wait to give your negative; it may build false hope.
- *Ask for and get feedback.* If something is bothering you, don't stew about it. Go directly to the source of your worries and ask for clarification. Then resolve the issue immediately. The unknown is a major source of distress.
- *Practice listening, really listening, to others.* This is what quality time is all about. It is the greatest validation of their worth you can give to people.
- *Take care of your health, and your significant other's.* Caring is not enabling.
- *Get enough sleep every night.* Sleep needs vary from person to person, so test your requirements. When you really feel awake and energized upon waking, you have had enough sleep.
- *Make the time to relax every day.* This is not as easy as it sounds. What relaxes one person may not relax another. Investigate until you find your thing.

Summary

The high cost of high achievement may be burnout, unhappiness, broken people, and disconnected relationships. Ask yourself:

- What do I really want out of life?
- What must I do to get it?
- What are my options?

There are several conditions necessary for a less stressful, more meaningful life. Make a sincere commitment to the belief that quality is more important than quantity. Learn not to confuse the quality of your life with your standard of living. Reassess your lifestyle to determine whether one quality automobile will serve your needs as well as an entire fleet. Do you really have to have two vacation homes? Do you need one at all? Many have found that renting is wiser because it takes less of your physical and financial resources, which reduces anxiety. Less anxiety results in more quality time to enjoy life while pursuing your goals, thereby reducing anxiety still further.

Problem-solving skills can of course help to reduce stress. Here are a few tips on how to spread them around.

- Provide new problem-solving skills for everyone involved in your organization, family, or social structure. A commitment to improving quality without the means to bring about improvement will be of little value to you or anyone else. If you are to solve problems, you must have the skills to solve them (consult Chapter 7).
- Build in rewards for successful problem solving. Whenever you are able to work smarter, not harder, reward yourself by truly relaxing or turning on to any activity that will give you a change of pace.
- If you find yourself having to make the same decisions or solve the same problems over and over, something is wrong with your system. Look into the causes. What happens just before this problem occurs? How could it have been prevented? Who needs to be involved in the solution?
- Hold people accountable. Give others ownership by letting them experience the negative and positive consequences of their behavior. Stop attempting to be the magic rescuer. Remember, if you always do what you've always done, you'll always get what you've always gotten. If you don't like the outcome you are getting, try something different.

If you always do what you've always done, you'll always get what you've always gotten. If you don't like the outcome you are getting, try something different.

When employer policies are implemented and organizations change their attitudes toward work/family issues, will there be less stress? Perhaps. But the paradigm must shift in all areas of human interaction. Employer attitudes are not the only influence on what happens to you. Coworkers, friends, and family have a major influence on stress levels as they relate to lifestyle choices for working couples. You must learn how to overcome resistance from others who may not approve of your lfiestyle choices. This resistance can come from anywhere, at any time, and from anyone with whom you associate. Chapter 9 will help you deal with resistance from others.

Chapter 9

They Work: Gaining the Support You Need

It's natural for people to disagree, but when disagreeing becomes disagreeable, there is a problem. When that happens, you need to investigate the barriers that are negatively affecting the relationship. Why do people disagree? Can you successfully manage disagreement? Sure you can. Not all of the time, of course, but you can certainly raise your percentage of wins.

How to Handle Disagreement

Some people disagree as a way of calling attention to themselves. They have a strong need to control their environment and feel that "going against the grain" gives them power. Others disagree because they feel threatened by any potential change in the status quo. These people feel powerless in a rapidly changing environment and want to put off decisions that may bring about even more change. Others disagree because of a sincere belief that their values and value judgments are right.

Most people tend to think of disagreement, of opinions that differ from their own, as a form of criticism of themselves. This causes them to engage in defensive behavior, which, in turn, triggers defensive behavior on the part of the other person. This can turn into what has been referred to as a "trained seal act." You throw an insult at me, then I throw one at you. Back and forth you go, trying to hurt the other person as much as he or she is hurting you. We have observed people bringing up events that happened ten years ago to support their opinions and prove that the other person is always disagreeable, hostile, inadequate, or manipulative.

Staying Out of Defensive Styles

Most people have a favorite defensive strategy. When confronted with conflict (and disagreement *does* cause internal conflict), they resort to their tried-and-true defensive mechanisms. These become habitual behaviors because they work. They used a particular kind of behavior when they were young and people reacted in a particular way. They liked what happened. It yielded the kind of results they wanted, so they tried that behavior, purposely, the next time they wanted the same outcome. Robert Bramson, in his book *Coping with Difficult People,* has identified four styles of defensive behavior: (1) blame others/fight; (2) distract/make nice; (3) blame self/give in; and (4) clam up/withdraw.

Blame Others/Fight

People who favor the Blame Others/Fight *style* appear to think they are personally perfect. We believe that these people are actually egomaniacs, with an inferiority complex. Nothing is ever their fault. If it weren't for the rest of the world, they could accomplish more things in a shorter amount of time and always do them right. They come across as hostile-aggressives and operate by putting everyone else on the defensive. Their manner is usually short, direct, and to the point.

> Alex is slamming doors from room to room as he swears, "Where are my keys? You always move my stuff! Why can't you just leave my things alone!!?" Maria is distressed, feels guilty, and wonders if she really did move the keys. "I didn't move them. Did you check the hook?" "Yes, I checked the hook!" Alex mimics her unflatteringly. "Damn it! Now, I'll be late." "Don't get so upset," replies Maria. "You go through this every morning. Why don't you learn to put things in their proper place?"

Now they are both angry, blaming each other and fighting. It's the trained seal act. When we operate from a defensive position, we put others on the offensive. The only recourse is for them to rebound and attack.

Distract/Make Nice

Most people cannot handle conflict at all. It goes against their nature. They crave peace even if it means that the conflict is *never* resolved. These people figure that if they can just get you to laugh or turn your focus somewhere else, the conflict will resolve itself. Part of their philosophy is correct. What we can laugh at, we can cope with. But distraction can turn destructive when we refuse to face our disagreements.

> Barbara, who is working two jobs in addition to being the psychological parent to two children, is tired. She is sitting and watching television after the children have been put to bed, sadly contemplating the typing she still has to finish by tomorrow. Her significant other comes to sit next to her and says, "Why do you look so sad?"
>
> Barbara replies, "I'm just so tired, Ed. I don't know how much longer I'll be able to hold down two jobs and take care of the children and the house, too." "Oh come on, pretty lady," soothes Ed. "Here, let me give you a little neck rub. There, isn't that better?" He starts to tickle her. She starts to laugh. After the laughing stops, he pats her on the shoulder and says, "I'm going to bed, hon. Got an early appointment tomorrow."
>
> Barbara is furious as she surveys the unwashed dishes in the sink. "The least he could have done was offer to do the dishes," she thinks. But how could she have asked him in the middle of her laughter? Ed may think he has resolved the conflict, but all he has done is help bury it, a little deeper, under another layer of resentment.

Blame Self/Give In

Part of the reason Barbara gives in and suppresses her justifiable anger is because she feels guilty about not being able to handle it all. She is also aware that she and Ed had agreed that it would be financially difficult while he was starting a new career after a layoff. She chastises herself for not being more understanding. "After all, he *is* trying," she reminds herself as she continues intellectually to blame herself and gives in to the situation. But she still feels tired, angry, and resentful.

Clam Up/Withdraw

A common defensive strategy of both men and women is to clam up and *not* talk at all, not even to argue.

> Bruno drags himself up the flight of stairs from the garage. It's 7:30 P.M. and he is exhausted. One of the machines broke down at work and he has been scrambling all day trying to keep up production and meet deadlines. All he wants is something quick to eat and then bed. Tomorrow promises to be even more hectic than today. He opens the door,

throws his coat on the chair, and heads for the kitchen. Louise is sitting at the kitchen table with her arms crossed.

"Hi, what's for dinner?" Bruno asks. Louise gets up, goes to the oven, and retrieves the hardened pork chops and soggy baked potato, places them on a plate, and takes it to the table. She does not say a word and her teeth are clamped together.

"I'm sorry I didn't call," says Bruno. "We had a machine go down on us and it was a hell of a day." Louise says nothing as she pours his coffee.

"Did you have a nice day?" tries Bruno. Louise says nothing as she leaves the kitchen and heads for bed. Bruno thinks to himself, "To hell with her! I'm doing the best I know how," as he chokes back his resentment.

Louise is clamming up and withdrawing as a form of control. She's playing the martyr, hoping Bruno will feel guilty and inadequate. Bruno *does* feel guilty and inadequate and resents Louise for making him feel that way. This couple is playing lose/lose.

Manage Yourself First

Learn to manage your own defensive behavior. The next time you find yourself in a disagreement or feel threatened by a criticism, analyze what you do. Each of us has special "hot buttons" or sensitive areas that, when pushed, tend to throw us out of control. Try to discover what your hot buttons are. Stop for a moment and try to identify the worst possible criticism of you that you can imagine. Perhaps you hate to be told that you are disorganized. Knowing this, be prepared to handle feedback on that subject without becoming defensive. When you know what you fear hearing, you can take constructive action instead of waiting to react.

Once aware, learn to interrupt your own defensive reactions. When you hear an unwanted criticism, stop! Don't say or do anything. Ask yourself, "Am I taking the criticism or disagreement personally? Could there be some element of truth in what the other person is saying? What is the cause of the criticism? What happened just before the criticism or disagreement? What is the other person saying or doing that annoys me?" Since the most effective thing you can do when confronted with a disagreement is to learn to control your own behavior, memorize, practice, and implement the FAA method of gaining control of your own negative emotions and begin to resolve the conflict.

Freeze, Analyze, Find Alternatives

When confronted with a criticism or disagreement, *freeze* your behavior. You know what's coming. You've been there before. We like to defend our own negative and ineffective behavior by making such excuses as, "I couldn't help myself! I just lost control!" Maybe that's the way you used to be. But wouldn't you like to be sufficiently in command of yourself to be able to control how you react? When you are about to lose your temper, just *freeze*. At first, this freezing technique will make you feel as if it's going on for hours. The actual time involved is only seconds and it will give you time to *think*.

Analyze what's going on. Ask yourself a series of questions: "Why am I feeling threatened? What's at stake here? My job? My ego? My relationship? My whole life?" Usually nothing more is at stake than that you don't like to be criticized. It's that Perfect/Worthless Syndrome rearing its head again: "If I can't be perfect, I must be worthless." While you are in the frozen state, begin to ask yourself:

- Could I be causing my partner (colleague, friend, child) to feel threatened?
- What do I really want out of this situation?
- Am I harboring hidden resentments from the past that I feel were caused by this person?
- Do I have a need to be right? Why?
- Do I want to get even? Why?
- How important is this issue, really?

Alternatives are the keys to handling disagreements. Ask yourself, "How else could I present my point of view? What's in it for my partner? What options are available to make us both look like winners? What are some workable compromises? How can I help my partner save face if I am able to change his/her mind and turn this disagreement into agreement?"

While the freezing technique takes only seconds, the next two steps may take more time. Therefore, you may have to freeze your behavior, put your mind in gear, and ask for a recess to disconnect in order to get your thoughts together. You might make a statement such as, "Look, can we agree that our objective is to fashion an agreement that is acceptable to both of us?" How could your partner disagree with that? Then suggest a time when you can get together to discuss the matter in more detail. Do your homework. Analyze the situation, develop alternatives, and present possible solutions.

Control Formula

<u>F</u>reeze
<u>A</u>nalyze
<u>A</u>lternatives

Be ready for that next meeting. Keep in mind, there are some opinions that will never be changed. That's okay. How important is it? Ask yourself, "Will I care about this disagreement three hours from now?" Pick your issues carefully or you'll wear the other person down. Most disagreements can be brought to a workable compromise for the mutual benefit of all involved. Remember to bring issues to closure. Don't keep rehashing the same gripes.

Dealing with People Who Don't Approve of Your Lifestyle

Disagreements tend to arise in a number of specific areas. Often the cause of disagreement boils down to the fact that your friends, relatives, bosses, or co-workers simply disapprove of your lifestyle choices. It's impossible to be happy or to feel fulfilled when just one element of your life is going well. You may be swinging sweet in your career, but if your marriage is falling apart, you will feel off balance. Or everything can be right on plan with your partner and your career, but your genetic family isn't talking to you, so you feel saddened. It's when everything is in balance that you feel good.

A major problem in our rapidly changing, mobile society is that couples are often isolated from their relatives and long-term friends. Too often we are relocated, either by choice or by the needs of our careers, to distant cities far from the people and places we know and love. You can communicate by phone and mail, but it isn't the same as being there to hug someone. If you have family close by, consider yourself blessed and take care to keep these support systems active and healthy.

We understand that it is sometimes difficult to get along with a bossy and overcontrolling mother-in-law or a jealous sister. Getting along with *anybody* takes vigilant awareness and effort, but parents are *there*. You can fight and fuss, but they take you back. A friend of ours once said, "Home is the only place you can go and they have to let you in." If you believed the messages coming from television and the movies, you would be forced to assume that all families are downers full of self-involved, uncaring parents who use their children. We've known a few such cases, but they are the exception, not the rule. Most parents love their children and want the best for them. That's why they are always so full of advice, suggestions, and judgmental attitudes. Patricia sums this up nicely:

"We have pressure in our commuter marriage. The pressure here is that the people around us don't understand it. Just think about the people we work with. My husband tells me, all the time, that most of the people he works with think it's bizarre that he lets his wife do whatever she wants. *He* doesn't care, but he must constantly listen to people say, 'Why doesn't your wife *move* here?' or 'Why don't you get a job there?'

"Then there's my mother-in-law, who is a very traditional home-maker. She doesn't understand why I even want to work, let alone why I want the two-career paychecks that most people need just to get by today. She figures that she struggled through on one paycheck, so everybody else should have to struggle through. Life is different today from when she grew up."

So what do you do? It's simple, ask them for help. People love to give help; it makes them feel important, as if they have influence with you. Use our **HELP** confrontation system to ask them in a structured and un-emotional way. Unfortunately, there is no way to get it over with all at once by gathering them all together. You must deal with each of your friends and family members separately, one by one. Start with your father. Ask him to hear you out, before he comments. Here's the scenario:

Confrontation System
Happening—specific events
Explain how you feel.
Left as is—consequences
Plan for change.

Happening:
"Dad, here is what's *happening*. I love you and Mom, but I also love my husband (wife). We want to please you, but we also have goals and commitments on which we have agreed. We are both working because you just can't make ends meet on one salary anymore. I'm really frustrated with the disapproval I am sensing from the family."

Explain:

> "Let me *explain* what I mean. The other day, when I mentioned I had to go out of town on business, you said . . ." [*give two or three examples*].

Left:

> "*Left* as it is, I'm afraid we may begin avoiding your visits, since they make us feel guilty and we don't want to displease you . . ." [*develop two or three negative consequences if this attitude continues*].

Plan:

> "What I'd like to do is develop a *plan* or a system for how we can lovingly accept our different lifestyles so that we can all look forward to being together."

Once all this has been said, summarize by asking for his **HELP** in arriving at a workable compromise. It also helps if you give him a hug.

Resistance usually occurs because of certain attitudes and blind spots people have. People fear what they don't understand. Strive to bring about an understanding of the reasons behind your lifestyle. It does help to take the time to explain. Think how often your parents took the time to explain things to you.

You may have to implement **HELP** several times with the same person. Be diligent. Each time s/he shows disapproval, take him/her aside, give a hug, and ask for **HELP.** Do this with each of the important people in your life, including your partner.

Requesting Their Help With Activities and Obligations

Ask in-laws to help when they come to visit. It will make them feel useful, wanted, and important.

Jaine used to try to please Mother Carter by doing everything whenever she came to visit. Mother Carter would ask, "Can I help?" Jaine would say, "No. Just sit and relax." After about three years of this, Jim explained to Jaine that she was making his mother feel excluded.

"What do you mean, '*excluded*'? I'm wearing myself out trying to be her maid. I make the bed after she sleeps in it, rush to get breakfast, take her shopping, and wash her clothes. What do you want from me?"

"Just ask her to help you make dinner," Jim suggested. "Make her feel a part of our family."

And so Jaine did. Once she started asking her to help, it was unbelievable how warm and loving everyone felt. Not only did Jaine stop feeling resentful because she was doing all the work, but Mother Carter eventually took over all the cooking, darning, cleaning up after meals, and entertaining the children. What a help she was!

Jaine began to really appreciate her mother-in-law and hated to see her go. Then, too, Mother Carter was one of a kind. She never resented helping and *never* made a negative comment about Jaine to others. If more in-laws would give up being critical and endeavor to become *real* supportive friends to their children and their partners, marriage would be a universal partnership.

His/Her Friends and Our Friends

Don't keep your partner from his or her friends and don't allow your partner to keep you from yours. Friends round out our lives. It's naive to believe that you are each going to like the same people. In fact, it's a miracle if you both like one whole couple. If you like him, she doesn't like her or vice versa.

Friend-test by looking around for people with whom you both can connect. When you truly connect, you feel more relaxed and can enjoy yourselves more. Try a couple out and if it doesn't click, look for another couple. In the meantime, each of you should keep your own friends and enjoy their company even if you have to schedule lunches or exercise excursions together. Then stop being jealous of each other's friends. S/he does not like them more than s/he loves you. S/he likes and loves them in different ways. Friends fill a separate space in our lives. They round us out and make us whole.

Taking Sides

A classic partnership dilemma is the issue of taking sides. When you are in a conflict situation, it is natural to look for support. When you do this, you are creating the classic double-bind dilemma for your friends and relatives. If they agree with you, out of love and loyalty, you are bound to flaunt this to your partner during a disagreement and s/he will never feel comfortable around these people again. On the other hand, if they agree with him/her, you will feel that you are being ganged up on. So, what should friends and relatives do to ensure that you both still value them at the end of a disagreement? They should *not* butt in. Assure them that when you complain about your partner you are not looking for advice—you are merely looking for a shoulder to cry on. Give them permission to say, "I love and value you and trust that you will eventually work this out with your partner. I will still love and value you, no matter what the outcome." That said, they should stay out of it.

Overcoming Resistance to Change

Researchers have concluded that resistance can be overcome by getting the people involved to participate in problem-solving activities. Participation cannot be conjured up or created artificially. It is a *feeling* on the part of people, not just the mechanical act of being called in to take part in discussions. People become resistant when they feel they are being asked to compromise their values. Tune into these values. They also become resistant when they feel you are being unreasonable, unfair, or authoritarian. Strive sincerely to value your friends' and relatives' unique contributions to your life.

Mending Fences and Building Bridges

We think that the trend toward blaming parents and breaking family ties is coming to an end. At least we hope so. You need all the support systems you can get. Of course, if your or your partner's parents are truly abusive, then you are wise to stay away from them. Media stories aside, most parents never mean to hurt us. They do the best they know how. If they could do better, they would. Remember that when your children are grown, and the phone doesn't ring nearly enough.

It is normal for families to go through trials and tribulations, have arguments, swear that they will never talk to one another again, and then make up. It's also true that older people tend to get on younger people's nerves, at least once in awhile. We see it with our own children, and we are pretty with-it people. One of our sons will call home, ostensibly to ask for advice about a career move or strategy, or to run an idea past us. Sometimes we fall into the trap of treating him as we would treat participants in our classes who have paid money and *want* advice. Our sons don't. They want our support. They want us to listen and to approve of the moves they have already decided to make. We used to worry about this because we know we could save them a lot of heartache and expense. Our parents felt the same way about us. They wanted to save us from the trauma of experience, but we didn't listen to them either. We had to go through the heartache, the pain, and the expense. Perhaps we are all slow learners or perhaps a lesson is not an experience until you try it out. Give parents, yours and your partner's, a chance. Here's how:

- *Deal with the issues that may be interfering with your relationship with them.*

• *Pay them back for what you have borrowed.* Too often we borrow from our parents and then act as if they can wait indefinitely for the return of their money. Even if they appear wealthy to you, they are probably trying to stay afloat, just as you are. If you are not in a position to pay them back, discuss a payment schedule that is acceptable to all.

• *Appreciate their individuality.* They are unique human beings and have their own fears and problems, lost opportunities and regrets. After Jim's mother died, we found a book of poems she had written. They were quite good, but we never even knew she was a writer. Jaine's father also wrote but hid his writing in the bottom drawer of his filing cabinet. Where on earth did he ever find the time to write? These poems and letters reveal the loneliness of unfulfilled dreams and the longing for . . . something.

Loving Your Parents
Accept them as they are. And always keep in mind that inside their aging bodies is the heart of a sixteen-year-old being held captive, longing for release.

• *Accept them as they are.* And always keep in mind that inside their aging bodies is the heart of a sixteen-year-old being held captive, longing for release.

• *Forgive them.* Clear up past arguments and resentments. Apologize for your role in misunderstandings and be prepared for them to act as if it was all your fault. Most of our parents don't read books like this, so you may have to play the adult in these instances. What difference does it make? Will it matter three years from now?

• *Listen to their advice and experience.* You may actually learn something. Sure, things have changed, life isn't as it used to be, but people are pretty much the same. We still want love, understanding, acceptance, and warm fuzzies. Remember the old bumper sticker that read, "Have you hugged your child today?" Well, go ahead and hug your child, then let your parents hug their child. It will make you both feel good.

• *Keep in mind that your partner's parents want to accept you and be accepted by you.* Let them. It will make everyone's life easier. Don't keep your partner from his/her parents. If you determine that you simply cannot visit with them as often as they would like, then suggest s/he go alone occasionally, but don't make phony excuses to them. Call them and say, "Hi, folks, I can't make it today. This is your chance to spend time alone with your favorite child." They will love this opportunity so long as they know you are not angry with or avoiding them.

• *Work out an arrangement for holidays.* Develop equitable trade-offs like one holiday with his family and the next with hers. The little three-day holidays don't count. They are for you and your family. All of us need those long weekends to catch up on our own lives. Just divvy up the big ones.

Children Need a Sense of Family

All of the above goes double for children. If this is the second time around for either of you, keep these cardinal rules in your heart and mind forever:

- Don't keep your partner from his or her children by a previous marriage!
- Don't force your partner to choose between you and his/her children. Even if you can't stand your partner's children, they are still his/her children. Make space and time for them. These children would probably prefer being alone with their parent, so allow this. They will not convince your partner that you are an offense to humankind and cause him/her to leave you. They may even learn to like you, if you give them time.
- Don't force the children to call you Mommy or Daddy. If they want to, let them, but don't consider it an affront if they want to reserve that endearment for their genetic parent.
- It is best to allow the genetic parent to administer discipline. Agree on the boundaries and then ask for your partner's support and commitment to help you maintain them.
- Don't be harder on your stepchildren than you are on your own children. It is sometimes difficult to recognize that you just don't feel toward them what you feel toward your own.
- Remember, they are human beings. They are not perfect and they are afraid. Make a place inside your heart for them.
- Don't try to fake it. Kids have an intuitive "knower" that can sense faking. If you can't find love for them, work on liking or respect or acceptance. The best gift you can give them is acceptance.
- Don't let them manipulate you. Treat them as you would your own children with regard to manipulation.

What About "Our" Children?

Issues centering on children are the most important challenges confronting working couples today. Having children has always been the major

challenge. As a result, many working partners have chosen to put off having children or not to have them at all. This is not a decision to take
lightly. Combining work and children is a large and difficult responsibility and a lifelong obligation.

If you already have children, consider taking a parent effectiveness
training course. It will help you to understand what is happening to children today. You need to ask yourself some serious questions:

1. Whose values do you want your children to grow up with?
2. Whose values are they growing up with?
3. How do they spend their time during the day? What do they do?
   If they are watching television all day, what are they watching?
4. Is what they are watching what you would like to have them *do*
   with their lives? (Children learn not from what we say but from
   what they see *done*.)
5. With whom do they spend time after school?

Children take a lot of time, and need constant and consistent attention. Leaving them alone after school is not a solution. Find another alternative. Howard D. Chilcoat, a researcher in the Department of Psychiatry
at Detroit's Henry Ford Hospital, tracked nine hundred third and fourth
graders in Baltimore. After two years, Chilcoat concluded that children
whose parents are home or reachable after school are less likely to try
tobacco, alcohol, or drugs. Parents who make an effort to know where
their children are and what they're doing can prevent their children from
starting drug use. Enforcing curfews was one of the most effective efforts.
Don't be afraid to search their rooms for drugs and other harmful sub-
stances and then make the necessary interventions. Do not allow them to
manipulate you when they ask, "Don't you trust me?" It is not a matter
of trust. It is a matter of love. Children, even though they object, want to
be monitored. It shows them that you care.

Do not take out your frustrations on your children (or anyone else's,
for that matter). They are doing the best they know how. Unconditional
love, however, is not the same as unconditional acceptance. When their
behavior is not up to your standards, think and act, "I love you just the
way you are. It's your *behavior* that is unacceptable."

Recently, Naples, Florida, had a proposition on the ballot for a one-cent
tax to be used to upgrade the city's children's services. As we went
around campaigning for its approval, we heard again and again, "I already raised my children. Children are no longer my responsibility."
That attitude saddens us. How will these retired people feel when a

teenager knocks them down and steals their wallet? Sure, it *should* be the parents' responsibility to teach their kids the difference between right and wrong, but ultimately children are the responsibility of all of us. Save the children and you make a better future for yourself.

> *Save the children and you make a better future for yourself.*

Sticking to Limits and Setting Boundaries

When you wear the cloak of guilt, it is easy to be manipulated by others. But parents do a lot of manipulating themselves. Sometimes manipulation is the only way parents know to manage children. The ultimate manipulation is conditional love and approval: "If you are good, I will love you. If you are not, I won't." Perhaps parents don't come right out and say these words, but children feel them. Manipulation is real. It's the way many relationships survive. Some manipulations are so common and acceptable that they become part of our daily interactions. "Go to bed now and I'll read you a story," parents and baby sitters promise. The fact that manipulation is used by almost everyone does not make it right.

Manipulation can be mild, like hinting, "I'm so tired! But I still have to fold the wash." Or it can be very destructive, like parents pretending heart attacks, or Jaine's mother with her series of operations. The bottom line is that people use manipulation to control others and to get their own way. The person being manipulated feels guilty, powerless, and resentful. Understanding manipulation, its moves and its counter moves, is important in order to maintain healthy connections and keep partnerships strong.

John manipulates his wife, Elke, by complimenting her on her independence. Whenever he is talking with someone and Elke is within hearing distance, he will admiringly mention the fact that Elke is her own person. "Elke is a very unique individual. She doesn't mind being alone; in fact, she enjoys it. She is the most independent person I have ever met."

Elke apparently revels in this. She goes out of her way to appear independent and not to need attention or warm fuzzies from others. Because of her need to appear an independent loner, Elke wouldn't think of questioning John about his need for frequent career changes, most of which have taken him to other countries, leaving her alone, at home base, for large stretches of time. Perhaps Elke is aware that John is manipulating her and assumes that acceptance is the only way to keep him. But perhaps she doesn't know and has waited her whole life for John to come home.

Serious coercions include the "divorce argument," which boils down to, "Since I can't get you to do what I want you to do, we might as well get a divorce," the "nobody likes you" argument intended to make someone feel alone and unloved, and the threat of suicide. When people resort to these ploys they are in serious trouble. They and the partnership need help. Don't toss such threats off as just another argument. Too often people follow through on their threats.

Actually, manipulation is an indirect way of asking for what you want. Some people simply do not know how to ask to have their needs met in an honest and direct way. To stop manipulative behavior, try this system.

1. *Recognize what is happening.* Analyze the moves. Don't jump to conclusions or try to take corrective action until you understand the whole process. People manipulate in different ways, in varying degrees, and for different outcomes.

2. *Ask yourself who uses manipulation on you?* What are they trying to gain? Why do they use manipulation instead of directly asking for what they want? We have found that children learn this behavior from watching their parents interact. All behavior is learned behavior, so if you notice your children using manipulative moves, attempt to discover where and from whom they learned it.

3. *Use the* **HELP** *confrontation system to call unwanted behavior to the attention of the manipulator.* Be gentle and considerate. Most people are not aware that they are being manipulative. Tell your partner, "I value you and I am interested in pleasing you, but you must ask directly for what you need and want from me."

4. *Learn better ways to connect.* Your reactions in response to manipulation may be what has allowed it to continue. New behaviors are required by both of you, but don't expect the manipulator to change overnight. It takes time. Be patient and hang in there.

5. *Once you recognize the moves involved in manipulation and your part in the dance, discipline yourself to stop unwanted behavior.* Ask, "What better way could you have asked for what you want?"

6. *Recognize manipulative behavior in yourself and stop using it.* These behaviors include crying, clamming up, getting angry, blaming others,

pacifying others, doing things for others while expecting something in return, and handing someone else the cloak of guilt.

7. *Remember to stay calm while you are attempting to stop manipulation in yourself or others.* Getting you angry, so that you are more likely to act negatively, is the work of a champion manipulator. After you have cooled down, you feel guilty for your negative actions and can then be manipulated into atoning for your mistake. Of course, as you make up, you are giving the manipulator exactly what s/he wanted in the first place.

Just like master salespeople, most of us have several manipulative strategies. If one doesn't work, we try another. If that one doesn't work, we try a third, and so on. The person with the most moves wins. The point of trying to stop manipulative behavior—in others and ourselves—is that what we really want is a situation in which everyone wins.

Jim is a member of Rotary International. One of its major goals is to raise funds for worthy causes. During a particularly busy period, Jim came home from a Rotary meeting all excited and asked Jaine how she would like to go to the Professional Golf Association (PGA) tournament. Not being a golfer and having spent a lifetime avoiding the sun, Jaine was not excited by the prospect, but she was excited by Jim's excitement and so she said, "Gee, that sounds great! When is it?" "It's next Sunday. We can get a group of friends together to work one of the concession booths. The proceeds go to the scholarship fund. Won't that be fun?"

Jaine didn't really think it would be fun at all and felt that she was being manipulated. She didn't want to throw cold water on Jim's enthusiasm, however, so she said nothing. Jim called several couples who apparently thought it would be fun and so got his group together. Jaine then told Jim she didn't think it would be the best use of her time owing to a deadline she had to meet. She felt her time would be better spent writing. Jim agreed, but Jaine felt guilty that she wasn't supporting her partner in his endeavor to make money for the scholarship fund.

Can you recognize the moves? Manipulation is sneaky. We were playing manipulate/manipulate and didn't recognize it until Jaine started wearing the cloak of guilt. Once recognized, we stopped the game.

"Jim, see what we are doing to each other. You want to go to the PGA and work the booth with your friends, but you feel guilty because you know you should be focusing all of your energies on our joint assignment. You thought you would feel less guilty if you got me to want to go so we would both be playing hooky. But I don't want to go. If I agree to go, it would be a double sin. I would be doing something I don't want

to do in order to please you *and* I won't be doing something I really
need to do. You go to the PGA and have fun. I'll stay home and work
on the assignment and I'll feel much better about myself. I will not be
angry or judgmental." And that is what we did.

Summary

Gaining the support you need from others begins with learning to recognize all the moves involved in manipulation and then mutually developing a system to eliminate partnership-defeating behavior. When you do
this, you will have more time to devote to your real priorities, free of
resentment and guilt.

The most effective strategy for dealing with disagreement and/or
resentment is to stay out of defense. While a good defense may help win
football games, it destroys open, honest feedback. Learn to manage your
own defensive behavior by analyzing what you do when you feel you are
being criticized. Then don't do it. Instead, freeze your behavior, put your
mind in gear, and begin to analyze what is really going on. Why are you
feeling threatened? Why is the other person upset?

Find alternatives to defensive behavior. How else could you handle
this situation? How can you help both sides save face? How important is
it, really? Be sure not to devalue or discount the other person's perceptions. Just don't overreact.

It isn't always easy to deal with disapproval. Often disagreements
and resentments arise because your friends, relatives, bosses, or co-workers simply disapprove of your lifestyle choices. You may never gain their
approval, but a good foundation is created when you give them the right
to their own perceptions and values, even if you have to agree to disagree.

A good relation with both sets of parents is important to partnership
happiness. Find a way to get along. Appreciate their individuality. Some
of their advice may actually save you heartache and hassle.

Children, too, need a sense of family. Somewhere along the line our
values have gotten muddy. As a society, we have to accept the fact that
the most important job we do as human beings is preparing the next
generation to live happy and ethical lives. Child rearing is the number
one job we do. We are not doing that job well. Children may be only 25
percent of our population, but they are 100 percent of our future. We must
change our focus. When couples look upon their children as so boring,
redundant, or demanding that they throw themselves into their work to
avoid them, they are literally failing at their number one job. Raising a
child is not self-sacrifice; it is a meaningful and rewarding occupation.

Sure, there are difficulties in raising children, but we are not talking about widgets here; we are talking about human beings. We have to get back to some fundamentals with regard to the family. There are certain responsibilities and accountabilities couples must accept. If you, as a couple, are not committed to the long-term responsibilities that parenting requires, you should not have children. It's as simple as that. You have a choice. They don't.

We also need to watch the signals we sent to our children. When a mother says, "I'm feeling stressed because I *have* to work," she is making it sound as if work is not fun, that it is in fact hard, and that she isn't happy. A much more encouraging signal would be: "Mommy has an exciting job she has to get finished tonight, but I'll be able to spend time with you tomorrow." Then guard against those "tomorrows" running together into weeks, making the children feel inconsequential compared to the job.

Work can and should be a marvelous adventure. With the right attitude, it will be. Chapter 10 will help you fill in another piece of the priority puzzle.

Chapter 10

Working With What You Have

Do you ever wonder who is really running your life? Is it your demanding boss, your out-of-control teenagers, a client, or a neighbor who is driving you crazy, or is your life being run by fear of losing your job or your significant other? We believe that successful, happy, well integrated people understand that they work for themselves, first.

When we ask people why they are working, the most common response we receive is, "We need the money!" That may be. But we don't think that is a good enough reason to spend forty, fifty, or more hours a week involved in any activity.

Bob is in his mid-thirties, with two children ages 1 and 3. His wife, Brenda, has been talking about going back to work in order to help with the family's financial needs. Together they did a cost/benefit analysis. This is important in making many decisions. When they looked at the financial side of her reentering the workplace, they discovered that it wouldn't really be cost-effective. Her reentering the work force would put them in a higher income tax bracket, which would mean higher taxes. It would also involve increased auto expenses, child care costs, an improved wardrobe, a need for cleaning services, and a probable increase in the dollars spent eating out.

After they had computed all these increased costs, they realized that the addition to their income made possible by a second earner wouldn't be enough to justify Brenda's working outside the home. Their conclusion was that it would be better to give up an extra pizza on Friday night than for her to go back to work.

Are You Working to Live or Living to Work?

Of course, there are other issues to be considered, but the idea of extra money needs to be considered carefully. When people are working just for the money, they are working to live. In other words, they fail to consider whether or not the particular work they are doing does or can lead to self-fulfillment. Whenever we are working simply to get the money to pay the rent, to buy the food, to pay for necessities, the work itself becomes a real downer. Those workers who live for Fridays and dread Mondays are literally cutting from their lives five full days of every week. That doesn't leave them a great deal of time to enjoy life.

We live to work. Our friends, children, and relatives accuse us both of being workaholics. That may be true. But, in preparation for this chapter, we asked ourselves the same questions we will be asking you. Why do we work so much? If we could eliminate all of the annoying little details necessary to running a business, we would each enjoy everything we are doing.

What would we change? Jaine says she would change having to do everything we are doing during the same time frame, under such strict deadlines. But all the tasks and parts feed into each other. They are all interrelated. Jim says he loves implementing but doesn't like getting involved in the design and production process. Both of us feel that the answer would be to have a staff of a hundred assistants, running around in a hundred different directions, taking care of all the annoying little details, planning our itineraries, designing the programs, and producing the shows. All we would then have to do is show up and do our thing. We would also need our own private jet with sleeping quarters and an exercise room!

The point is that work is very important to us. We live to work. Our work helps us to achieve our own mission and purpose in life, and we try to work for clients whose missions and purposes complement ours. We are motivated internally, not externally. Our motivation stems from our internal mission statement, which is the driving force in our lives.

How Important Is Working to You?

Turned-on people have these characteristics in common:

1. *They take personal responsibility.* These people take control of their lives. They know that they cannot always control the events in

their lives, but they can and do control their individual reactions to these events.

2. *They have a sense of purpose in life.* They have decided who they are and what they want out of life and are committed to an ongoing search for fulfillment.

3. *They have an energetic attitude toward life.* They don't just get the job done but do it elegantly and appear to have greater impact with less effort.

4. *They have developed behavior adapt*-ability. These people have the ability to adjust and to adapt their actions to fit the needs of the situation, and the people within those situations, so that they can arrive at mutual wins.

In order to be successful in your career, you must first truly believe that you do work for yourself every day, throughout your life. You can choose to work for someone else or you can choose to work for yourself. The choice is yours. But you cannot enjoy life while pursuing your goals unless you are completely honest about what you want out of life, and for whom. Many of the couples with whom we have talked readily admit that their careers are more important to them than having children. Therefore, they have wisely chosen not to have children, at least at this stage in their lives.

What Do You Want Out of Your Career?

Some people have the capacity for multilevel thinking. They can think about what has to be done today to cope with the here and now and they also have the ability to think about the ramifications of today's actions ten or fifteen years from now. They have a greater ability to think globally. You need to develop the ability to do this because your career will be affected, either positively or negatively, by these outside forces. You can't commit yourself to an organization that thinks only of the short term because that kind of organization will not be around in the long term. That will negatively affect your economic stability. Too often, working couples are caught up in the here and now and are not dealing with issues that will have an impact on their careers, and therefore their lives, downstream.

What Do You Want Out of Your Job?

The truth is most people want more than one thing. Jaine wants to be able to create and follow through with her ideas. She wants to be successful at and rewarded for bringing these ideas to fruition. However, she also wants a harmonious and fulfilling personal relationship with her significant others. Throughout the years, she has found herself torn between her career and her relationships. A satisfying relationship can be a full-time job. Add some children to the significant other mix and you've got several full-time jobs. Now, throw in a meaningful career and anyone would burn out.

In retrospect, she would have preferred taking on each of these meaningful activities one at a time. It doesn't make much difference which one you go for first. You can marry young, have children, then pursue a meaningful career after they're grown. Or you can give all your energy to achieving your career goals first and then focus on your significant others. Sticking to your choices is difficult, because opportunities don't always present themselves at the most convenient times. You have to be prepared to accept or reject those opportunities on the basis of your overall life plan.

Margaret Ann, a child psychologist with a master's degree, married Rick when she was in her thirties. Her life plan included children. After several serious marriage conferences, she and her partner committed themselves to living on his salary while she devoted her time to having and raising their children.

Margaret Ann knew herself well enough to understand that she would feel undervalued and unproductive if she didn't receive compensation for what she considered a full-time, meaningful occupation. Therefore, they agreed to pay her a salary out of his income. This salary was not to be considered as an allowance or household funds. It would be Margaret Ann's separate income to do with as she pleased.

Their children are now in middle school and Rich feels that his career is sufficiently well established that he can easily help with such chores as picking up the children from school and taking them to Little League practice. Margaret Ann is now focusing her energies on redeveloping her career. She says she is happy with her choices, so far, and would not have given up those early development years with her children.

Twenty years ago, we met a woman consultant who was beginning to be in demand on the speaker circuit. Just when her popularity started to climb, she retired to raise her children. Many of us at the time thought that this was a negative career move and that she would live to regret her decision to drop out. We didn't hear much of her until about five years ago, when her name started to appear in seminar brochures around the country. Suddenly, she was popular again. Jaine couldn't resist calling her to ask if she was sorry about her original choice. But this woman, like Margaret Ann, said she would not have changed her decision.

Both these solutions worked because both sets of partners leveled with each other about their needs, discussed the alternatives, and committed themselves to living within the constraints of their chosen lifestyles.

Do you have to schedule your career sequentially? No! We didn't, but it was hard. Very hard. We realize now that fear is what motivated us to keep accepting all those golden opportunities whenever they appeared. We witness that same fear, today, in hundreds of career couples. "Jobs are not that plentiful," they lament. Or, "It's easy for you to say. You've made your mark. We've got a long way to go." Keep in mind that it is never easy to turn down an opportunity, and you may never feel as if you have made it. People are always looking for another opportunity, another challenge. And who knows? Jobs may be more plentiful ten to twenty years from now.

Why Are You Working at the Job You Are Working?

Once you have decided that you are going to work and when, make a further decision that you are going to be working at a job that turns you on. Find that job by conducting a career investigation. There are so many careers from which to choose, and each offers the possibility of achievement as well as its share of anxiety and boredom. Many people select a career with little thought as to whether it will fit their abilities, strengths, or interests. It just sounded like a good idea at the time.

Do a helping/hindering analysis (explained in Chapter 5) on yourself. List every conceivable reason why you feel that you cannot succeed at the career you really prefer. Be completely honest with yourself. You will accomplish nothing if you try to con yourself. If you have children who prevent you from traveling, put that down. If you need a degree of some kind, put that down. If you tire easily, put that down, too. Take your time and list all of the barriers to achieving your career preference. This is an excellent opportunity to brainstorm with your partner. You both need to be aware of the factors that could hinder your career success.

Once you have completed a comprehensive list of perceived barriers, the next step is to create alternative solutions to eliminate these hindering factors. Contemplate each of the barriers you have listed. Imagine alternative solutions to each. What possible things could you and your partner do to eliminate the obstacles? Take your time and come up with at least one solution to each problem. Try for more.

What Do You Have to Offer?

There are hundreds of books and training programs that tell you what you *should* do. They urge you to add something new to yourself—a new technique, a new attitude, a new style. The implication is clear: You lack something. The fact is that your most important resources are already there, within you. Most adults are not going to change the essence of themselves very much; nor should they. A more useful quest would be to look for better ways to use what you already have. A realistic approach to your own growth can start with asking yourself, "How do I get the most out of what I have?" This question can be answered as you become more aware of the gap between what you are currently doing and what you are capable of doing. You can then choose what and how to change. Change within this frame of reference involves identifying and utilizing your resources rather than trying to impose behavior characteristics and styles upon yourself that are not consistent with your uniqueness as an individual. Utilizing your resources involves:

- Being aware of and comfortable with your own gifts.
- Understanding how you currently use these resources.
- Knowing the options that are available to you as you translate your resources into effective actions.
- Taking the steps necessary to achieving your career objectives.
- Learning how to work successfully with others.

The last item is the biggie. There is nothing more important to your success in life than your ability to work and interact with people. No two people are quite alike. Since this is the case, we would be foolish to treat all people exactly alike or to expect them to be motivated by the same techniques. What works in one situation, with one person, may not work with another person in the same situation. There is no best style of interaction. Research supports the conclusion that the most effective people are those who know themselves, know the demands of the situation, and *adapt* their personal actions to meet those demands. This takes awareness and flexibility. The person who has the most options available will be the person who has the greatest chance of winning with people.

How do you become aware of your options? The best way is to know your strengths and weaknesses and to learn how to blend your behavior style with that of others in your work or personal environment.

Behavioral Preferences

One theory is that a person's weaknesses are actually excesses, or overextensions, of personal strengths. Most people never connect the two and find it hard to understand that a fine strength carried to excess can account for a so-called weakness. For example, your strength may be that you are very fast and organized, able to accomplish tasks in much less time and with much less effort than it takes many of the people with whom you are associated. However, you may also be very impatient with the disorganization or slowness of others, expecting a great deal of them and requiring them to work as hard as you do. Your impatience is an excess of your speed and organization tendencies.

Everyone has *tendencies* toward specific behaviors and you may have strengths and excesses in several areas. Find out yours by going through and ranking the statements in the following Personal Preference Profile. Give a 4 to the statement that best describes you and a 1 to the statement that least describes you. The Personal Preference Profile will also give you an idea of how you tend to come across to others.

PERSONAL PREFERENCE PROFILE

INSTRUCTIONS: Please rank-order the statements below. Give a 4 to the statement you most prefer and a 1 to the statement you least prefer. Then choose between the two remaining statements for the 2 and the 3. There can be only one 4 and one 1 in each A-B-C-D series.

1. I prefer:

   A _____ Getting many things done, fast.
   B _____ Helping people get things done.
   C _____ Doing one thing at a time.
   D _____ Getting things done right.

Note: The Personal Preference Profile is only an indicator of preference or of style. It is not a validated instrument such as the Meyers-Briggs Type Indicator Test or the Personal Profile System.

2. I fear:

    A _____ Being taken advantage of.
    B _____ Not having people like me.
    C _____ Losing my job.
    D _____ Criticism.

3. I believe:

    A _____ Meetings are a waste of time.
    B _____ Meetings are an opportunity to develop relationships.
    C _____ Everyone's opinion should be heard.
    D _____ Information should be supported by provable data.

4. I generally:

    A _____ Have high expectations of others.
    B _____ Realize that people are only human.
    C _____ Know people need time to finish tasks.
    D _____ Believe people should be more careful.

5. I value:

    A _____ Completed staff work.
    B _____ Friendship and approval.
    C _____ Loyalty.
    D _____ Accuracy.

6. I look at:

    A _____ The total picture.
    B _____ The opportunity to make an impression.
    C _____ Stability in any situation.
    D _____ Logical sequence in things.

7. I enjoy:

    A _____ New experiences.
    B _____ Playing charades.
    C _____ Puttering around the house.
    D _____ Learning about my computer.

8. I prefer to communicate:

    A _____ One-on-one.
    B _____ In groups.

C _____ In a way that ensures no one is offended.
D _____ By written correspondence.

9. When correcting someone, I:

   A _____ Cut to the chase.
   B _____ Make people laugh.
   C _____ Beat around the bush.
   D _____ Look for information to support my ideas.

10. When reading the newspaper, I:

   A _____ Go through it like a buzz saw and leave it in a shambles.
   B _____ Always read Ann Landers and the obituaries first.
   C _____ Clip out the coupons.
   D _____ Look for misspelled words and grammatical mistakes.

11. When in the grocery store, I:

   A _____ Quickly move up and down the aisles, in order to get out fast. Sometimes I try to go through the "10 items or less" line with more than 10 items.
   B _____ Have social conversations with people in the checkout line.
   C _____ Use a list and come equipped with coupons.
   D _____ Carry a calculator in order to determine the price per ounce of each item.

12. When working with others, I:

   A _____ Have a tendency to be demanding.
   B _____ Want to talk out the situation with humor.
   C _____ Listen to and hear out all sides.
   D _____ Prefer to withdraw and not deal with people.

13. When traveling, I:

   A _____ Check into my room immediately and get on the phone for an update on all projects.
   B _____ Try to find out all the best restaurants in town and where the action is.
   C _____ Immediately unpack and get organized for the next day as soon as I enter my hotel room.
   D _____ Check to make sure the sheets are clean and count the towels.

14. When going on a road trip, I:

    A _____ Always drive the car.
    B _____ Ride up front and play travel director.
    C _____ Bring and label the food.
    D _____ Ride in back and control the map.

15. At elevators, I:

    A _____ Always push the button several times.
    B _____ Talk to everyone waiting.
    C _____ Take the stairs if I am late.
    D _____ Compare weight load capacity and the number of people
    waiting before entering.

16. I am:

    A _____ Results-oriented.
    B _____ Enthusiastic.
    C _____ Supportive.
    D _____ Analytical.

SCORING: Count and write down on the "Most" line how many A's you
    scored with a 4. Record these under the T. Count and write down how
    many B's you scored with a 4. Record these under the E. Count and write
    down how many C's you scored with a 4. Record these under the A.
    Count and write down how many D's you scored with a 4. Record these
    under the M.

    Then count and write down on the "Least" line how many A's you
    scored with a 1. Record these under the T. Count and write down how
    many B's you scored with a 1. Record these under the E. Count and write
    down how many C's you scored with a 1. Record these under the A. Count
    and write down how many D's you scored with a 1. Record these under the M.

T	E	A	M
A	B	C	D

	A	B	C	D
Most	_____	_____	_____	_____
Least	_____	_____	_____	_____

Look at the area in which you have the greatest numbers of 4's. This is the area in which you have the highest overall score. It would be either T, E, A, or M. If you have the greatest number of 4's in the M area, it indicates that you have a tendency to activities and interactions that exhibit more M characteristics.

T, E, A, and M are each symbols of different styles of behavior. Behavioral tendencies illustrate how people differ and how these differences affect them in different situations. The following grid provides a summary of the four behavioral styles.

Behavioral Tendency Grid

(T)ough *TO CONQUER*	**(E)nergetic** *TO PERSUADE*
"I'm a take-charge person! But I wish I could delegate . . . and mean it."	"I LIKE people and can adapt to their needs. But I'm also a people-pleaser."
(A)daptive *TO BE SUPPORTIVE*	**(M)ethodical** *TO AVOID CONFLICT*
"I'm a very trusting and loyal person. But I feel so obligated and guilty if I have to say no."	"I need to consider all aspects of a situation. But it's difficult for me to know when I have enough data."

Let's look at an overview of each style. **T** stands for *tough*. People who exhibit **T** behavior place an emphasis on controlling the environment by meeting the opposition head on in order to accomplish results. These people have tendencies that include doing things now, getting others to do things, accepting challenges, making quick decisions, taking over, and solving problems.

Each of us tends to have a backup style that we use when we are under stress or when our self-esteem is low. This is what we refer to when we say that our weaknesses are only the excesses of our strengths. It's the excesses in people that irritate and exasperate us. Unfortunately, we don't seem to have the strengths without the excesses. Your objective is to identify, develop, and manage your personal strengths and to control your excesses.

Let's look at this excess concept more closely. Think of the excess as a caricature of an individual's style. The high **T** personality would have strengths that include the ability to take control, confidence, persuasiveness, a sense of time urgency, willingness to take risks, and forcefulness. Here's what happens when these characteristics become exaggerated. Controlling becomes domineering, confidence becomes arrogance, persuasiveness becomes impatience, risk taking becomes gambling, and forcefulness becomes coerciveness.

People with high E behavioral characteristics are *energetic*. E's like to focus on working with people to accomplish mutual goals. On the positive side, high E's can be very flexible. Other strengths include sensitivity to others, good verbal skills, and enthusiasm. They are inspirational, tactful, and agreeable. But when pushed to excess, sensitive becomes emotional, flexible becomes inconsistent, enthusiastic becomes pushy, agreeable becomes two-faced, inspiring becomes unrealistic, and tactful becomes mere people-pleasing.

People with high A behavioral tendencies are *adaptive*. The A places emphasis on cooperating with others to get things done. A's strengths include being very family-oriented, dependable, loyal, helpful, and good at listening. Under stress, or when involved in conflict, however, A's resist change, family-oriented becomes self-sacrificing, dependable becomes gullible, loyal becomes obligated, and helpful becomes enabling.

High M people are very *methodical*. They have a specific method for everything they do and expect compliance with their standards. High M's place emphasis on working within the boundaries of policies and procedures to promote quality in products or services. M's are accurate, budget-oriented, logical, introverted, tenacious, and analytical. When pushed to excess, accurate becomes perfectionistic, budget-oriented becomes stingy, introverted becomes unfriendly, tenacious becomes stubborn, and analytical becomes obsessive.

Once you get an idea of your own behavioral tendencies, it's great fun to observe the behaviors of different people, so make this an ongoing project for yourself. For example, in a grocery store, high T's are a show in themselves. They are the people who leave the checkout line, at least once or twice, to run back and get something. They never use a list and are always trying to sneak through the "ten items or less" line with twenty items. High E's have a social conversation with all the people in the checkout line as well as with the cashier. High A's come equipped with their envelopes full of coupons, arranged in the way the store is laid out. They always have a list. High M's carry calculators and work out mathematical equations as to the price per number of ounces or grams. They also have a list; however, it is organized by product and aisle. Are you beginning to see yourself? Your boss? A significant other?

You have probably noticed that you feel more comfortable and successful with people who have certain types of behavioral tendencies. Usually you feel more rapport with those people whose styles are similar to your own. Unfortunately, in a work environment, having too many people with similar work styles may throw the team off balance. You will feel more rapport with people whose behavioral tendencies are like your own, but your productivity and efficiency may suffer if you are not aware of the need for creative balance.

How can you use this information to improve your relationships at work and at home? Information is power. Since information is power, the more you know about the people you live and work with, the greater will be your chances for harmony, cooperation, and acceptance. There is less hassle in your life when you can successfully predict how people will react. If I know you better than you know me, I can control the situation. If I know you better than you know you, I can control you. Awareness is the key. Always strive to know yourself at least as well as other people do.

> *Information is power. If I know you better than you know me, I can control the situation. If I know you better than you know you, I can control you. Awareness is the key.*

Let's draw some conclusions. No one style is right or wrong. Each style has its strengths and its excesses. You need to be aware of your dominant style as well as of your excessive style so you can plan to use alternative styles and strengths to help you in a variety of situations. Surround yourself with people whose behavioral styles are different from your own so as to augment your strengths and modify your excesses. Develop an understanding of each style, individual uniqueness, and what each can contribute to a specific situation. Instead of being critical and annoyed because a person wants to do something differently or doesn't excel in the ways you do, consider that that person's way may be equally valid and effective.

Successful people are *flexible* people. Flexible people are those who develop the skill of tuning in to the appropriate behavior for each situation they are in with others and adapting their own behavior accordingly. This puts them in *positive control*. Positive control is exercised by individuals when they actively facilitate effective communication (between themselves and others) by adjusting their natural style to whatever style is more comfortable for those people with whom they are interacting.

Summary

Unless you are independently wealthy, you will be involved in some kind of income-producing activity for the largest part of your life. It's a smart idea to figure out what you want to do with this block of your life and then find ways to turn your discovery into something that turns you on.

Turned-on people have these characteristics in common. They take personal responsibility for what happens to them in their lives and their careers, they have a sense of purpose in life, they have an energetic attitude toward life, and they develop behavioral adaptability. They know what they want out of their career and out of their job.

Many people can tell you what you should do but only you can decide what you want to do. Become aware of your options. Know your strengths and excesses; then learn how to blend or adapt your personality to meet the needs of the situation and the people involved in those situations. Develop **TEAM** relationships at work and at home by working with people, not against them.

In Chapter 11, we discuss ways in which the partnership can help each of you manage your career challenges.

SECTION THREE

Success Strategies for Working Couples

Chapter 11

Managing Career Challenges

Careers are an ever changing process. Numerous pressures from outside the family cause a need for periodic reassessment of where you are now and where you want to be. Without teamwork and a commitment to cooperate, a dual-career relationship will send one or both of you straight to burnout. Managing a two-career family can be equated with managing a small business, and each of you must move toward involvement in the choices you make affecting your future.

An old management axiom advises that nothing will work for the organization unless top management is committed to it. That's true. It's equally true that nothing will work, in any system, unless the parts work together. That's what a partnership is all about: making the parts work more efficiently so that the whole can function with maximum productivity. What you need in order to enjoy life while pursuing your goals is an effective strategy that can increase the quality of your life by maximizing your impact and minimizing your effort; a way of organizing your lives so that you can take control of your careers.

Healthy people don't make excuses or blame others. They take full responsibility for their lives. Underachievers feel that life is mostly determined by chance circumstances, which would account for being in the right place at the right time, or that people are somehow predestined to lives of success or failure. Margaret Mead calls personal responsibility the most important revelation in psychology and feels that attachment to the notion that we are powerless products of our environment is our biggest sin. So do we. Responsible people live in the present and pursue their own goals in life. They learn from the past and plan for the future but give up waiting for some miracle that will enable them to live happily ever after—without effort.

> *Attachment to the notion that we are powerless products of our environment is our biggest sin.*

Finding a Mentor

For years we lamented the fact that something was missing in the management training courses we taught internationally. Participants appeared to gain intellectual knowledge and were able to practice the skills taught during class, but when they went back to their work sites, they reverted to the old ways of doing things. There appeared to be little changed behavior. Then we discovered the missing link. That missing link was a personal coach. A personal coach is more than a mentor. A coach can guide you through practice, play the devil's advocate, and cheer you on.

Career people need someone they can talk with on a regular basis to help guide them through the business decisions they must make and the conversations and communications that must take place in order to plan with their bosses, their co-workers, and their peers. This career coach should be someone outside the organization (though having a few inside also helps) so that there is no risk of damaging an insider's opinion of you in the event that that insider ever becomes your boss. We at Carter & Carter offer this service, but the majority of career people will never have the opportunity to avail themselves of our services.

A psychotherapist won't fill the bill unless s/he has extensive business experience and understands the nuances of organization politics. A therapist can help you talk about your feelings, but a business career coach will help you develop strategies and techniques for achieving success within your organizational structure. *The perfect career coach might just be your significant other.* After all, your partner already knows you, your strengths and excesses, your limitations, and your personal style. When your partner is also a career person, s/he understands the trials and tribulations of working life. S/he too has a boss and co-workers with whom it is sometimes necessary to contend and knows the frustration of not getting that raise or promotion one has worked so hard for.

Get outside your old paradigms and establish new rules for using one another as sounding boards before a critical presentation or a confrontation with a co-worker. If you are the coach, give feedback in a constructive way that is designed to improve the presentation or relieve the stress of the confrontation. If you are the one being coached, it is enormously beneficial to know that someone is on your side, no matter what happens during the critical incident. But beware of enabling each other to continue in the same old ways. Sometimes being on someone's side means to level with them about the role they are playing in creating their own difficulties. Don't kill the messenger who brings such valuable insights.

> *Sometimes being on someone's side means to level with them about the role they are playing in creating their own difficulties.*

Relighting the Fire in Your Belly

If you have decided that a job working for other people is what you want, get busy and start making a career out of your job. It isn't easy to get ahead when there are 76 million baby boomers competing for the same jobs and, at the same time, organizations have become obsessed with downsizing. But it can be done if you learn the rules of the game.

People who run companies know that there are really only two critical factors in business. One is to make money and the other is to generate cash. As long as you do these two things the organization is going to love you and support your efforts. Companies want to make money and if that means pushing their employees to work harder and longer, so be it. CEOs claim that they don't ask anything of their employees they don't ask of themselves. In a *Fortune* magazine survey (March, 1990), CEOs were asked how many hours a week they expect high-level executives to work. Fifty-eight percent of those surveyed reported that they expect between 50 and 59 hours a week, and 53 percent expect middle managers to put in those same hours. Another 62 percent reported having to work longer hours than they did ten years ago, with 45 percent spending between 60 and 69 hours at the job themselves.

If you want to get ahead in this rapidly changing environment, stop feeling sorry for yourself and learn to think like the CEO of a well-run organization. Put in the time to learn the rules of success, both the written ones and the unwritten ones. Organizations want creative people who can make a decision and then act on that decision. The leaders of tomorrow cannot afford to sit on their haunches expecting to get by on past knowledge and experience. Whatever it is that got you where you are today will not be sufficient to keep you there.

Learning and flexibility are the major requirements for profitable survival in today's lean and mean organization. Be a sponge. Read constantly. Underline key ideas and trade off with your significant other. Share ideas at dinner, while you do the dishes, or at business lunches you have together. The most important skill you must learn is how to stay close to the bottom line, keeping a close eye on profit and loss. Look around for where you can make your greatest contribution and take personal responsibility now to ensure that your projects produce outcomes the company can measure in dollars and cents. This will take help.

Learn the Rules of the Game

Can you still get ahead in today's downsized environment? Sure. One way is to look for a position that is one of a kind in an organization. This will give you more negotiating room at salary time. If necessary, try to rewrite the position's responsibilities so that they better reflect what you are actually doing. Too often, job descriptions were written years ago by someone in personnel who couldn't realistically know what actually goes on in a position when various people perform its responsibilities. Each individual brings unique talents and experience to a job. Often these talents result in an expansion of the job's tasks. You may not be getting your fair share.

Do jobs no one else wants to do. You probably don't want to do them either, but the best way to make a mark for yourself is to find an empty niche and fill it. Certain jobs have to be completed in order for all the other jobs to be integrated. You'll have more power if everyone needs to come to you for coordination.

Read everything. It's hard to decide what is just "nice-to-know" information within an organization when you are trying to get ahead. What if department B is one you have identified as not critical to your information base but you later discover that department B is in need of an ability or function at which you excel. That may be your opportunity to shine. Or, what if you decide that the company picnic is nice to know about but not something in which you need to get involved, only to discover, after the picnic, that Mr. Big attended, which would have given you an opportunity for visibility. The secret is not to drown yourself in reports and studies or even to know all the answers. It's to know what's knowable and where to look to *get* the answers. Here is where your partner might be able to help. Depending on his or her time restraints, you may be able to divide and conquer.

> Jaine took a sabbatical for a year after our second son was born. During that year, in order to keep up and to help Jim with the volumes of material he was required to read, Jaine skimmed reports to determine what items were necessary for Jim to read in greater detail. After the children had gone to bed, they would discuss what she had reviewed and she would make suggestions and recommendations for actions to be taken. This was a successful routine because Jim respected Jaine's knowledge and experience and because Jaine had a desire to learn more. Perhaps it also worked because we were in similar fields, but it could work for couples in dissimilar fields when knowledge of them would give you both the opportunity to grow. Of course the added benefit is that it gives you something meaningful to talk about besides dirty diapers and "the relationship."

What Are the Rules?

There are certain behaviors that are expected within every organization no matter what the specific culture. The following is an overview of those behaviors and suggestions on how to get around them if they are holding you down.

One of the unwritten rules of business is that an employee should never go around the chain of command. More and more businesses have *written* policies itemizing the steps you must take if you feel your boss is being unjust, unfair, or discriminatory. The truth is that upper management usually sides with middle management, so going over your boss's head is a high-risk move. Be sure the possible cost to your working relationship is worth the benefit you feel you will derive from going around him or her.

Your immediate boss is not the only problem. Let's hypothesize that you have been able to get transferred to another department because you complained about an unjust boss. The organization is running scared because of a recent union situation or a sexual harassment complaint, so it defuses your situation by transferring you to another department with a new boss. How do you think that the new boss will feel about you? S/he, of course, knows about your situation and is going to handle you with kid gloves. If that is your objective, so be it. But if your objective is to establish a partnership based on mutual trust and respect, you have just riddled your path with broken glass. Are there alternatives? Try these:

1. *Use a variation of the time management tips suggested by Alan Laikin in* How to Get Control of Your Time and Your Life. Divide the request for change into small pieces. For example, if you are requesting a change in the way a task has previously been completed, don't present it as a major change in procedure. Instead, ask that you be allowed to change one small aspect of an entire system. Once you have proved that this new way of doing something is efficient and cost-effective, try another small aspect.

> Frank wanted to move into financial sales. His boss was determined that he serve his time in research analysis. So Frank decided to work toward the opportunity to move into sales gradually by requesting permission to help existing sales personnel develop their sales presentations. After he had successfully prepared several written sales reports, one of the financial associates suggested that he be allowed to sit in on one of the actual presentations in case he, the associate, was asked about something with which he needed help. Soon Frank was included in all customer presentations to answer questions or suggest additional analysis. He was the only one in the organization with an in-depth knowledge of how the system worked and had now expanded its utilization.
>
> He currently has the ability to research and prepare customer presentations as well as the opportunity to interface with clients. His only challenge is training someone to take over his expanded position when he decides to ask for a financial associate slot.
>
> Frank first divided his request into bite-sized pieces and then *offered to help out*. In that way, he made himself indispensable to his coworkers, who will now support the requests he plans to make to higher-ups.

2. *Offer to accompany your boss as he presents your proposal for the change.* Phrase this offer as a question: "Boss, do you think it would be a good idea to run this proposal past [*name a particular department or persons*] to see if anyone has ideas for improvement and to get an idea about how receptive they are? I'd be happy to accompany you to the meeting to field any questions they might have about the contents and technical aspects of the report. What do you think?"

3. *If you are getting nowhere, let someone else run with the ball.* Look for support for your idea in another department or from someone who is in greater favor with the boss than you are. Or ask your sponsor if s/he will test the idea on his/her contacts.

4. *Don't abandon your idea just because you can't find any immediate support.* Keep your proposal current and be prepared to make a spontaneous presentation in the event that circumstances change. And they will. You never know when the blockading boss will be transferred, promoted, or given the golden handshake. Be ready.

Avoid Becoming an Example of the Peter Principle

Too swift promotions are the enigma of *The Peter Principle* (by Laurence J. Peter and Raymond Hull), a condition in which people rise to the level of their own incompetence because of too frequent promotions. It isn't likely that people will be promoted quickly in today's competitive job market, but it doesn't hurt to be forewarned. You won't get promoted or be given greater responsibility unless you have the flexibility and know-how necessary to perform at the next highest level in your organization. Be ready. Don't keep putting off that night class or finishing that book on management or learning how to make your computer dance and sing. In short, make yourself more valuable to the corporation and to yourself.

> *Make yourself more valuable to the corporation and to yourself.*

Factoring in the Plateauing Trap

If too swift promotion was the problem depicted in *The Peter Principle*, under-promotion, or plateauing, is the phenomenon treated by Judith Bardwick in *The Plateauing Trap*. In this, she examines the three types of plateauing: structural, content, and life plateauing.

Plateauing in life is when nothing seems worthwhile to you anymore. Everything has lost its color, meaning, and excitement. These feelings pervade every area of your life. How you feel about your work and what is happening in the organization can significantly affect how you feel about your life. Structural and content plateauing may lead to life plateauing.

Structural plateauing is when you've gone as far as you can go within the organization and you are stymied in your career. We all have to face the reality that with 76 million baby boomers actively competing for the same available jobs, only a few of us will make it to the top of existing corporate structures. Promotion ends, despite your ability to cope with greater responsibilities, simply because there is no place to go.

All but one percent of us will eventually reach that plateau. The rest of us must find ways to protect ourselves from allowing structural plateauing to lead to content plateauing—when you feel that you've learned all you can learn about your job. Some people refer to content plateauing as burnout. We burn out when we view our lives as a series of recurring crises demanding the same decisions on the same sorts of issues. One man complained, "If I have to make that same decision one more time, I'll scream." The challenge is gone. What a desperate way to live a life! You may not have much control over structural plateauing, but you certainly have total control over content plateauing.

When you know everything there is to know about a job, look for another job, inside or outside the organization. If you feel you are too old to take that risk, look for other challenges. Let your boss, mentor, sponsor, or anyone else who might be able to help guide you in looking for a new challenge. Then don't sit on your hands, investigate. Look around the organization and find a niche that needs to be filled, a problem that needs to be solved, or a glitch in production you think you could handle.

Ask for what you want. Go in prpared with a proposal, complete with bottom line statistics, proving the need for your intervention and showing the results for which you would be accountable. Don't expect more money. Remember, you wanted the extra challenge. The organization may not be ready to hire a special person just to resolve this issue. Suggest that a bonus be forthcoming if you are able to improve the bottom line. One way to help the organization improve the bottom line is to become a work/family expert.

Encouraging Management to Participate in Achieving Your Partnership Goals

In the early eighties, Lillian Buchanan and her husband, Mike Clary, decided that they would alternate, every three years, whose job took priority over the other's. During the first three years, she would be the career person and he would work at something he could do from the house while he cared for their children. During this time, he wrote the book *Daddy's Home*, a ground breaker at the time but too early in the paradigm shift to have much impact on business organizations. Things have changed.

If there comes a time when the two of you decide that career advancement is not all it's cracked up to be and you want to begin spending more time with each other and your children, realize that there is no "win" in it for management to give you special treatment. We know that less stress makes for more productive employees. Upper management may talk a good game, but in practice, it wants committed team players who are there when they are needed.

Instead of getting angry and feeling wronged, look at the issue from management's point of view. Survival in the nineties depends on the ability to react to change promptly and productively. In order to be competitive, managers need to lower costs and increase positive outcomes. As a manager, if I'm there, but my key man or woman is not there because of flexi time or maternity leave, I'm at a disadvantage. I may want to be compassionate and help out with work/family issues, but the day-to-day realities of running a department prevent me from having much sympathy. I have my problems, too. So if you want to be considered a valued member of the work team, and you do decide to campaign for the work options that follow, be sure you are carrying your load. Don't take advantage of an already stressful situation. Companies do not owe you flexible schedules. You owe them an honest day's work for an honest day's pay. Companies are responding. Smart employers are paying attention to their employees' concerns.

> *Companies do not owe you flexible schedules. You owe them an honest day's work for an honest day's pay.*

There are some problems that need to be addressed when employees choose work/family options involving flexible scheduling. Workers without children or elder care responsibilities are beginning to voice their resentment at having to cover for absent employees, no matter what the reason or the company policy. It is true that employees who are at the job site are expected to answer phones, deal with customers requiring immediate attention, handle emergencies, and interface with the boss on a regular basis. Employees who have no children still require time for a personal life and dislike relocation transfers as much as do employees with children. Is it any wonder they feel that since they are committed 100 percent to the organization, they should be considered for promotion and salary increases before nontraditional employees?

Theoretically, childless employees should have the same options as workers with children and other family responsibilities. In addition to the growing response by companies to the need for child and elder care alternatives, larger organizations are beginning to offer other flexible schedules to workers who are snowed under by the dual responsibilities of work and family needs.

While flexible scheduling can benefit any worker, it is especially appealing to dual-career couples who can join together to make flexible arrangements work. Many couples have already created their own versions of flexible scheduling by alternating shifts. She works days and he works nights. She works weekends and he works Monday through Friday. We created our own workable schedule by starting our own business (see Chapter 13). No doubt we would both have stayed in traditional organizations if child care options had been available at the time we made our decision.

Investigate the alternatives your company may be offering by contacting your human resources department. Ideally, managers should describe such benefits to their immediate employees, but, as we pointed out, most managers have not yet determined what's in it for them and are therefore reluctant to encourage their workers to utilize flexible scheduling. Even if your company doesn't offer flexible scheduling, you may be able to work out a mutually beneficial arrangement with your manager by doing your homework.

Put together a proposal showing the benefits to the manager and to the organization of allowing you more flexibility in delivering your work. Keep in mind that the biggest obstacle to overcome is the perception of other employees. The old "if I do it for one, I'll have to do it for everyone" attitude has some basis in fact. Employees do get jealous and resentful if they think someone else is getting a better deal than they are. What wins people over are results. When teammates can see that you are still carrying your fair share of the work load, they will be more willing to accept the situation and cooperate with you.

The truth is that you will probably be working harder, but more productively, than you were when you had a traditional schedule. There are fewer interruptions when you come in earlier or later than the rest of the crew, less chance of bumping into them in the elevator or at the water cooler. If you've opted for a compressed work week, for example, you will still have to get the same volume of work completed that you did when you were working five days. The trade-off may be worth it. Then again, it may not. Discuss all these options with your partner before deciding to approach your boss. What are these options?

We envision a future when organizations wake up to the need to redesign jobs to fit both the needs of the work force and the work that has to be done. Mammoth amounts of duplicated effort and wasted time will be eliminated when we learn to do only what needs to be done and stop trying to fill up employee time with unnecessary and annoying little details. We also see a trend toward employment by contract—hiring people when you need them for as long as you need them. If this trend continues, it will be useful to make yourself more valuable to a corporation by focusing on a specific specialty, one for which there are not already large numbers of employees competing. Market these skills to companies on an "as needed" basis. This concept is referred to as *contingent employment* and includes permanent part-time, temporary, or contracted employees. In order to participate, you will have to do your homework.

Investigate skills that are needed in today's market. Study trends and forecasts to get an idea of where the economy, government, and business will be moving over the next three to five years. This will not be an easy task, but information is available through sources like the *Nesbitt Trend Letter* and *Workplace 2000—The Revolution Reshaping American Business*, both by Joseph Boyett and Henry Conn. The challenge is in trying to predict the direction corporations will be taking in the years to come. What will customers need? What wants will have to be filled? The old adage was to "find a *need* and fill it." A better direction is to find a *want* and fill it.

What Are the Flexible Workplace Options?

The following overview is not intended to be an in-depth explanation of your options. For a more in-depth analysis, consult *Creating a Flexible Workplace* by Barney Olmsted and Suzanne Smith. Think about which option may be most helpful to you in managing your career challenges.

Flextime

One of the most widely used options is *flextime*. The objective is to vary starting and quitting times to meet the preferences and needs of employees within a core base of operation. For example, if the organization must have its employees available between the hours of 8 A.M. and 6 P.M., a manager must schedule his available employees to be present within these core hours. Once that has been established, employees may choose to start earlier or leave later so long as they still put in the required number of daily work hours. It is a bigger hassle for the manager but allows employees to choose hours that best fit their individual needs and biological clocks.

Jaine would like to start each day by 7:00 A.M. and quit working by 2:00 P.M. She does start early, but she is rarely able to quit early. Jim, on the other hand, would like to start work around 10:00 A.M. and is just hitting his stride by 4:00 P.M. He often works until 8 or 9 o'clock in the evening. When the children were young, we had to discipline ourselves to work according to the schedule they were on, if we were going to connect as a family. Now that they are grown, we do our own thing, which is terrific. During the week, we have lunch together as often as possible, when we are both in town, but realize that we aren't going to get much quality personal time together until the weekend.

Flexible scheduling might include compressing the work week by squeezing in ten hours of work a day for four days versus eight hours a day for five days. The advantage for employees is a three-day weekend every week. The drawback is that the organization's existing policy may require overtime pay for anything over eight hours a day. Check with your human resources department. Another disadvantage is that you will probably be exhausted after working ten hours a day in addition to traveling to your place of business and tending to personal responsibilities. If you have children, contrary to helping your family, flexible scheduling may result in your having less time with your family and certainly less quality time.

Flexiplace

Flexiplace is the new term for telecommuting or the "electronic cottages" predicted by John Nesbitt in *Megatrends* and Alvin Toffler in *Future Shock*. This option looks similar to the contingent worker arrangement except that, in most cases, this is a permanent arrangement that allows certain employees to work at home while communicating with the office through computer/phone modems, fax machines, and telephone. The advantage to employees is that they can combine working with caring for the children at home.

The disadvantages are similar to those of the compressed work week option. Managers like to see their employees and to have them available for spontaneous meetings or regular conferences. It is also a delusion to think that you can adequately care for children at the same time you are attempting to perform telephone sales and service, accounting services, word processing activities, editing responsibilities, or any number of tasks that require concentration.

You simply cannot concentrate when children are running around, vying for your attention, or getting into trouble. We know, because we have attempted to combine these roles. The result has been duplication of effort as you try to figure out where you were when you were interrupted for the hundredth time and now need to read everything you have just done so you can recover your train of thought. It also results in hurt children, who are told repeatedly not to bother you because you are occupied with important business matters. They get the message: "I am not important."

In the event that you are successful in talking your boss into trying this option, build a system in which you don't attempt to do the impossible. Get up earlier than everyone else and put in a couple of hours before you play spouse and parent. Then interact with the children while you throw a load of wash in the washer, prepare the lunches, and get dressed. When the children take their naps (and all children should take naps until they are ninety-five), hustle back to the professional work you are supposed to be doing and work nonstop until the children wake up. After a little snack, put them to work entertaining themselves for an hour. Do some work-work. Then take a break and give the children some quality time, and then back to work.

In this way the children know that they will be getting your attention and will be more likely to let you work for an hour at a time. None of this snatching for time will equal a full day's work for a full day's pay, so when everyone is in bed for the evening, you will have to put in another couple of hours of professional work. You will be tired and harried. When you do a cost/benefit analysis on this option, you may find it is costing you as much time as, and more energy than, if you had gone to work during the day and performed your parenting tasks in the evening. The big difference, however, is that *you*, rather than a day care center, will be raising your children.

The other big disadvantage is that when you are out of sight, you are out of mind. Even the most progressive manager is not inclined to think of you in the same professional terms as he or she does employees who are *there* every day. It's just a fact of life. But if that fits within your lifetime goals, so be it. The objective is to be happy and feel good about yourself and what you are doing.

Job Sharing

Another option is *job sharing*. In theory, the concept includes two or more people sharing the same job. For example, Mary shows up for work as a computer operator on Mondays, Tuesdays, and Wednesdays, while Helen works the same job on Thursdays and Fridays. We have tried this option with women who want to do word processing. The difficulty we encountered was in coordination and communication. Mary never appeared to know where Helen had stored data, did not like her system of labeling, and thought herself superior to Helen, who felt the same way about Mary. These women were friendly when the arrangement started, but unfriendly when we finally had to face the fact that we were spending too much of our time arbitrating disputes. Of course, not all job sharing situations result in fiasco. But if your manager has had difficulty with this or any option in the past, s/he will be more reluctant to experiment in the future. You have to prove yourself.

We have even suggested that couples would make excellent job-sharing partners for organizations that do not have nepotism rules.

Alternatives

Two other possible solutions to the problem of wanting more time with your family are:

- He works nights, she works days. You never get to see each other, but your children will have the advantage of having a parent around most of the time (more on this in Chapter 12).
- Start your own business. There are many advantages to this option (consult Chapter 13 for suggestions).

What about on-site child care? In 1992, Catalyst was awarded a grant by the Pew Charitable Trusts to examine the quality of corporate-sponsored child care programs. Its research indicated that corporate-sponsored care has many benefits, including increased ease of employee recruitment, lower employee turnover, improved productivity, and reduced absenteeism. Get the report and present it to your manager.

For a few years Jaine worked for an international restaurant and hotel chain as its training manager. This job, too, required travel but not as extensively as when she became a free-lance public speaker and program designer. If either of our jobs had had quality, on-site child care, our lives would have taken a different direction and so would have our careers. Child care was our number one challenge for over eighteen years. Eighteen years may seem extensive to you. What child needs child care after the age of 12 or 13? All of them. At least, that's what *we* believe. At seventeen, a boy should no more be left alone overnight than at seven months. The problems and risks are just different.

Summary

The notion that we are powerless products of our environment is our biggest sin. Manage the challenges in your life and your career. You are not a victim of the big bad corporation or government. But it does help if you have a coach who can help you negotiate the minefields created by corporate politics and government regulations.

Your partner can and should help you with your career by being on your side. Your partner can successfully act as your mentor-coach, committed to giving you open, honest—even distasteful—feedback about how you may be sabotaging yourself and hurting your career chances. Develop this valuable resource, and don't shoot the messenger.

Make a career out of your job. Learn the rules of the game. Be a sponge and soak up information, advice, classes, and anything else that will help you succeed. Do jobs no one else wants to do, and don't complain about them. Get management to support your ideas by following the strategies suggested in this chapter.

If you want to encourage management to participate in achieving partnership goals, make it easy for them to say yes. As with making any major suggestions to management, do your homework, gather all available information, and analyze it. Don't just gather barrels of information and dump it on your manager's desk. Go through the information with your partner and whittle it down to the pertinent facts.

Check references and talk with other organizations that are using work/family systems. Talk with providers. Talk with mothers. Then put together a written summary of the data and make your recommendation. Ask for an appointment and then present your findings. As always, there is power in numbers, so the more support you can find within the organization, the better it will be for you. How many employees would actually avail themselves of the work/family options you are suggesting? How much would they cost? What are the benefits to the organization?

All this takes time, you say? Of course it takes time. That's why organizations, and managers in particular, keep putting it off. Remember, organizations do not *owe* you on-site child care, work/family referral services, or flexible scheduling. If *you* want the options, take the responsibility for your own welfare and discover what's in it for them to give you what you want.

Chapter 12

Working Realities: Resolving Critical Issues

New working realities require constant adjustments for working couples. Increasingly, couples must find very creative solutions to stressful job requirements. Some of these ideas sound good at the time they are developed, but many couples have found that the extra pressure such arrangements cause can have a devastating effect on the partnership. For example, if your job requires that you leave on Sunday evening and not return until Friday night, it will put pressure on the partnership. Partnership pressure may lower your productivity at work, which puts your job at risk. It's an unpleasant cycle.

While you are considering these arrangements, keep in mind that the goal should be to find solutions that help to release the pressures on both of you. Always implement a new strategy on a trial basis and then constantly evaluate what these new arrangements are doing to the relationship. When the arrangement works, it may keep couples from having to relocate or change jobs, or allow one or both partners to be more readily available to their children or aging parents.

These include situations in which one partner may work in a different city from the other; he works days and she works nights; one or both have to travel frequently; job relocation turns one partner into a "trailer"; one partner is paired with a member of the opposite sex; and even "flip-flop" arrangements in which he works from the house one year and she works at home the next. There is also the issue of who earns more money. What if it is the woman? Can his ego accept being on the bottom?

Can personal partnerships survive the additional stresses resulting from increased competition for jobs? Of course, they can if both partners know the rules and agree to focus on mutual objectives. Their special needs must be discussed from the point of view of feelings, financial advantages, and loneliness. Special guidelines and boundaries need to be worked out and commitments made, by both of you, that if the arrangement begins to threaten the well-being of the partnership, alternative lifestyles will be created.

Gene Landrum, author of the book *Profiles of Female Genius—Thirteen Creative Women Who Changed the World*, writes that really successful women, the kind who have changed the world, chose not to have children. They needed to focus all their energies on their careers. Our challenge, while interviewing for this book, was to find career-oriented couples who had children. In several instances, the male partner had children by a previous marriage, but didn't have any in this partnership. The reasons women gave for not having children varied:

- "I can't have children, so I can be flexible. My work is my life."
- "We didn't have children so we could focus on our careers from Monday through Friday."
- "If we had children, we couldn't travel like we do."
- "He told me, at the beginning, that he didn't want any more children. I accepted that."
- "I want children, but it isn't feasible in a commuter relationship. I worry that the biological clock is running out."
- "I observed how he treated his past wives. As soon as the children arrived, he found a position in another country. *He* is my child."
- "My career was always too demanding to think of having children. Then it was too late. There are many times when I think I made an irreversible mistake."

Choices. We are constantly presented with choices, and the decisions we make affect our whole lives. Most choices are reversible—for example, where you live, what kind of job you take, career decisions, and whom you marry. Even the choice as to whether or not to have children is reversible until the biological clock runs out. With recent medical advances, this too may turn into a long-term choice. And consider the reality of our overpopulated world. You can wait to adopt children until after your careers are established and then make your choice.

> *We are constantly presented with choices, and the decisions we make affect our whole lives.*

Euphoria soon turns to ennui with the daily responsibilities of work and family. Sometimes you begin to feel as if there is no joy at all in your life. So if you have not yet had children, consider your choices carefully. Children are not a temporary responsibility you can take on and then change your mind about. They are a lifetime commitment, or should be, for both of you. And they are not always cute and cuddly. They are often selfish and demanding and jealous and irritable. Children also cost a great deal of money, so don't be fooled into thinking that your cousin's hand-me-downs will suffice forever. They want their own stuff, and while you are purchasing their stuff you will have to be content with only a new dish towel or toilet plunger for yourself once in a while. You have to be very dedicated and very much in love with them to put up with it all. We were. And you have to make serious adjustments in your lifestyle. We did.

> *Children are not a temporary responsibility you can take on and then change your mind about.*

For us, having children was never a question of *if*, it was a question of *when*. We had them early in our partnership, which filled us with joy. But if we could do it over again, we would make every conceivable adjustment to keep from having to send Jaine back to work until the children were in school full-time. We were fortunate in that we could plan our work schedules around the children— most of the time. Our plan was for one of us to be in town if the other was out. This didn't always work out, so we called upon Jaine's mother as an overnight baby sitter. If you are lucky enough to have relatives who will help out on a regular basis, and if you have a good relationship with them, use this valuable resource. Usually grandparents love the opportunity to bond with their grandchildren.

If you don't have family you can call on for help, try to find one you can trust. Several universities around the country are attempting to merge child care and elder care facilities. Most elders still have a lot of bang in them. Having children around keeps them active and alert by giving them something to do, and children love hearing stories of "when I was a kid." It's only when we get older that we hate to hear them.

Also investigate community housing arrangements. These are a form of clustered houses surrounding a common "town hall." While they can be arranged in a variety of ways, the objective is to allow each family its own quarters while focusing all activities in and around the town hall. Some of these arrangements include meal preparation trade-offs. One day a month your family cooks for the rest of the community and then sits back and enjoys life until the rotation gets back to you. Most communities also include child care trade-offs. You'll find a resource guide in the back of the book.

Whose Job Is More Important?

Both of your careers are equally important. That does not necessarily mean that each job is equally important to the well-being of the partnership. Agree in advance that you both work because you need and want to. Both add to the financial and emotional well-being of the partnership. Set boundaries and guidelines for how decisions are made.

> Jaine had a viable and important career as the training manager for a national hotel and restaurant chain when we met and married. During our courtship, we agreed that having children was an important need for both of us. She wanted to take a sabbatical after the birth of our children until they were both in school full-time. That was the objective. Therefore, no matter who was making the most money or how important the title or function was for each, we knew that our personal objective was to free Jaine to stay at home. During that period Jim's job was considered the more important because he was the one who would have to advance and succeed in order to support the family alone. Partnership efforts therefore went toward enhancing Jim's promotability and profitability.
>
> A glitch in our plans came when there was a downsizing in his organization. Those who survived were given a cut in pay. This caused financial strain on the Carter budget, so the partnership investigated ways to bring in extra money while still maintaining the primary objective of allowing Jaine to stay at home. As mentioned in Chapter 2, Jaine began promoting workshops for working women. These workshops were an immediate and profitable success, because the timing was right. So we went back to the drawing board. Whose job was more important now?
>
> More money was flowing in through Jaine's business than was flowing in through Jim's job. Jaine needed help keeping the momentum going, so we both focused on the new business while holding on to the steady income provided by Jim's job. It was hard. Jim was literally doing two jobs. So was Jaine. Then came the big breakthrough. Jaine and her seminars were in such demand that she simply couldn't handle them all.

We went through a cost/benefit drill and decided to take the plunge. Jim quit his steady job.

This flip-flop scenario has gone on throughout our partnership. At times, Jim's career is more important. At other times, Jaine's is the focus. Decisions depend on what is going to help us toward our overall life goals at the time.

What If She Makes More Money?

Surveys show that a growing number of women are outearning their spouses. In 1992, 30 percent of women who worked full-time earned more than their working spouses, according to the Bureau of Labor Statistics. Among professional women, the percentage is higher. A survey of 4,500 readers of *Working Woman* magazine found that 42 percent earned more than their male partners.

With most of the couples we interviewed in the course of planning and writing this book, there were times when she made more money than he did. At other times, he outearned his partner. This flip-flop in earning is more usual than unusual. In several partnerships, she has always made more money. How do they manage this nontraditional arrangement? Unfortunately, most couples, in our select survey, have not addressed the issue. They just act as if nothing unusual is happening. On the surface, this appears to be commendable, but our observations are that they have gone underground with their feelings. Men and women *must* discuss the perception of role reversal that friends, family, and their own conditioning make apparent. Men have been conditioned to function in a hierarchial environment. The guy with the most marbles is the leader. The man who can run the fastest, throw the ball the farthest, or make the most money is the winner. It's a power issue.

From the woman's point of view, our research indicates, they are still protecting their partner's ego. When asked how they handle their separate salaries, most said that they put their entire salary into a joint checking account. When asked if they had any separate rainy day funds, most said they didn't. All of the women who have an open shared banking arrangement have separate, well-paying careers. Yet they have no fallback account of their own.

All of the men feel this is the way it should be. When asked if it bothered them that their partners made more money, they responded in a variation of, "No. More power to her." Another interesting observation is that all of the men whose partners made more money felt that the situation was only temporary: "It's just while I'm going to school," or "I've hit a rough spot in my career, but I'll be making more than she does within the year," or "I've started my own business and it takes a couple of years to get the show on the road." For some, the "year" flows into five, even ten.

We have noticed a growing trend toward women supporting men. We used to refer to this as the "Naples phenomenon." Many of the men in the Naples/Marco Island area are not working. Some say they are over-qualified and that Naples is just not the place to get jobs in their chosen field or specialty. They claim they are spending this time to discover themselves and to decide what they want to do with the rest of their lives. On first inspection, this would seen a commendable commentary on our times—men finally coming into their own, attempting to develop the sensitivity their women have always wanted of them. How is this affecting women?

Women confess that, at first, they were proud to be able to give their partners the opportunity to take time off to plan the rest of their lives. But the burden of supporting the family gets heavy after a while. A thirty-five-year-old former schoolteacher with tenure told us, "He wanted to move here as much as I wanted to. I gave up a good job to relocate, but I went back to school to become a massage therapist. That was two years ago and I'm still the only source of income. He just goes from idea to idea and never follows through with any of them. I feel used!"

A director of a not-for-profit agency complained, "He opened a business, but he doesn't *do* anything. He gets up, goes out to breakfast with "business associates" who also don't do anything, goes to the office on which I pay the rent, and then goes to lunch. He has not even made the money to pay his own office phone bill."

These are only a few such laments. Women are feeling used and resentful, but they don't change anything. They confess that they complain to their partners, suggesting that they look for paying jobs. The forty-two-year-old husband of the massage therapist remarked, "Who would hire me? Nobody wants a forty-two-year-old any more. They want the young hotshots they can get for peanuts!"

These issues are not going away and until the paradigm completes its shift, old rules will have to be rewritten. Is it right for women to support men? Just as men may be paying for the sins of their fathers, are women required to pay for the sins of their mothers? Is it time that women support men? Or is this just another form of abuse?

Men who are allowing their partners to work while they make half-hearted or no attempts to contribute to the partnership are controlling women in a different way than they did in the past. In the past, men were the keepers of the money. They wrote the checks, made the investments, and delivered the allowances. Even when women earn more money, most men still control the money.

What Do You Do If His/Her Job Requires Relocation?

Relocation opportunities require a serious revisiting of your partnership plan. Relocation can wreak havoc on your partnership. We have several stories told us by an ex-IBMer, who related that IBM stands for "I've Been Moved." The situation may have changed some, but frequent relocation is still the domain of large organizations. For example, another branch is opened in the Far East and key personnel from the New York headquarters of your company are reassigned to form the opening team. Who fills the positions left open by their relocation? It may be you or your partner. Employers are hiring and promoting more women and in the process doing more to narrow the spread between what men and women are paid. These possibilities should have been discussed while you were doing your partnership plan or when you considered taking the job.

Even when you have discussed the possibility of relocation and have planned for it, it never seems to come at an opportune time. There are endless consequences to be considered. If you have children, what about their schooling and friends? What about your spouse's job? Can s/he find a comparable job at comparable pay in the new location? Is the new job worth the hassle it will cause the family? What will happen if you turn down the request for relocation? Major decisions must be made. Let's look at them.

> *Even when you have discussed the possibility of relocation and have planned for it, it never seems to come at an opportune time.*

First, we want to dispel the myth that children are very adaptable and will adjust easily to change and relocation. They are not and they will not. Once a child is in school, relocation to another school requires a total readjustment. Children have only a limited frame of reference. Unlike you, they don't *know* that the future location will turn out beautifully, that they will eventually make new friends, and that the teachers in the new school are not ghouls. Consider their needs, very carefully. And if you decide to avail yourselves of the new opportunity, take cautious steps to prepare your children by giving them time to adjust to the *idea* of another life before you actually flip-flop their world. Let them make choices that affect their lives. Visit the new location with them to view the living quarters, to examine the new school system, and to experience the community. Give them control over as many decisions as possible that will affect their lives.

Second, let's dispel the myth that you have control over whether or not you accept the relocation opportunity and still stay on the fast track at your present company. It's okay to refuse top management's request to relocate just as it's okay for management to compute your refusal into the equation the next time an advancement opportunity comes around. It is not equitable for you to refuse all the undesirable positions while holding out for the prizes. It doesn't work that way, except by some miracle. Most of us have to serve our time, which means that we have to play by their rules, like it or not. And don't scream that it's not fair. It is fair. It's their company and they have the right to call the shots, just as you did when you were young and owned the football. An associate of ours is fond of saying "Them who gots gets" or "The golden rule is: Those who have the gold, rule."

> *"The golden rule is: Those who have the gold, rule."*

So here are the challenges:

1. If you agree to the relocation, it will not be easy for the family to adjust.
2. If you refuse to move, you will find yourself plateaued—or out.
3. One of you will be without a job.
4. You will probably not be able to enjoy the same lifestyle on one salary in the new location.

The best advice we can give you is to take this all one step at a time. Don't make any drastic moves, but accept the request. Temporarily turn your partnership into a *commuter marriage.* Negotiate with the organization requesting the relocation to provide you with living quarters for an indefinite length of time at the new location. Also negotiate for air fare every weekend until a permanent decision can be made. Tell the relocating firm that this arrangement must last until you can sell your present home, or until the school break, or until you can find a comparable home at a comparable price in the new location. Also negotiate with them to reimburse you for the money you may lose from the sale of your present home. Ask their help in finding your partner a job comparable to the one s/he will be losing.

Once negotiations are successfully concluded with your relocating organization, start your analysis. Instead of the relocating partner coming home every weekend, the partner still at home should go there to get the lay of the land. What are the job opportunities at the new location? What are property values doing? What about crime? Consider all the angles, but keep an open mind.

> Ron lives in Boca Raton with his wife, Pat, and their children. He was offered a job in Houston doing what he loves to do. But Houston was just recovering from a depressed economy, whereas property values in Boca were continuing to go up. So he and Pat decided to commute. She stayed in Boca and he got the Houston firm to pick up the tabs for his housing in Houston as well as his weekly trips back home. After nine months of this see-saw, they decided the job was not worth the hardship that commuting was causing so they looked around for options.

We fear that too many of us are living lives of quiet desperation because we look into the future and see closed doors. Stop negatively projecting. It may be a depressed economy riddled by competition and low wages today. But things can and do turn around. During our careers we have had both good years and bad. The trick is to average them monetarily. When things are good, put as much away as you can for the time when things won't be so good. And these times will come. They always do. The job you hold now is *not* the last one available in the whole world unless you give up and make it just that.

Trailer Partnerships

If your decision is to accept the request for transfer and your partner has agreed to relocate, consider the consequences to the trailing partner. Chances are s/he will not be able to replace the income, seniority, and/ or status s/he had in the old job. Therefore, face the fact that his/her career opportunities will most likely decrease.

This can be especially devastating to the man if it is his wife who is offered the promotion. Factor this into the equation carefully. How will his decrease in earning power affect the partnership? Will she eventually become resentful of having to provide primary support for the family? You can never really predict how you will feel in the future; but if you go in with your eyes open, you will at least make a more informed decision.

The Commuter Marriage:
When His/Her Job Is in Another City

When we first started researching the commuter phenomenon we assumed that its characteristics would be similar to those that exist for frequent travelers. But couples who live and work in different cities, while they do experience a great deal of travel, also experience a whole separate set of challenges. In essence, these partners lead two separate lives—the one they have together and the one they have apart. There must be two permanent residences, two sets of utilities, phone hook-ups, automobiles, wardrobes, appliances, furniture. You name it, each partner has to have it. A few of these relationships try to survive as if they were temporary arrangements. One partner lives out of furnished facilities to maintain the illusion of nonpermanence. In the beginning, the "temporary worker" is the one who makes the long trek home each weekend. This wears thin.

> Gene Landrum, the author of *Profiles of Genius—Thirteen Men Who Changed the World*, and his wife Dedra have had a commuter marriage several times in their eleven years together. Gene admits, "The only way our commuter marriage has worked is because Dedra is an extremely independent woman."
>
> Dedra adds, "Since Gene and I have known each other we have lived in three states and seven houses and we've had fourteen jobs. Not everyone would go for that. But I have the security of my own job and my own thing, so he's kind of the excitement in my life."

In interview after interview, couples claimed that communication was their number one problem. This is especially true of commuter marriages. One woman said this on the subject: "I think marriage is a difficult situation to begin with. It has some inherent stressors. But the biggest challenge in a commuter marriage is that you have to plan more and you have to communicate more because you don't have the luxury of saying, 'I'm going to grab this person tonight after dinner or after we wake up tomorrow.' In a commuter marriage, you are not in the same city on the same day. We do communicate, but it doesn't always mean that it works. Talking is important. Planning is key."

Some people believe that a commuter marriage isn't really a marriage but merely long-distance dating. One person who strongly disagrees argues, "That's like saying that marriage is not a significant factor in your life. I don't know anybody who would purposely go out and have a commuter marriage. Things happen that you can't always control. You have to evaluate your careers and make difficult decisions. I don't think I'm going to do this forever. I could see where we could, but I don't want to." To survive such a partnership, use the same strategies suggested for frequent travelers.

> *"I don't know anybody who would purposely go out and have a commuter marriage."*

When Work Requires Frequent Travel

Frequent travel has its perks. It also has its pains. Depending on the strength of the partnership, the one left at home may begin to feel abandoned. It appears as if the traveling partner is never around when you need him/her. We had the added challenge of having to flip-flop our travel schedules. Because of the children, one of us needed to be home while the other traveled.

Give or take a couple of years, Jim traveled more than Jaine. There were weeks on end when he would leave on a Sunday afternoon and not return until midnight the following Friday. Every tragedy in our family seemed to happen between Monday and Friday. Children needed stitches, parents had emergencies, and life went on. If your partner must travel frequently, resign yourself to the fact that you are a single person/ parent when he or she is away. You must entertain yourself, protect yourself, and generally enjoy yourself as if you were alone, because you are. Don't put yourself on *hold* and wait until the weekends to live. If you do, you will one day turn around to discover that five-sevenths of your life is gone and you did nothing in it but survive. Develop a network of friends and relatives who are willing and able to help you in the event of a crisis and who are also willing and happy to include you in their lives.

Console yourself with the perks. Our family has never had to purchase a bar of soap. That's pretty good for twenty-five years. We must have saved at least $198 this way. Small consolation for being gone so often, you say? Okay, with the advent of frequent flyer miles, our whole family became connoisseur travelers. The Carters have been all over the world together, to places we could never have afforded if we had had to pay for the trips ourselves.

Set ground rules or you will find that instead of frequent traveling careers adding to the financial well-being of the partnership, they will be a drain. Most couples involved in a frequent travel partnership say that they supported AT&T until they learned to discipline themselves. It gets lonely, and the stay-at-home partner wants some form of connection every day. The trouble is that you are loath to cut the connection. You get each other on the phone and you want to share everything that happened that day in minute detail. If there are children, each child wants to play on the phone for fifteen minutes. Then there is the issue of the hurt feelings you had just before you left.

When you are setting ground rules, agree on a general time limit for each call. You will need more than the basic, "Hi, how are you." "Fine." But rehashing grievances on the phone is futile and dangerous. The traveling partner is helpless and alone. S/he has no friends or family on the road, no one to talk with or to listen to imagined injustices. It's not fair. So bite your tongue and be entertaining and loving. Besides, if you rehash injustices on the phone, you will soon find that the traveler doesn't call home as often.

So save your gripes for the day after the traveler gets home. It's okay to ask your partner to give you moral support for something you have to do at work or an action you took with the children or another relative. This is what connection is all about. It's also permissible to discuss pending plans or needed decisions over the phone. Generally, though, the purpose of phone connection is to connect—just connect.

> *So save your gripes for the day after the traveler gets home.*
> *The purpose of phone connection is to connect—just connect.*

Betty and Bill are both frequent travelers, though Bill's job requires more time away from home base. Betty says that the only way she has successfully survived Bill's prolonged and continual absences is to develop a network of friends with whom she can interact and share dinners, shopping sprees, and movies. They also have relatives nearby, which helps tremendously. One of their rules is that they connect every day, no matter where they happen to be. Usually, this is in the evening after each finishes his or her respective assignments, unless one or the other is running for another plane to the next location. In that event, knowing each other's schedule, the result of a two-calendar system closely coordinated, they arrange to connect during lunch breaks. This does take a conscious effort, especially when he is in California and she is in Florida. Different time zones are tricky. "You really have to love your job to put up with all the grief and the unhealthy environment on the planes. Otherwise, it would be intolerable," Bill says.

Call with, "Just checking in. How are things going?" It keeps the partnership moving and alive. In the twenty-five years we have been married not a day has gone by that we have not talked, either in person or on the phone. Sound corny? Well it has worked, hasn't it? Take it from there.

How do you handle the situation when the traveling partner has been on the road all week and the stay-at-home partner is bored and itching to go out to dinner or to socialize on the evening of his/her return? Have a heart! The road warrior is weary. We used to say that all we wanted when we got home were some vegetables, our own bed, and not to have to smile.

Give your road-weary partner some space, some time, and consideration. Contrary to the belief that they have been catered to all week, consider that they have been *on* all week, talking to clients, prospects, participants, and bell people. They have lived out of suitcases, waited in lines at airports, hotels, taxi stands, and restaurants, and generally been treated badly. Wait and go out the next night with a now grateful partner.

Don't blame your partner for traveling. Too often we encounter partners of frequent travelers who believe that the traveling partner could travel less if s/he wanted to. It's as if the nontraveling partner believes that the traveler is using travel as an excuse to get away from home. There is always the possibility that people use work-related situations to avoid their responsibilities, but it is the exception, not the rule.

Work with whatever situation you are given. Renee says that she uses the time when Richard is away or involved in a particularly heavy work mode to visit her parents, who are ill. In this way, she gets the opportunity to play dutiful daughter without having to worry about Richard and his needs. Richard also uses work travel situations to visit his folks whenever possible. That way his family has the chance to see him without having to worry about including Renee. It works for everyone. We did the same thing. Wherever Jim was close to Toledo, Ohio, he took the opportunity to route himself so he could visit with his mother. We will always be grateful for that last trip to Toledo because it was just two weeks before an aneurysm took her life.

Get friends and family to cooperate. We were finally able to arrive at a time in our lives when close friends and family would schedule their parties, weddings, and special events around our mutual travel schedules. Since they wanted us to be there and we wanted to be included, we worked it out so that they would check with us before they booked the church or the caterers.

> *There is always the possibility that people use work-related situations to avoid their responsibilities, but it is the exception, not the rule.*

Your Partner Wants You to Travel With Him/Her on Certain Business Trips

Traveling together can be a great perk in the frequent flyer partnership. You can combine business trips with time spent together if it can be worked out to the mutual satisfaction of both you and your partner's employer. Sometimes it works and sometimes it doesn't. The important thing is not to create an issue over it and make the partner who can't accompany you feel guilty.

When Ginny and Winn merged in a partnership, Winn made it quite clear that he expected Ginny to accompany him on business trips as much as possible. Ginny explains, "At the time, I didn't think of my career as being viable. It was just something to augment our high lifestyle. Since I worked for a small firm, they had no objections.

"At first I went with Winn every time he asked me. After a while, that got old hat. It wasn't fun anymore to sit in a hotel and wait for Winn to finish with his business appointments. I began limiting the times I went with him to the supervacation spots of the world or when he felt I would be a definite business advantage. This worked until my career took off and I wasn't able to get away."

He Works Days, She Works Nights, or Vice Versa

In order to manage child care responsibilities, many couples have chosen to flip-flop their working schedules. Whether or not a couple has children, day/night shifts are part of a growing business trend to around-the-clock staffing. Today's consumers want a customer service representative available whenever they want to order merchandise, check their credit card balance, make travel arrangements, or fulfill any other need. How does this affect the partnership?

Flipping schedules presents the same problems that are faced by frequent travelers or partners in a commuter relationship, with the added challenge that partners in this kind of relationship seldom find enough time to sleep.

> Pam and Peter have three children. As a nurse, Pam has always had a rotating schedule, while Peter has always worked days. During the early years of their relationship, Pam would come home from a midnight shift, straighten the house, get the next day's lunch ready for the children, find something to eat, and go to bed as soon as possible.
>
> "I never got more than six hours of sleep, because Peter had to be at work by seven in the morning. I wanted to get up, get his breakfast, and have a few minutes to connect. This was never the best arrangement, as he was always just half awake. Over the years, I have been able to adjust my schedule so that it is more tenable. I have chosen to work the midnight to seven shift. This gives me time with the children in the morning before they go to school, and after school, all through dinner. It also gives me time with Peter in the evening."

Trying to work and sleep during the day while the children are young just doesn't work. They can get into as much trouble while you are sleeping as they could if you were not there. In truth, you are not there. The only way a night shift worker can get enough sleep to survive is to arrange child care for the children during the day, even if this is just for six hours. Several shift workers said that the best schedule for child care is when one partner worked nine to five and the other five until midnight. That way, you need a sitter only during the one or two hours between parents. That is, of course, if one of you doesn't have to work overtime. One night shift worker suggested that both partners work nights so they could be available for the children during the day. But this works only if you have a trusted relative who is willing to sleep in the house while the children are sleeping. As for partnership connections, you will have to put them off until your days off. Just make sure those days off fall on the same days.

What if S/he Is Required to Team and Travel with a Member of the Opposite Sex?

Teaming with a member of the opposite sex is a reality of this decade. Male/female attractions and flirtations are also a reality. It is unreasonable to pretend that his/her teams will not be confronted by male/female issues. Even if, at first, you are totally turned off by your work teammate, it stands to reason that when you work together and experience the same challenges and overcome the same barriers, mutual respect and admiration will develop. You would soon learn to detest your job if you had to work with a person you despised. That's the reality.

What do significant others do? The same things that men and women have always done. Work with it. Women may have more meaningful careers than they did in the past, but they have always been present in the workplace. Restaurants have always had waitresses, executives have always had secretaries, doctors have always had nurses. It's true that some of these male/female teams have succumbed to mutual attraction and dallied with doing dangerous things. That's life. This history lesson doesn't make it any easier for you to swallow when it's happening to you, but there are no rules you can set to prevent it if it's going to happen.

What you can do is take care of *you*. Too often, when straying occurs, strayed-upon partners feel that it is their fault, that there's something wrong or lacking in them. Give that up. If your partner strays, it is not because you are working too much or because you were a witch the evening before or complained because he didn't take out the garbage. We don't believe that it is even because the boredom of doing the same thing day after day starts to wear you down. Attraction, plain old physical attraction, is what lands most of us in a compromising position. And fear of consequences that we don't want to happen is what helps us exert the necessary restraint to resist temptation.

When you want what is in the partnership you already have, you will be less inclined to risk losing it. If the partnership is not giving you what you want out of life, then nothing will help keep it together. This, too, is as old as both sexes. Should we not put male/female teams together? That doesn't make much difference from our point of view. If a partner is going to disconnect from the partnership and reconnect with another, working together in teams just makes it a little easier, that's all.

Summary

Working couples today encounter career challenges that require the development of creative solutions. This takes cooperative effort by both partners. The decision as to whether to participate in these challenges depends on your value systems, the strength of your partnership, and the determination of how these challenges will enhance your long-term goals.

Frequent travel, day/night shifts, and commuter relationships all cause extended separations. Most women dislike these times of disconnection. Some even begin to feel abandoned. Men need to understand their partners' need for connection and make every effort to reach out and stay involved.

Women, too, need to accept that the demands of their partners' jobs may require compliance. While the traveling partner may be turned on by his job, it does not mean that he is turned off by his partner.

All it takes is a shift in attitude and a consistent commitment to stay tuned in to each other's feelings and needs. When the career begins to threaten the relationship, you need to design new options. Working together may be one of them.

Chapter 13

Working Together: Co-preneurs

An estimated one out of every six middle managers and executives who have lost their jobs as the result of downsizing have started their own small companies, many with their spouses. Can personal partnerships successfully develop into business partnerships? Ours did and we have just celebrated our twentieth anniversary. Starting your own business may give you more control over your future, but unless you consider all the ramifications of working together, it could also drive an irreparable wedge into the relationship.

When significant other partnerships work, they can bring financial success and enrichment to the personal partnership. Family-owned and operated businesses are being formed to combat the insecurity caused by downsizing and organizational plateauing and to provide couples with work/family options that are not available when they work for someone else.

Most family businesses are started with the entrepreneur's own money or money borrowed from relatives, but some types of small businesses may actually be financed by larger companies that are looking to develop suppliers of specialty services or products they don't want to provide internally. The advantage to entrepreneurs of this kind of setup is that they have a ready-made customer as well as venture capital. The funding company also has a vested interest in seeing the new venture succeed. Another form of entrepreneurial enterprise, called an "intra-preneurial" venture, is started within a larger organization but functions as a specialty unit to research and supply new ideas of interest to the "mother" company. You should research these options. If they are available, it will take much of the risk out of breaking away. If not, decide whether you want to start from scratch, purchase an existing company, or be part of a franchising organization.

Crawl, Walk, Run

If you are considering starting a business together, we recommend that you start slowly and don't burn your bridges. Lifestyle changes require a great deal of research and planning before it is safe to take the plunge. Don't just decide that you always wanted a dry cleaning business, for example, and go out and sign a lease on some space. Look around. How many dry cleaning establishments already exist in your area? How much can a dry cleaning business expect to earn? How many hours a day will each of you have to devote to this business? What activities are involved? Will you enjoy being surrounded by steam and dirty clothes all day? How much start-up capital will it take to get going? How long will it be before you can expect to start making a decent living out of the business? Where will you find financing? The list is endless.

Where can you find information to help you answer these questions? Start in the library. There you will find listings of business categories with references for gathering more information. Also contact your local and federal Small Business Administration (SBA). They provide a wealth of information, including advice on how to go about getting financing. Most communities also have SCORE contacts comprising groups of retired executives and business owners who donate their time in order to help small business entrepreneurs get started and avoid the pitfalls that await every new business. They may be able to help you avoid business failure, the fate of more than 77 percent of new start-ups that are no longer in operation after five years. Many universities have centers for small businesses offering counseling and classes on how to start a business.

How Should You Structure Your Company?

A partnership is an arrangement between two or more people to carry on a business. Choosing the right partner is critical to success. It also presents legal considerations you need to think about. Just as with any working relationship, it is important that partners understand the other's behavioral tendencies, values, goals, and expectations.

The most significant feature of a partnership is that each member can legally bind and obligate the other. This means that the actions or conduct of one of the partners can make the other personally responsible. Obviously, if you have any doubts about the integrity or capability of your potential partner in the business, you shouldn't do it, but there are advantages to a partnership. Legally, a good partnership can help divide the work and responsibility. In addition, the "double tax" and many of the statutory regulations imposed on corporations are avoided.

How about the disadvantages? A bad partnership can ruin a marriage and divide families. The stress can be enormous. Legally, as with the sole proprietorship, there is unlimited personal liability. Even worse, each partner is now on the hook for obligations of the business, even if they are incurred by only one of the partners without the knowledge of the other. Another difficulty lies in the death or withdrawal of one of the partners, which can cause the partnership to be dissolved.

With proper planning, these obstacles can be overcome. Love and trust are not the issues here. Good business practices are merely a matter of common sense. Sadly, too many partnerships are established without any thought given to death, disability, or divorce. A buy-and-sell agreement may prevent this particular problem from occurring. A buy-sell agreement gives the remaining partner the right to buy out the interests of the disconnecting partner. This concept is important in the event of a divorce. It is rare for divorced partners to function effectively in a co-venture once they are divorced. Making arrangements to buy from or sell to the other will prevent hassles should this unfortunate event occur. Of course, you are not entering this co-preneurial venture anticipating an end to the relationship. No one does. Be sure to consult with an attorney and tax adviser concerning structure and buy-sell agreements.

Since buy-and-sell agreements are so closely tied in with insurance, insurance agents encourage partners to set up some sort of plan. Many agents have taken special courses and are well read on the requirements. But be wary if they offer to draw up the agreement. Keep in mind that insurance, not law, is their specialty. This is a highly complex field, and no two situations are identical.

Many partnerships exist without any formal written agreement. The parties trust each other and understand their relationship. This is not an effective or anticipatory problem-preventative way to form a partnership of any kind, however, even in a partnership between significant others. If one of the partners died or became disabled, the survivor would be tangled in a web of legal problems. It's better to have a written partnership contract and to plan in advance for future contingencies.

The partnership agreement should also cover the duties of the partners. Who is supposed to do what? This is one issue that would benefit from formal position descriptions. When dissension begins, it is usually because one partner perceives that s/he is doing more than the other partner and begins to feel resentful. Just as in the corporate environment, each partner would benefit from formal standards of performance being developed during a joint planning session. Regular sessions should be scheduled to monitor outcomes for each partner in order to prevent grudges or resentment from building up.

Develop and utilize an advisory team. This team should include your accountant, your attorney, your business consultant, and your insurance adviser. You need each of these professionals to help guide you toward making the right decisions for your business. A good business consultant can also help you develop mechanisms for airing disagreements and guide your team through the formulation and implementation of your business plan. While developing your business plan, you should identify an objective outsider who can serve as a resource in case there is serious disagreement, now or in the future, to help you find the middle ground. Remember, these advisers are like out-sourced employees. They look at you as a customer and will go the extra mile to help you be a success.

Power Plays: Who Will Really Be the Boss?

Who is really in control? Who calls the shots or makes the final decisions? Whose name is listed as chairman of the board and whose as president? Making a personal business partnership work takes a comprehensive plan that includes an understanding of individual vision, a joint mission statement, agreement as to how the business is to be operated, how decisions are to be made, and who is responsible for what. Spell out in advance every detail you can think of that might interfere with the smooth operation of the business as well as with the harmonious functioning of your personal lives, so there can be no room for misunderstanding.

Why was the business formed? What does each party wish to accomplish? How will goals be established? Prepare an inventory of skills. Decide whether additional skills or knowledge will be necessary for the success of the business. Then decide how, when, and where the skills, knowledge, or information can be obtained. Couples contemplating a business partnership should also decide whether they have personalities that will mesh well in a business relationship. People who have terrific personal relationships can't always transfer these compatibilities to a business partnership (consult Chapter 10).

Separating Business Issues From Personal Issues: Can It Be Done?

If appropriate planning and controls are not established at the outset, the working relationship may destroy the personal relationship. The things you admire, like, or love in a personal partnership may be annoying and unprofessional in a business partnership. Business success depends on your partner's ability to get results. Your partner's propensity for being cute may be destructive in customer or employee relations.

> *If appropriate planning and controls are not established at the outset, the working relationship many destroy the personal relationship.*

When the business is not going smoothly, business partners tend to bring that negative home to the personal relationship. Obviously, your views can conflict in many instances. This natural conflict can be aggravated by partners who have no talent for money or business or who have different visions for the company.

Openly and mutually, establish a trial basis for working together. We always recommend that you keep your present jobs, if at all possible, until the business is making enough money to support at least one of you at a level comparable to what you are currently earning. This is the most stressful time for any co-preneurial venture. Both of you will be working two full-time jobs while you are attempting to get your new business started. If you can get along during this trial-by-fire period, you will probably be able to make it work when the time comes for full-time togetherness.

If crawling hasn't hurt too much, and you are both still committed to the new business, one of you may begin to walk. The next step will be for one of you to take the plunge and quit your job. The equation is simple. The person making the most money working for someone else should be the person who continues working. Are things still looking good? Then gradually bring the second partner into the new business, at first on a part-time basis and then full-time. This is when you are ready to run. Give it all you have and don't look back. You will need all your combined energies to make your business a success.

From Mom-and-Pop to Big-Time Shop:
Do You Still Have the Same Vision?

Today's co-preneurs do not fit the traditional Mom-and-Pop model of a decade ago. Today's personal partners are more complicated, which contributes to business partners being more volatile. As business consultants, we witness the whole range of potential and existing problems that are created when partners have different visions for their company in combination with their personal partnership.

When the children were in school full-time, Nadine started a dress salon. She loved to design and make unique custom fashions for a select clientele. Her business prospered. Within two years, Nadine's little business was bringing in more profit than her husband, Jefferson, was making from his position as a manager for an engineering firm. They had often talked about the possibility of Jeff quitting his steady and secure job and joining Nadine in her business. Jeff was a good enough business professional to realize that they would have to expand the business if they were to make enough to match what they were both making individually. Nadine couldn't imagine how she could produce designs any faster than she already was if she were to continue to produce the one-of-a-kind fashions that had earned her a unique place in the copy-cat world of fashion. Jefferson mapped out a plan showing Nadine that she could continue her specialty while he expanded the business to include unique accessories. She agreed to his plan and Jeff quit his job.

After only six months, with business flourishing, Jeff suggested that they expand again to include a ready-to-wear line of resort fashions. Nadine didn't like the idea of adding ready-to-wear clothing to her exclusive products but finally agreed. Their existing space was limited so Jeff leased the space on either side of the original salon. They also needed additional personnel. Because Nadine was usually too busy to get involved in personnel problems, she delegated all management issues to Jeff, which seemed the expeditious thing to do in that Jeff had been in management most of their married life. This arrangement appeared to be working until Nadine's star designer and two of her seamstresses started to complain about the other employees. They reproached Nadine, telling her that they felt she had lost her vision.

Nadine attempted to discuss this with Jeff, but he always put her off with, "You worry about the custom end of the business and I'll worry about the rest." Nadine worried that they had expanded too quickly. They had lost their uniqueness. This was a constant source of friction between her and Jeff. They fought all the time at home and at work. Employees were divided. Nadine's custom business began to decline.

Nadine begged, threatened, and complained to Jeff, who started to take steps to ease Nadine out of the business. One day she heard Jeff talking with one of the employees about another expansion. "What expansion?" Nadine yelled. "I absolutely will not tolerate another expansion. This is *my* business. I started it. I made it a success! You are ruining my dream. I want you out. Just get out of my business!" Jeff tried to explain that the business was no longer just her baby. They had changed the structure of the business from that of sole proprietor to a corporation. He now owned fifty per cent of the company.

Who was wrong? Was Jeff a terrible person for horning in on Nadine's business? Or was Nadine thinking too small, limiting their potential by insisting on operating as they had in the beginning? We think that neither of them was wrong. They just had different visions for their business.

For couples to become successful business partners, they need the characteristics that anyone must have to set up a partnership: a commitment to hard work, a good working relationship, lots of energy, tolerance for risk, a sense of adventure, and a set plan for handling disagreements. Since couples are immersed in the business together, they can't go home and complain to some uninvolved third party. Each partner, in advance of the co-preneurial venture, must structure a method for letting off steam and getting impartial advice. Everyone needs to develop a no-risk sounding board. Having a mentor is just as important when you are operating your own business as it is when you are functioning inside someone else's corporation. When you are in business together, it must be someone outside the family.

> *Everyone needs to develop a no-risk sounding board.*

Basically, the management problems that face members of a family-owned business are the same as those that confront the owner/manager of any small company, but emotion is an added dimension when significant others work together. It is difficult to make objective decisions about each partner's skills and abilities. Another aspect of this emotional atmosphere is that often nonfamily employees avoid giving objective feedback. They may base their decisions on their knowledge of how their bosses are likely to react. This is not the best basis for producing sound decisions affecting your company.

Recognize that differences exist. Go over the Personal Preference Profile in Chapter 10. These differences may actually be advantages in the operation of a business. For example, he may be more results-oriented, a risk taker who is good at making fast decisions. She may be more detail-oriented, good at weighing the pros and cons of business opportunities.

While both styles may annoy the other at times, both strengths are necessary in making cost-effective decisions. Recognize, respect, and utilize
these differences.

There are other differences to consider. She may be a day person and
he may be a night person. This is advantageous only if you have formed
a business that will be operating twenty-four hours a day. Metabolism is
usually something that cannot be changed. One must learn to work with
it.

> Jim is not fully awake until about ten in the morning. Oh, he walks
> around and gets involved in business activities, but you never know if
> he has actually *heard* what you have to say. Jaine, on the other hand, is
> usually up and ready to climb mountains by six in the morning. Instead
> of fighting these differences, we have learned to work with them. If we
> have a choice, we never schedule an important meeting before ten in
> the morning, when Jim is fully awake, or after four in the afternoon,
> when Jaine has begun to wilt. Of course, when we conduct workshops
> or planning sessions, we have to dance to a different tune, but we can
> arrange our presentations to fit our metabolic rhythms. Jim puts partici-
> pants into morning team activities, while Jaine structures them for the
> afternoon.
>
> Another difference is that Jaine is an organized neatnik, whereas
> Jim's desk looks like an exercise in free association. We have had to
> make arrangements to protect files and other important documents from
> Jim's briefcase, where they have a habit of disappearing.
>
> Both of us are creative, results-oriented, type A, polyphasic people.
> As a result, we each have to help the other stay focused on the task at
> hand until it is completed. Our preference would be to come up with a
> great idea, get other people excited about the idea, and then let them
> carry the ball. Often, the only people who can carry that ball is us. That
> takes discipline.

Learn to Treat Each Other as Who You Are, Not Who You Wish Each Were

Using your inventory of skills, differences, and preferences, divide the
work that needs to be accomplished according to each person's abilities,
education, and experience. Since this is your own business, formed for
the purpose of enjoying life while pursuing your goals, also consider
what each of you *likes* to do. While it is not always possible for business
owners to do only what they like to do, it may be possible to divide the

annoying little details in such a way that neither of you hates doing what needs to be done.

Create boundaries between business life and personal life. Co-preneurs need to create a personal plan as well as a business plan (consult Chapter 6 for details on planning strategies). The business plan explains how the business is to function. The working couple's plan outlines how the co-preneurs will work/live together. While we do not advocate a "do not talk about work at home" rule, working couples who are in business together may find that if they do not set aside some hours in which business is taboo they will never be talking about anything else.

> Marvin and Julia are in the beauty business together. Both are too busy during the day to discuss problems or make necessary decisions. Julia has a great need to resolve issues that she feels are important when they are alone in the evening. "It is the only time that I can discuss things with him without twenty pairs of ears listening to everything we have to say." But Marvin has a "do not talk about work" rule and he is constantly reminding Julia of it. The rule is actually the source of frequent arguments.

Although we understand the rationale behind Marvin's feelings, we also understand that business issues must be discussed at the most convenient time for both partners. Julia needs someone to whom she can confide, complain, and connect. A more effective arrangement should be worked out stipulating the specific times when work is not to be discussed. For example, we try not to talk about work on Saturday mornings and Sundays. We also attempt not to talk about work after eight in the evening during the normal week. It is not always possible to adhere to these boundaries, but having set guidelines, we are more conscious of the need to limit our work talk in favor of personal connection.

Should You Work at Home?

The American Home Business Association estimates that there are more than 13 million full-time home businesses operating in the United States, with another 14 million part-time corporate homeworker or homeowner businesses. That number is increasing every year. A growing number of companies are running experimental programs to determine if telecommuting is a viable option for some workers. Government is also looking at the feasibility of allowing certain government workers to perform their jobs from their homes. The United States Chamber of Commerce indicates that more than 25 million businesses list their home address as their office address, and the World Future Society estimates that by the year 2000 one-third of the American work force will be telecommuting. It's an option.

There are several advantages to working from your home, especially if you have children or elders who need monitoring. We have run the gambit. Jaine started our business out of our home while the children were young and still prefers working out of her home office, where she can be alone to concentrate. Once Jim came into the business, it was obvious that we needed more space along with the prestige that comes with having a commercial office. As the business grew, so did our office needs, so we expanded and expanded until one day we had eighteen professional consultants running around to every state in the Union plus Canada, three secretaries, two consultative sales types, plus Jim, and a full-time accountant.

As is often the case with entrepreneurial companies, some clients still preferred to do business with us personally, so we were still on the road. Besides, we had to increase income to the corporation to handle the increased overhead and salaries. One day Jaine sighed, "We have to bill over a half million dollars a year before we can start taking money out for us. I don't feel as if we're getting ahead."

We called a conference with our advisory board and Jaine presented her case. If we downsized, we could work less and still earn more disposable income. We weighed the pros and cons and made the decision. We explained the situation to our staff and offered to use their services as independent contractors. They weren't happy, at first. They felt it was better to have a secure salary than to take the risk of being on their own. Today, each of these people is in business for himself/herself, making far more than they would have made working for someone else.

Over the years, substantial contracts have come into the business that required us to rev up, hire personnel, and expand out of the house. The cycle would begin again. We finally faced the fact that the biggest motivator for getting bigger and requiring plusher office space was our egos. Big egos get pretty heavy to carry around.

The advantages of working from your home include far lower fixed costs. You also don't have to waste time commuting and you save money on your wardrobe, though we suggest you dress well enough to greet customers if they decide to drop by. The best thing about working out of your home is that you are in control of your life and your time. You can work at your own pace and vary the work you do to fit your needs. It also gives you the advantage of being available to your family, but don't be lulled into believing that you can concentrate on your work or talk freely on the phone while small children are underfoot.

> *Don't be lulled into believing that you can concentrate on your work or talk freely on the phone while small children are underfoot.*

The biggest disadvantage of working from your home is the loss of prestige. Most people we know who work out of their homes still get defensive when you ask them where their office is. "I am working out of my home temporarily until I find the right space," or "I have an office in town, but it is more convenient for me to meet you at my home," they will say. You also have the problem of limited space and the difficulties of separating work and family. It's just too easy to keep working when it is all right there. Home workers still don't feel as professional as people who have an office to go to, but it is definitely the way to go when you are first starting out. Be sure to check zoning requirements and other restrictions affecting your area.

If the two of you do decide to work out of your home, have separate work areas. You spend at least eight or more hours at work. Being with one person for eight hours every day can drive you up the wall, no matter how much you love him or her, especially when you are with that same person all the rest of the day. Separating your work spaces is a good way to keep from interrupting each other and from causing minor annoyances, like talking to your partner while your partner is on the phone talking to someone else. People tell us that their greatest annoyance is when their significant other insists on making comments to them about a conversation they are having on the phone with another person.

If you absolutely cannot arrange for separate offices, place your desks at the opposite ends of a room. Office landscaping will also help keep you separated and dull the noise. A good rule for preventing co-interruptions is to agree to interrupt each other only once every quarter to the hour. That way each of you will have some undivided time to complete necessary activities.

Speaking of time, build in some time away from each other. This is especially important if you are living and working in the same place together. You are bound to get on each other's nerves occasionally. While we do not usually recommend separate vacations, this may be the exception to the rule. Still schedule and take time off together. Maintain vacation time for the entire family to unwind together, but also think about separate fishing or spa trips, visiting your parents without your partner, and special nights off to do your own thing.

Whether or not you are working out of your home, develop and agree to problem-solving techniques. This will help keep resentments from forming. No two partners will solve problems the same way. Address a problem as soon as it occurs and search for a compromise. We know a couple who ran a printing business. Ed had a quick temper and could really get bent out of shape. We asked Barbara how she put up with Ed's ranting and raving. She told me it was easy. "With Ed, if it's hysterical, it's historical." Learn to laugh at yourselves. Don't take everything so seriously. Running a business is a big responsibility, but it is not the end of the world. If you lighten up once in a while, it will lighten the load. What you can laugh at, you can cope with. Humor changes the expectation.

Stay focused. Too often we get bored and plateau out after a few years of operating a business that has a steady, if not exciting, growth potential. That's when small business owners may get themselves in trouble. They may decide to try something new for which they have no experience or track record. If excitement is your goal, go ahead and take a risk. But if security, stability, and steady growth are your goals, stick to your knitting and be persistent.

Knowing When to Give Up

When Winston Churchill was asked the secret of his success, he replied, "I can answer that in seven words. Never give up. Never, never give up." That's good advice if you are not losing money, have not lost your mind, and your partnership is working better than ever. If not, you may need to know when to throw in the towel. Answering that question is exactly what having an advisory team is all about.

Review your profit and loss statement monthly. If you find that you haven't made enough over the past year for both of you to take a reasonable salary, it's time to get serious . . . and honest. Often we find that partners fool themselves into believing that their business is profitable by loaning their salaries back to the corporation. It is not unusual for us to find that while partners continue to take a monthly salary, it is the same salary they loaned back to the company last month. In other words, they are paying themselves a salary on which they have paid taxes, social security, workman's compensation, and other deductions. They then turn around and use that same money to pay themselves again. Talk about double and even triple taxation!

Pay Yourself First

We have a cardinal rule. *Pay yourself first.* When you are co-preneurs, that means both of you. How do you arrive at how much you should be earning? Research similar companies in your area to find out the going rate, or call the association that caters to your industry. You will find most of these associations listed in the Washington, D.C., or New York areas. If you can't find one that is related to your industry, contact the American Society of Association Executives in Washington, D.C. Remember, although self-fulfillment is great, you still have to put food on the table. If you are not making a decent living out of your business, it is a hobby, not a business.

Summary

Keep growing. Take every class you can find on communication skills and conflict resolution. It is critical that you each adopt a no-blame attitude; otherwise, you will allow every business failure, lost customer, employee or vendor problem to drive a wedge between you and your love for each other. Develop a system for resolving business annoyances in a clear, nonaggressive manner.

Decide, in advance, who will be responsible for arranging for household chores such as child care, elder care, car maintenance, grocery shopping, and doctor's appointments. These chores should be divided just as if each of you were working for someone else. Do not fall into the trap of believing that one partner has more time than the other to accomplish these necessary activities. Both of you bring unique contributions to the partnership. Therefore, both of you are needed on the job as well as in the home.

Don't allow employees to talk negatively to you about your significant other. You don't want to fall victim to a three-way complaint in which you are forced to take sides or pacify an employee at your partner's expense. If an employee feels that s/he has a valid complaint, suggest that the three of you meet to discuss the issue. Then discipline yourselves to remain cool and in control. Remember the old rule about not killing the messenger. Reward open, honest feedback. It may be your road to profitable growth.

Chapter 14

Ways the Partnership Can Help Achieve Greater Success

We are often asked questions about the functional aspects of a significant partnership. These issues may appear unimportant to couples who are not having a specific problem at the time, but it is the seemingly little things that frequently cause a partnership to disconnect. Elephants don't bite, mosquitoes do. It is when too many "mosquitoes" have nibbled away at your relationship that you feel you have no alternative but to dissolve the partnership. Contrary to the slogan, "Don't sweat the small stuff," and, by the way, it's all small stuff, we advise you—if you want to keep the small, trival things from building into an impenetrable brick wall—to get a fly swatter.

> *Elephants don't bite, mosquitoes do.*

You Need Someone to Talk With, but Your Partner Has a "Do Not Talk About Work" Rule

This is a ridiculous rule. You are partners. You have merged your talents, experience, and dreams for the mutual attainment of lifetime goals. With whom are you supposed to talk? Your co-workers don't understand your personal arrangements. Your best friend doesn't understand your job *or* your personal situation. S/he can only speculate and offer subjective advice. Your relatives have their own agendas. Your partner is your confidant. Since you are both working, you have different strengths and perspectives to bring to conversations and problem-solving sessions. Connect with each other.

If you need to talk immediately after work, consider timing. Perhaps your partner is the type of person who needs a few minutes to change gears before interacting with you. Jaine used to fantasize that the perfect life would be to have fifteen minutes of uninterrupted, uninvolved time after she walked through the door of our home in order to go to her room, change clothes, and switch gears. She would then be ready to bubble over with enthusiasm as she listened to the children's successes or traumas, made dinner, and threw a load of laundry into the washer. Jim would then move into his role and interact with the children as Jaine got ready for the next day. Unfortunately, children don't have that kind of patience, so we had to wait eighteen years to make that fantasy come true.

Should You Use Each Other as Sounding Boards?

Yes! This is a partnership, remember? When you are in a partnership with someone, you run things past him or her. We even play devil's advocate for each other, taking the role of a prospect or client, pounding the other with any and all negatives we think may crop up in future meetings. When one of us doesn't think an approach is effective, we share this thought, give advice, and send the other back to the drawing board. Then we role-play again. We can't imagine how a partnership can survive without your using each other as sounding boards.

Enabling Can Destroy Personal Responsibility at Home and at Work

Enabling is the buzzword of the nineties, taken from the vocabulary of self-help groups that teach us how to deal with addictive relatives and significant others. To "enable" people means to allow them to continue their self-destructive behavior by covering for them, doing their work, or interfacing with their superiors in such a way as to make excuses for them. An enabler says, "S/he can't come to work today because s/he has the flu," when the "sick" person is really hung over. Too often, we enable in the name of love.

Enabling prevents the recipient from having to take behavioral responsibility. We also do this when we make excuses for a partner and blame other people for his/her behavior. Saying "Your boss is stupid, you are great" only encourages behavior blindness. The problem with enabling is that although it is meant to help, it too often hinders personal growth. People remain behaviorally blind because they want to and because they can't see what they are doing to sabotage themselves. That is why we recommend giving your partner permission to function as your mentor, to give you open, honest feedback. Then, don't shoot the messenger.

Raoul came home exhausted and angry. He was in the mood to kick the dog, if they had had one. He was infuriated because his boss had given him a lukewarm performance evaluation that day. "I work my butt off for that guy," he shouted. "I do everything he tells me to do. He is just prejudiced, like all the rest of them. That's the second time it's happened to me!" Juanita knew, from experience, that this was not the time to be Raoul's mentor or to give constructive feedback. What Raoul wanted was someone to *be on his side*. So she made appropriate comments like, "I know how frustrating it must be. I don't blame you for being upset." But Juanita was careful not to denigrate Raoul's boss or toss the experience aside by saying, "You are right. He is an idiot." This would have enabled Raoul to avoid looking at the underlying causes of his predicament and at how they could structure a plan to prevent this kind of thing from happening in the future.

Later, when Raoul was calmer, Juanita approached the subject by asking: "Raoul, what do you think are the reasons you are being given lukewarm performance evaluations? Perhaps your boss is prejudiced, but it may be something you are doing that is turning him off. Let's make a list of possibilities and then figure out what we can do to change this situation."

As the conversation progressed, Juanita used the "I" approach. "Raoul, remember when a similar thing happened to me? When I was really honest with myself, I realized I was coming across as having a chip on my shoulder. I know you don't mean to, but could *that* be the problem with you and your boss?" She listened and responded and kept steering the conversation back to "What was *your* role in this situation?"

We have found that enabling is also what keeps partners from picking up their fair share of home responsibilities. When she first falls in love and gets married, she wants to impress her new partner with how well she can take care of him and his every need. This enables him to sit back and get used to being catered to. Or he wants to protect her from the realities of budgeting and paying bills, so she won't worry. By doing this, he enables her to live like an ostrich with her head in the sand. Enabling destroys lives. Guard against it.

Using Scapegoats to Avoid Confrontation

How do you handle the situation when you don't want your significant other to join you at a work event? Too often, when we don't want to be the bad guy, we make someone else the bad guy. "Gee, I would love to have you join me, but the boss has limited this function to employees only." Or, "I don't think the boss likes you very much, so you weren't invited." Or even, "I'd love to have you, but Sally doesn't have anyone to go with, so we kind of agreed we'd go together, just the two of us. You don't really mind, do you?"

> Several years ago, Jaine was giving a presentation to a group of VIP wives entitled *"How to Live With a Workaholic."* During that workshop she divided the group into smaller teams of four each to discuss issues they would like to discuss with their spouses. We are always amazed at the intimacies women will share with other women and Jaine was concerned about how strongly the CEO's wife felt about his weight. "When I married him, his pant size was a 34. Now he wears a size 40! This bothers me very much." Jaine asked why it bothered her so much. The wife calmly stated all the acceptable reasons: "It isn't good for his heart. I'm afraid for his health. It makes him too tired to do anything in the evening but sleep."
>
> As is Jaine's habit, she continued to ask, "And what else?" As the wife's list of rational reasons ran out, she started crying and said, "It's embarrassing! I feel it's a reflection on me when people see me with this grotesque man! I used to be so proud of him. Now I can't stand the thought of going to bed with him!"

This is not only the lament of VIP spouses, and weight is not the only issue. What people are referring to when they talk about "embarrassment" involves the whole package. We want to be proud of our partners, to feel confident that they will make a good impression and reflect favorably on our judgment. This is usually the case at the beginning of partnerships. Then something happens. It may be the stress of the job, anxiety, or even resentment.

Many people who are caught in the web of addiction are there because they blame other people for their unhappiness or feelings of inadequacy. They drink or eat or take drugs and even overspend to get even with these people they blame. They drink *at* someone. "Okay, you are not living up to my expectations, so I'll get even with you by hurting myself."

If you think you may be caught in one of these webs, run, don't walk, to the nearest twelve-step meeting. There are hundreds of these meetings each week, in every county, city, suburb, and community in the world. They include, but are not limited to, Alcoholics Anonymous, Overeaters Anonymous, Narcotics Anonymous, and a variety of recent self-help groups like Emotions Anonymous, Healing the Child Within, Letting Go of Shame, and groups designed to help participants raise their self-esteem. No one can do this for you. You have to do it for yourself and by yourself. Don't put it off. There is light at the end of the tunnel and life after addiction.

What if it's your partner who has the problem? Remember that we all function within a system. What affects one part of the system affects all parts of the system. There are self-help groups for people who are involved with people who have an addiction. Check your local phone book and call any one of them. They will refer you to the one best suited to your needs. A support group will also help you learn how to cope with these situations.

We feel issues such as these need to be addressed through positive confrontation. Use the HELP confrontation strategy discussed in Chapter 9 and talk with your partner about how you feel. In the meantime, don't invite your addicted partner to social functions that may reflect negatively on your career. Don't lie or try to make up stories about how you have to go alone. Level with him/her and ask for his/her suggestions on how these uncomfortable situations can be managed.

What if you are not embarrassed, but you feel that your partner needs some help interacting with your co-workers and bosses?

Scott and his wife were invited to the annual Christmas party his organization gives for employees and their families every year. He was anxious to make a good impression on the power brokers so he asked Susan what she was planning to wear. A recent college graduate, Susan didn't have a whole lot of choices. After she had modeled her entire repertoire for Scott, they both agreed that they needed some alternatives, so the next day Scott asked women on the staff what they would be wearing. They stated that this was to be a dress-up affair, and one of his associates agreed to go with him at lunchtime to help him select appropriate apparel.

Scott wasn't stupid and was certainly not going to make the final decision for the woman he loved. He had the department store hold several outfits that were within their budget from which Susan could choose. She was delighted with the choices and selected the one she felt would best suit her style. They both felt confident as they attended the gala and had a terrific time.

The lesson to be learned here is that they worked together to help enhance a partner's career. There were no hurt feelings or recriminations. Their objective was to fashion a solution that was workable for each of them. Always keep in mind that whatever enhances the career of one enhances the life of both.

Rules to Follow at Office Parties and Other Social Functions.

Business functions such as conventions, meetings, office parties, and entertaining co-workers are not really social occasions. They are opportunities to learn, to network, and to make a good impression. What is the rationale for business social functions? People like doing business with people they know. The objective of these events is to allow people to know you better so that they will feel more comfortable doing business with you. Don't drink at these functions. If you want to drink, wait until the event is over. Ask your partner not to drink or indulge in party drugs, even if everyone else is doing it. If you feel that either of you will feel sorry for having passed up the "free" booze, consider this: Nothing is free.

> *Nothing is free.*

It is not worth the risk you will be taking if you drink too much and make a fool of yourself. Even if you don't drink too much, you may still make a fool of yourself, but the odds will be more in your favor. Of course you will be nervous. Jaine admits that these aren't her favorite activities. She knows they are necessary and is always supportive. When her appearance is expedient, we agree that we will attend, make a good impression, talk to everyone, and then depart as soon as is socially acceptable. Those who socialize a great deal know that it's not how long you stay that's important but the quality of the contacts you make. People who stay too long and overindulge are not the connections you need to cultivate.

What About Office Romances?

We discussed this issue in the section covering opposite sex work teams in Chapter 12. Here we would like to caution you that these liaisons can be very destructive to your career. In the movies they either end in murder or in the underpaid secretary marrying the CEO and becoming the corporate president. Unless the CEO owns the business, you are not going to be promoted to the second top slot because of an office romance.

When Jim was in his first position, his boss warned: "Keep your zipper out of the payroll." That advice is as good today as it was then. You cannot supervise someone you are sleeping with. When you are sleeping with someone, that person expects preferential treatment. When you give preferential treatment to your lover, everyone else will be resentful and uncooperative. Productivity will go down and you will not look good to upper management, and you've also set yourself up for a possible sexual harassment suit. If upper management is full of playboys and playgirls, so be it. But you can't afford to play.

Your significant other is bound to find out either from a "friendly" co-worker or the spouse of a friendly co-worker, or even from you when you can no longer stand the cloak of guilt. So, for a little passion, you have jeopardized both your career and your partnership. Of course, it is not always easy to stay monogamous, even if you are still very much in love with your partner. Temptation lurks behind every desk. But trust is what commitment is all about. It's being mature enough to consider the long-range consequences of your behavior and strong enough to resist a little flirtation, which may lead to a little romance, which may lead to. . . . You get the picture.

What About One-Night Stands?

We don't advise infidelity. The risk is too high. Fooling around to inflate your ego or to add a little variety to your life is a sucker's play. You can add risk and variety to your life by taking up skydiving or bungie jumping.

What if you have promised not to engage in affairs but find yourself consumed by passion during an out-of-town convention? We are not perfect human beings. If it's a one-shot encounter and you don't plan to see that person again, don't risk the partnership because of a one-night stand. You were wrong. Don't do it again. But don't go running home to the confessional. Confession may be good for the soul, but it is poison to partnerships. Some partners are more forgiving than others, but you will have planted the seeds of doubt. "If you have done it once, you'll do it again," goes the mantra in your partner's brain every time you walk out of the door.

A divorce attorney advises that partners should carefully think through the advantages and disadvantages of confession. Assess the partnership and ask yourself what is important in the total scheme of things. "It isn't honest not to tell," you say? Where was your conscience during the convention?

How to Protect Your Private Time

When you are in a career-building mode, it is difficult to protect your private time. We know. Ground rules have to be set so that both of you consider alternatives to requests for your time. Your partnership will not survive successfully if you always put your career before your significant other.

Don't overcommit yourselves. There are some activities that will enhance your career and others that are just annoying little tasks that nobody else wants to do. We are constantly amazed at the activities in which organizations get involved in the name of employee relations or charity. We have each been a part of companies that have had an annual outing, the planning of which took the better part of some employee's time for a whole year. This was a poor use of resources. Besides, most employees to whom we have spoken say they would rather have the money and/or the time off than attend these affairs.

Don't volunteer for such assignments. They are not good for your visibility for several reasons. First, you cannot please all of the people all of the time. Co-workers are bound to complain about the food, the location, or your "uppity" attitude. Second, while you are working on the outing, you are not concentrating on what you are supposed to be doing. This is a bad move, so get out of these activities whenever possible.

A continuing private-time issue is scheduling social engagements with personal friends.

Cindy comments: "Even though we tried not to work on weekends, we were always out with friends on Friday and Saturday nights. Sundays we were with one group of relatives or the other. We suddenly realized that we weren't spending any time together, just the two of us. So we decided that Sundays would be just our day: no friends, no relatives. We weren't going to go out and we weren't going to have anyone in. We blocked out every Sunday for the next year. We would deal with exceptions as necessary."

The same holds true of personal involvement. During the year that Jaine took her sabbatical, she formed a baby sitting exchange in which parents exchanged points for watching each others' children. It was actually a simple and effective alternative to baby sitters, but it took an enormous amount of Jaine's time. Our church also asked her to run the annual fund raising fair, which brought in more money than it ever had, and she donated her time to narrating children's stories. She was so involved and busy that she actually felt relief when she finally went back to *work*.

When we first moved to Naples, Jim was asked to coach the Little League. Missing the days when local children would ring our door bell to ask, "Can Mr. Carter come out and play?" he gleefully agreed. At about the same time, our new church asked if he would be a visiting pastor. This also turned him on, so he agreed. As we were both traveling constantly at the time, these extra activities were almost impossible to schedule if we were still to have any time left over for our family. We rationalized that "somebody had to do it." This is true, but that somebody doesn't have to be you if your career is already taking up the bulk of your time.

Private time is just that—*private* time. Private time should include time to be by yourself to recharge. Schedule time for yourself and then zealously guard this time from intrusions. This time will be what keeps you from burning out.

What About Bringing Work Home?

This is unavoidable on occasion, but try not to make a habit of it. The old-time management rule that states "Work will expand to fit the time available" is true. If you fall into the trap of feeling that you can always bring work home, you will not make productive use of your time at work. We have found, however, that one hour of uninterrupted time in the evening (or, in Jaine's case, in the early morning) brings enormous rewards. It's nearly impossible to get certain tasks completed during the workday when you are constantly interrupted. In our job, seminar participants who have questions want answers, and there is no time to complete paperwork during the day.

Plan for business work at home. Discuss with your partner the best time for each of you, and other members of your family, to do this work. Ideally, the work should be scheduled at a time when children are in bed.

You have precious little time with them as it is. Put limits on this time. For example, only work for one hour every evening. Or limit focusing on the job to Mondays, Wednesdays, and Thursdays. Whatever works for you.

> Cindy and Chris decided early in their partnership that, until they had children, they would focus on their careers exclusively from Monday morning until Friday night. "What we have agreed to is that from Monday through Friday evening at six we will be in our work modes. We agreed not to complain to one another because we were not able to go to a movie or be available for dinner. Of course, we were not able to adhere to this rule all the time, but that kind of agreement gives you guidelines to work within."

We structured the same kind of agreement. Our goal was to be home every weekend, which gave us a framework when booking assignments. For example, when an organization asked us to do a three-day seminar, we would suggest that they schedule it on Wednesday, Thursday, and Friday so that neither of us would have to travel on Sunday. This didn't always work out, but it helped us eliminate 80 percent of weekend travel.

Summary

When the two of you have done an adequate job of communicating mutual goals and planning for the future, you will find that almost every challenge can be overcome when you answer the question "How will this help us move toward our goals?" Assess every action in terms of your mutual goals. Each should be asking of himself or herself, "What can I do to help the partnership achieve greater success?"

Chapter 15

Work, Work, Work: Enjoying Life While Pursuing Your Goals

Stretched-to-the-limit couples complain that they never have enough time for the partnership because of the constant demands of the job. Frequently, an analysis reveals that certain people do prefer work to involvement in the relationship. Those of us who prefer work to interpersonal involvement may be considered workaholics, or we may just be compulsive workers. It is socially acceptable to be a workaholic, so people often brag about being one. Work does provide many of us with a sense of self-worth, and others respect people who are involved in their work. When you ask workaholics who they are, they will describe themselves in terms of their jobs. They enjoy work. It is who they are. They feel more comfortable working than at any other time and are only really turned on when they are working.

What about those workaholics who don't enjoy working all of the time? Compulsive workaholism may be as addictive as alcoholism and a disease that is responsible for the disintegration of the family, according to Lotti Bailyn of MIT. Some people are compulsive workers because they feel it is expected of them. This perception may have started in their youth when parents admonished, "Don't just sit there, *do* something!" These children may have found that they were rewarded with warm fuzzies when they were involved in continual constructive activities.

Once people discover that they are accepted for what they accomplish, they may begin to suffer from the Perfect Worthless Syndrome: "If I can't be perfect, I must be worthless" (see Chapter 4). It is a reality of our society that we are rewarded for staying busy. This becomes our goal in that it serves many objectives. It can help you avoid intimacy: "If I'm too busy to get involved with people, they won't find out I am worthless." It may also help you to play the martyr and get sympathy. Sympathy is negative recognition but recognition nonetheless, and negative strokes are better than no strokes at all.

Are You a Workaholic?

Are you a workaholic or a compulsive worker? Answering the following questions may help you decide. This is a forced-choice assessment. Choose the statement in each pair that best describes how you feel.

1.	a. I stay after working hours to get caught up.	
	b. I get so caught up in my work that I forget the time.	
2.	a. I get bored if I don't keep busy.	
	b. I would rather be working than interacting.	
3.	a. I stay busy with all of my responsibilities.	
	b. I enjoy the challenge of my work.	
4.	a. I prefer vacations with many activities.	
	b. I prefer vacations that can be combined with work.	
5.	a. I feel guilty if I'm not working.	
	b. I find it difficult to envision a life without work.	
6.	a. I have feelings of anxiety about work.	
	b. I feel most alive when I am working.	
7.	a. Many times I am too busy and exhausted to have sex.	
	b. It is difficult for me to concentrate on making love when I am involved in a project.	
8.	a. I would rather do things myself than risk someone else's mistake.	
	b. I do things myself because I like to stay involved.	
9.	a. I will pass up social events if I have work to do.	
	b. I would rather work than go to a social event.	
10.	a. I would rather work than argue.	
	b. I am too involved in work to have time to disagree.	

If you answered *b* to six or more statements, you may be a workaholic. You work because you are actually turned on by what you do. You work because you *want* to. Your challenge will be in maintaining balance in your life. Find other things you like to do and then discipline yourself to stop working and start playing.

If you chose *a* for six or more of the statements, you may be a compulsive worker. You work because you feel you *have* to. Analyze the drivers in your life. Who or what pushes you or your partner toward compulsive activity? Negative drivers can lead to other binge behaviors. When people work long and hard and still don't get the warm fuzzies and recognition they expect, they may reward themselves by way of binge behaviors involving alcohol, drugs, or food. There are other avoidant behaviors such as overspending or gambling that act as pacifiers for bingers who fear inadequacy, rejection, or abandonment.

Many significant others actually perceive continuous work as a rejection of them personally. This is especially common among couples who are involved in commuter partnerships, marriages that require constant travel, and work schedules that keep them from interacting with each other on a daily basis. Perceived rejection and feelings of abandonment are reasons women give for their growing resentment. Men also become resentful when they feel that women don't understand how harried they are. Resentment leads to disconnection. Don't let prolonged disconnection lead to divorce.

Start talking. Define the real problem. Too often the partnership and the extended family are perceived as a burden—just one more problem to have to think about, one more shackle weighing you down. Couples aren't talking and they aren't touching. One man happily remarked, "This weekend I got lucky for the first time in weeks!" Why is this such an occasion? It should be a regular event. Is she holding out because she is carrying resentment or is she simply too tired to have sex? What happens when she keeps putting him off? He starts thinking, "Who needs this relationship? I'm not getting sex, I'm working all the time, and she always has a honey-do list that would choke a horse. I come last."

Most couples mask the reasons they have for not wanting to have sex. Something else is going on in the relationship that they are not addressing, but it shows up in the bedroom, in the checkbook, when one goes out and buys something without consulting the other, or in an uproar over how to discipline the children. The CD, television, house, furniture all become pacifiers for what couples are not getting out of the partnership. The mutually enable each other to believe that these things *are* what they need in order to take the focus off the real issue. They start looking for ways to pacify themselves for the real hurts. They think, "I don't feel fulfilled. I don't feel relaxed. I don't feel loved because of all the responsibilities I have. Throw me a cookie." So they focus all their energies on carpeting the apartment or building a house or buying a new car. Cookies are costly. These pacifiers cause more debt, so they have to work more. More work means they have even less time for each other. The domino effect is at work again.

If this is what is happening in your relationship, you need to go into a room by yourself to analyze if this partner is really the person with whom you want to spend your life. Make a list. What is positive in the relationship? What are the negatives? If the positives outweigh the negatives, you decide that this partner is as good as any other with whom to build a life. It's better not to get a divorce because until you work it out for yourself, you are going to make the same mistakes the next time around. It is much less stressful to grow within a comfortable, organized, cooperative partnership than it is to continually search for a new partner. Our divorced friends engage in an endless search for mates, joining singles clubs or parents without partners groups, getting friends to fix them up, going on blind dates. Talk about risk! Starting all over again is not what it's cracked up to be.

Give time a chance. Schedule a private, uninterrupted one-on-one. Without blame, discuss how you both really feel about the partnership. Remember, there are three elements in a partnership: the He, the She, and the We. You may discover that you both still love the He or the She but that the We is not making it. Try the "what if" technique. What if you didn't have all this work. What if you didn't have the children. What if you didn't have the house, or worked somewhere else. Would you still want each other? Most relationships can be saved when partners sit down together and clean out their dirty clothes baskets. Each of you needs to participate, to risk taking off your masks.

Maintaining Intimacy on a Busy Schedule

It's difficult to nurture an intimate relationship when you are working all the time. There are too many things requiring your attention and no time for each other. Pulling into the driveway to get the children organized, getting the groceries from the car into the refrigerator, putting the food on the table, settling disputes, helping with homework, washing the dishes all become responsibilities that have to be fulfilled. By the time these things are done, you collapse into bed and rush to fall asleep in preparation for another day doing more of the same. This treadmill can continue for years if you don't set boundaries for and with each other.

Unrelenting responsibilities, balanced by no renewal, will eventually burn out the partnership. Forget "there is always tomorrow." Intimacy is critical to the successful accomplishment of your mutual goals. Make the time to be intimate again, talking and touching and connecting in the old ways, before the outside pressures push you to the breaking point. Without your partner, professional success can be a hollow victory.

Put thoughtfulness back into your relationship. Check in on a daily basis to let your partner know you are thinking of him and value his presence in your life. Women are better at this than men. If men want a happy and fulfilled partner, they need to reach out and make that connection. A phone call just to say "hi," an invitation to lunch, a circled article in the newspaper, or a sincere compliment to show you noticed are all ways to connect. Men may think about these things, but generally get too busy to actually do them. Be attentive and supportive during hard times. Too often we live together and yet lead totally separate lives. Your goal is to establish a healthy independence within a framework of mutuality. Search for activities you can enjoy together on a regular basis.

> *If men want a happy and fulfilled partner, they need to reach out and make that connection.*

Renee and Richard gave each other kayaks for Christmas. They like to take them out on Sunday mornings and spend an hour on the sound kayaking side by side. They stop on the shore, open up a picnic lunch, and talk.

Gene and Dedra are ardent skiers and tennis players. Every chance they get they hop on a plane to go skiing. While it's not practical to go skiing every weekend, they make sure that they are on the tennis courts sharing something they both enjoy.

We take a daily walk around a lake in our neighborhood. Sometimes we are so busy that these walks come late at night, but we enjoy the lamplight as we hold hands and talk.

Without these connections, you can drift apart and away from one another. By the time you recognize the chasm between you there is a real problem. If you can't think of anything to talk about, walk through the elms of your past together. Share special memories—the discovery moments, the crazy coincidences, a favorite joke, or even a crisis you have overcome together. Develop a couple's heritage that builds a sense of mutuality, confidence, and trust. Eventually you will both come to realize that a one-night stand with anyone else in the world is colorless next to the depth of your dual history.

Reach out and touch each other. Maintaining nonsexual touching seems to be more of a problem for men than it is for women. When women feel that they will have to engage in sex every time they are touched, they will forgo touch until they want to have sex. Snuggling and hugging are extremely important to building intimacy in your relationship. Sex helps, but it isn't everything. Women hunger for touch, and men who touch frequently find their sex life improving.

> *Reach out and touch each other. Maintaining nonsexual touching seems to be more of a problem for men than it is for women.*

Scheduled Sex Is Better Than No Sex at All

One of the first things to go in a busy dual-career relationship is sex. It is difficult to get together when you live in different cities, work different shifts, are away most of the week because of your travel schedules, or have children who are up past nine in the evening. You pass on sex until a more convenient time. Perhaps you should ask yourselves that old question: If not now, when?

Larry says he hasn't had sex in two months. This is getting to him and he feels put down and undervalued. Luanne is working two jobs to help support the family while Larry is starting a new career. Larry also has paperwork to complete for the new job, but he is usually finished and ready for bed by 10:30 p.m. That's when he makes his overture. Luanne is feeling stress because she doesn't want to lose her accounts by missing deadlines, so she usually refuses. Larry goes to bed with a seemingly casual "Don't work too hard." Luanne types until one or two in the morning, when she finally crawls into bed exhausted. Larry tries again, but Luanne gets angry: "Larry! I need some sleep, damn it! Six a.m. is only four hours away." Larry rolls over with a groan and another day is added to his two-month celibacy record. Again, they have not connected.

A satisfactory sex life is important for good mental health. The results of an ongoing study of 37,500 adults at San Francisco's Institute for Advanced Study of Human Sexuality indicated that people with fulfilling sex lives tended to be less anxious, violent, and hostile and not as likely to blame others for their misfortunes. They have a greater sense of self-reliance, which helps bring out the best qualities in each partner and also helps them achieve greater success in their careers.

There is never enough time to do all the things that need to be done in life, but it is a tragedy when love, intimacy, and sex take a back seat to work, dinner, dishes, and children. Why are you together? Without sex, you might as well be same-sex partners or brother and sister running a business together. Make the time to connect. So spontaneity goes out the window. So what? If you are waiting for the magic moment when passion strikes, you will let the present pass you by. Get creative. Commit yourselves to a weekly rendezvous in your own home. Once a week? That's right! Our interviews over the years indicate that working couples consider themselves lucky if they connect once a week, and most of them admit that it does not happen spontaneously. When you are on a busy schedule, nothing is spontaneous. So, just as you do with everything else in your life, schedule a time to allow for connection. Search your schedules and those of the people in your household. What two- or three-hour block of time can you set aside each week just for the two of you? Get a baby sitter if you have to or exchange children with a friend or neighbor every other Saturday afternoon or evening. Then crawl into bed and cuddle.

What if you sense that something is missing? Is sex not as exciting as it used to be? Compared to what—television and movies? If that's our criterion, is it any wonder we conclude that our sex life is inadequate when we are not ripping off clothes and passionately falling over furniture to devour one another? While this may happen occasionally, it is not the norm. Quiet, tender connections will make you feel just as valued, warm, and accepted as robust, athletic assignations. The media have forced us to raise our expectations of performance level even in bed, from satisfying to explosive. No wonder we're tired!

Keep your appointments with each other. Don't let fatigue or other put-offs ("I have a headache," or "my parents are in the next room," or "this unexpected appointment cropped up and I have to run back to the office") keep you from this primary activity. Every put-off is a put-down. It loudly proclaims that your partner is not as important to you as all of the other activities in your life. Put-offs and put-downs can also be used as power plays. The person wanting the intimacy falls into the role of underdog. The person withholding the intimacy is in control. No one likes to feel controlled or to know that another human being has power over them. Any time you feel yourself falling into the trap of using the most intimate activity supplied to humankind to enhance intimacy in a manipulative way, realize that you are putting the partnership in jeopardy.

Could a Counselor Help?

Most of us would readily consult with a tax expert to help us iron out our financial problems. We use money managers to guide and direct our portfolios, and we run to physicians for even minor aggravations. However, some of us still see consulting a counselor as a sign of weakness. Statistics show that women are more likely to seek marriage counseling than men are. The male system of hierarchy supports the belief that asking for help is a sign of weakness. The fact is that seeking a counselor is a sign of strength. We are always amazed that couples will go through a divorce before joining a recovery group to help them cope with the trauma. Apparently the destruction of lives and the devastating division of assets divorce causes are preferable to talking about why we can't connect.

We know several people who are entering their third marriage. These people continually choose the same kind of partner, even to how the new partner looks. As a result, they regularly have the same kinds of problems. Seek individual therapy before you enter a new partnership, and if this partnership too goes on the rocks, seek professional advice. It is worth every dollar you spend. The life you save may be your own.

Here are a few tips to follow when you are looking for a counselor and want to make sure you find the right one.

1. Look for a counselor who is experienced in couples therapy.
2. Shop around until you find the right fit.
3. Ask about fees. Your insurance may reimburse you.
4. Listen to your feelings. If the relationship doesn't feel right, look some more.
5. Ask how long it will take. Therapy should not be a lifetime commitment.

Sex or Sleep?

Make sure that your schedule allows for enough sleep. Fatigue makes crybabies of us all. In our fast-paced, rapidly changing society, we are working more and sleeping less. Sleeping less has even become a new power symbol of being on the fast road to success. Dr. June Frye, director of the Sleep Disorder Center at the Medical College of Pennsylvania in Philadelphia, hypothesizes that people think that sleep isn't macho. The feeling is that if you can't work all night and still do the job well, you are not motivated.

There is much variation in how much sleep individuals actually need, but most of us need between seven and eight hours of sleep a night. Researchers estimate that the majority of Americans get between 60 and 90 minutes less sleep each night than they need. Working women already sleep about 5 percent less than their partners do and shouldn't cut back any further. When we don't get enough sleep, we become moody, irritable, and depressed. Some of us even suffer from what has come to be known as chronic fatigue syndrome. Therefore, when you are doing your time analysis, be sure to allow sufficient time to renew, recoup, and plan ways of staying together.

Summary

Sometimes, when our relationship is not all we had hoped it would be, we attempt to escape this reality by losing ourselves in compulsive activities and/or other people's problems. This takes the focus off the relationship and there is never enough time to touch each other or to connect. Too often, we put ourselves on "hold," waiting for some magical time in the future when we will allow ourselves to be happy. Don't do that to yourself.

Working couples need to develop the maturity and patience to give time a chance. Successful partnerships are not developed overnight or just because you are in love. Success takes time, commitment, and focus.

What are you doing, right now, to make your life and your partnership better? Decide now to embark on a self-development plan that will truly help you to enjoy life while you are pursuing your goals. Focus your thinking on what is really important to you. List your values and update this list on a regular basis. Updating it on a quarterly basis will help keep you and your partner focused on the goals that are really most important to the partnership. Prioritize these goals so you can concentrate on those of primary importance to you both today.

Life is an adventure. Enjoy it. You can't get out of it alive, so make the most of what you have going for you. Don't limit your life to passively watching television or a continual stream of spectator sports. Get out there and play. Don't take yourself too seriously. Care, but don't care so much that your world falls apart if you don't hold on to what you have, don't get what you think you should get, or have to correct a mistake.

Sometimes bad things happen to good people. No explanation. That's just the way it is. We all get our share. Don't sit around lamenting the negatives so long that you overlook the positives in your life. Stay off the pity-pot. Keep asking yourself, "Am I happy yet?" You may find that you are happier than you think.

Keep this in mind always. Both of you are doing the best you know how. If you could do better, you would. He works, just fine, and she works, just fine. The secret is to get the he and the she to work together.

Bibliography

Ambry, Margaret, co-author. "The Official Guide to American Incomes and the Official Guide to Household Spending," *New Strategist*, 1993.

Arcus, M. E. "Family Life Education: Toward the 21st Century," *Family Relations*. 41 (1992): 390–393.

Avery, C. S. "How Do You Build Intimacy in an Age of Divorce?" *Psychology Today*, May 1989, pp. 27–31.

Bailyn, Lotti, and E. H. Schein. "Life/Career Considerations as Indicators of Quality Employment," in *Measuring Work Quality for Social Reporting*, ed. A. D. Biderman and T. F. Drury. New York: Sage, 1976.

Bardwick, Judith. *The Plateauing Trap*. New York: American Management Association, 1986.

Barnett, Rosalind C., and G. K. Baruch. "Determinants of Father's Participation in Family Work," *Journal of Marriage and the Family*. 49 (1987): 29–40.

Barnett, Rosalind C., Aline Sayer, and Nancy Marshall. *Gender, Job Rewards, Job Concerns and Psychological Distress: A Study of Dual-Earner Couples*. Working Couple Paper Series No. 270. Center for Research on Women, Wellesley College, Wellesley, Mass., 1994.

Beatties, Mellody. *Co-Dependent No More: How to Stop Controlling Others and Start Caring for Yourself*. San Francisco: Harper, 1987.

Berk, S. F. *The Gender Factor: The Apportionment of Work in American Households*. New York: Plenum, 1985.

Berne, Eric. *Games People Play*. New York: Grove, 1964.

Biderman, A. D., and T. F. Drury, eds. *Measuring Work Quality for Social Reporting*. New York: Sage, 1976.

Bly, Robert. *Iron John*. New York: Addison-Wesley, 1990.

Bolles, Richard Nelson. *What Color Is My Parachute?* Berkeley, Calif.: Ten Speed Press, 1991.

Bombeck, Erma. *A Marraige Made in Heaven . . . or Too Tired for an Affair*. San Francisco: HarperCollins, 1993.

Bonderly, B. L. *The Myth of Two Minds: What Gender Means and Doesn't Mean*. New York: Doubleday, 1987.

Boyett, Joseph H., and Henry P. Conn. *Nesbitt Trend Letter* and *Workplace 2000—The Revolution Reshaping American Business*. New York: Dutton, 1991.

Bramson, Robert. *Coping With Difficult People*. New York: Ballantine Books, 1991.

Branden, Nathaniel. *The Six Pillars of Self-Esteem*. New York: Bantam, 1994.

Brown, Peter. *It's a Gender Thing*. Scripps Howard News Service, November 20, 1994.

California Industrial Welfare Commission. *Alternatives to the Eight-Hour Day Within a Forty-Hour Week: The Four/Ten Workweek*. San Francisco, May 1985.

Campbell, J. "Male Answer Syndrome," *Utne Reader*, January–February 1992, pp. 107–108.

Cardozo, Arlene Rossen. *Sequencing: Having It All But Not All at Once*. New York: Atheneum, 1986.

Carter, Jaine. *Stay Out of Your Own Way and Get the Job You Want*. Naples, Fla.: Carter & Carter Enterprises, 1984.

Catalyst. *Corporations and Two-Career Families: Directions for the Future*. New York, 1982.

———. *Cracking the Glass Ceiling: Strategies for Success*. New York, 1994.

Cetron, M., and O. Davies. *American Renaissance: Our Life at the Turn of the 21st Century*. New York: St. Martin's, 1989.

Clary, Mike. *Daddy's Home*. New York: Seaview Books, 1982.

Coveman, S., and J. F. Sheley. "Change in Men's Housework and Child-Care Time, 1965–1975," *Journal of Marriage and the Family*. 48 (1985): 413–422.

Cowan, A. L. "Women's Gains on the Job: Not Without a Heavy Toll," *New York Times*, August 2, 1989.

Craddock, Suzanne, et al. "Flexitime: The Kentucky Experiments," *Public Personnel Management Journal*, Summer 1981.

Demo, David H. "The Relentless Search for Effects of Divorce: Forging New Trails or Tumbling Down the Beaten Path?" *Journal of Marriage and the Family*. 55 (1993): 42–45.

Demo, David H., and Alan C. Acock. "Family Diversity and the Division of Domestic Labor," *Family Relations*, July 1993, pp. 323–331.

Deutschman, Alan. "The Upbeat Generation," *Fortune*, July 13, 1992, pp. 42–54.

DeWitt, Paula Mergenhagen. "Breaking Up Is Hard to Do," *American Demographics*, October 1992, pp. 52–59.

DuBrin, Andrew J. *Your Own Worst Enemy: How to Overcome Career Self-Sabotage*. New York: American Management Association, 1992.

Edwards, Paul and Sarah. *Complete Start-Up Kit for a Business With Your Computer*. Santa Monica, Calif.: Here's How, 1989.

———. *Working From Home: Everything You Need to Know About Living and Working Under the Same Roof*. Los Angeles: Jeremy P. Tarcher, 1990.

Einstein, Elizabeth, and Linda Albert. *The Stepfamily: Living, Loving and Learning*. New York: Macmillan, 1982.

———. *Strengthening Your Step Family*. New York: Random House, 1986.

Ekman, P. *Telling Lies: Clues to Deceit in the Marketplace, Politics and Marriage*. New York: W. W. Norton, 1985.

Elliott, Susan. *Becoming Self-Employed: First Hand Advice From Those Who Have Done It*. Blue Ridge, Pa.: Liberty, 1987.

Faber, Shirley Sloan. "Are Men Changing?" *Working Mother*, February 1993, pp. 49–51.

Farrell, Warren. *The Myth of Male Power: Why Men Are the Disposable Sex*. New York: Simon & Schuster, 1993.

———. *Why Men Are the Way They Are*. New York: Berkley, 1988.

Fisher, Helen. *Anatomy of Love: The Mysteries of Mating, Marriage, and Why We Stray*. New York: Fawcett Columbine, 1992.

Fletcher, Jan and Charlie. *Growing a Business—Raising a Family: Ideas and Inspiration for the Work-at-Home Parent*. Seattle: NextStep Publications, 1988.

Francese, Peter. "America at Mid-Decade," *American Demographics*, February 1995.

Fraser, Barry. "Adult Men: Happy Children, Miserable Mates," *Employee Assistance*, November 1992, p. 30.

Gabany, Steve G. *The Working Person's Survival Guide*. Terre Haute, Ind.: Hunt & Peck Publishing, 1990.

Gerson, Kathleen. *How Women Decide About Work, Career and Motherhood*. Berkeley, Calif.: University of California Press, 1985.

Goldberg, Herb. *The Hazards of Being Male*. New York: Signet, 1977.

Golden, C. *Understanding the Gender Gap: An Economic History of American Women*. New York: Oxford University Press, 1990.

Gottman, John. "New Ways to Tell If Your Love Will Last," *Glamour*, February 1994, pp. 145–146, 202–204.

Greene, Katherine and Richard. "Couples, Inc.," *Working Woman*, December 1994, pp. 33–74.

Harris, Diane. "16th Annual Survey 1995," *Working Woman*, January 1995, pp. 25–34.

Hayes, Christopher, quoted by Clint Willis, "Mind Over Money," *Working Woman*, February 1992.

Helmering, Doris Wild. *Husbands, Wives and Sex*. Holbrook, Mass.: Bob Adams, Inc., 1990.

Henry Ford Hospital. *The American Journal of Epidemiology*, January 1995.

"The Hidden Meaning: An Analysis of Different Types of Affairs," *Marriage and Divorce Today*, June 1, 1987, pp. 1–2.

Hill, Martha. *Patterns of Time Use in Time, Goods, and Well-Being*. Ann Arbor, Mich.: Institute for Social Research, University of Michigan, 1985.

Hochheiser, Robert M. *If You Want Guarantees, Buy a Toaster*. New York: William Morrow, 1991.

Hocschild, Arlie Russel, with Anne Machung. *The Second Shift: Working Parents and the Revolution at Home*. New York: Viking, 1989.

Internal Revenue Service. *Guide to Free Tax Services* (Publication 910), Washington, D.C.: U.S. Government Printing Office.

———. *Tax Guide for Small Business* (Publication 334), Washington, D.C.: U.S. Government Printing Office.

Israeloff, Roberta. "The Sleep Mystique: Could You Get By on Less?" *Working Woman*, September 1990, pp. 195–196.

Juster, F. Thomas, and Frank P. Stafford. "The Allocation of Time: Empirical Findings, Behavioral Models, and Problems of Measurement," *Journal of Economic Literature*. 9 (June 1991): 477.

Kaye, Beverly. *Up Is Not the Only Way: A Guide for Career Development Practitioners*. San Diego, Calif.: University Associates, 1985.

Kent, Margaret, and Robert Feinschreiber. *Love at Work: Using Your Job to Find a Mate*. New York: Warner Books, 1988.

Kern, Coralee Smith. *How to Run Your Own Home Business*. Lincolnwood, Ill.: VGM Career Horizons, NTC Publishing Group, 1975.

Klinman, Debra G., and Rhiana Kohl. *Fatherhood U.S.A.* New York: Garland, 1984.

Krannich, Ronald L. *Change Your Job, Change Your Life*. Manassas Park, Va.: Impact Publications, 1994.

Labich, Kenneth. "Can Your Career Hurt Your Kids?" *Fortune*, May 20, 1991.

Lampe, P. E. *Adultery in the United States: Close Encounters of the Sixth (or Seventh) Kind*. Buffalo, N.Y.: Prometheus Books, 1987.

Landrum, Gene. *Profiles of Female Genius—Thirteen Creative Women Who Changed the World*. Buffalo, N.Y.: Prometheus Books, 1994.

———. *Profiles of Genius—Thirteen Men Who Changed the World*. Buffalo, N.Y.: Prometheus Books, 1993.

Latack, Janina C., and Lawrence W. Foster. "Implementation of Compressed Work Schedules: Participation and Job Redesign as Critical Factors for Employee Acceptance," *Personnel Psychology*, Spring 1985.

Laurence, Peter J., and Raymond Hull. *The Peter Principle*. New York: William Morrow, 1969.

Lewis, Hunter. *A Question of Values: Six Ways We Make the Personal Choices That Shape Our Lives*. San Francisco: HarperCollins, 1990.

Liebowitz, M. R. *The Chemistry of Love*. Boston: Little, Brown, 1983.

Mayer, Anne. *How to Stay Lovers While Raising Your Children: A Burned-Out Parent's Guide to Sex*. Los Angeles: Price Stern Sloan Inc., 1990.

Mead, M. "Marriage in Two Steps," *Redbook*, July 1966, pp. 47–49.

Mead, W. W. "Changing Men, Changing Marriage," *Working Woman*, November 1986, pp. 170–171, 252.

Mellody, Pia. *Facing Co-Dependency: What It Is, Where It Comes From, How It Sabotages Our Lives*. San Francisco: Harper, 1989.

Michaels, Bonnie, and Elizabeth McCarty. *Solving the Work/Family Puzzle*. Homewood, Ill.: Business One Irwin, 1992.

Michaelson, Peter A. *See Your Way to Self-Esteem*. Naples, Fla.: First Prospect Books, 1993.

Morgensen, Gretchen. "Watch the Leer, Stifle That Joke," *Forbes*, May 15, 1989, pp. 69–70.

Nair, Mohan S., M.D. "Recovering Healthy Sexuality," *EAP*, December 1992, pp. 13–16.

Namka, Lynn. *Doormat Syndrome*. Deerfield Beach, Fla.: Heath Communications, Inc., 1989.

National Opinion Research Center (NORC). "The General Social Survey," *American Demographics*, November 1992, p. 50.

The National Report on Work & Family.Washington, D.C.: Buraff Publications.

Nesbitt, John, and Patricia Aburdene. *Megatrends 2000: Ten New Directions for the 1990's*. New York: William Morrow, 1990.

"1990 IRS Data," *Los Angeles Times*, August 28, 1990.

Olmsted, Barney, and Suzanne Smith. *Creating a Flexible Workplace: How to Select and Manage Alternative Work Options*. New York: American Management Association, 1989.

Pinson, Linda, and Jerry Jinnett. *The Home-Based Entrepreneur*. Tustin, Calif.: Out of Your Mind . . . and Into the Marketplace, 1989.

Pleck, J. *Working Wives, Working Husbands*. Beverly Hills, Calif.: Sage, 1985.

Plummer, Joseph T. "The Futurist," *Paine Webber/Young & Rubicam Ventures*, January–February 1989, pp. 8–13.

Reich, Charles A. *The Greening of America: How the Youth Revolution Is Trying to Make America Livable*. New York: Random House, 1970.

Roberts, Jeanne D. *Taking Care of Caregivers*. Palo Alto, Calif: Buell, 1991.

Seligman, Martin. *Learned Help Issues*. New York: Oxford University Press, 1993.

Shaef, Anne. *Escape From Intimacy: Understanding the Love Addiction—Sex Romance Relationships*. San Francisco: Harper, 1990.

Smedes, Lewis B. *Choices: Making Right Decisions in a Complex World*. San Francisco: Harper & Row, 1986.

Solo, Sally. "Stop Whining and Get Back to Work," *Fortune*, March 12, 1990, pp. 49–50.

Stautberg, Susan, and Marcia L. Worthing. *Juggling Love, Work, Family and Recreating*. New York: Master Media, Ltd., 1992.

Steere, David. "Freud on the Gallows Transaction," *Transactional Analysis Bulletin*. 9 (January 1970): 3–5.

Steinem, Gloria. *Revolution From Within: A Book of Self-Esteem*. New York: Little, Brown, 1992.

Steiner, Claude M. *Games Alcoholics Play: The Analysis of Life Scripts*. New York: Ballantine, 1984.

Stryker, Bingham, Mindy, and Sandy. *More Choices: A Strategic Planning Guide for Mixing Career and Family*. Santa Barbara, Calif.: Advocacy Press, 1987.

Swan, Helen L. *Alone After School: A Self-Care Guide for Latchkey Children and Their Parents*. Englewood Cliffs, N.J.: Prentice-Hall, 1985.

Tanner, Deborah. *You Just Don't Understand: Men and Women in Conversation*. New York: Ballantine, 1990.

Thompson, L. "Family Work: Women's Sense of Fairness," *Journal of Family Issues*. 12 (1991): 181–196.

Thorne, B. "Feminism and the Family: Two Decades of Thought," in B. Thorne and M. Yalom, eds., *Rethinking the Family: Some Feminist Questions*, rev. ed. New York: Longman, 1992, pp. 3–30.

Thownsend, Bickley, and Kathleen O'Neil. "Women Get Mad," *American Demographics*, August 1990, pp. 26–32.

Tingley, Judith C. *Genderflex: Men & Women Speaking Each Other's Language at Work*. New York: American Management Association, 1994.

Toffler, Alvin. *Future Shock*. New York: Random House, 1970.

U.S. Department of Health and Human Services. *A Parent's Guide to Day Care*. Washington, D.C.: U.S. Government Printing Office.

U.S. Department of Health and Human Services, Bureau of Labor Statistics. "1986 Divorce Profile," *Vital Statistics of the United States*. Washington, D.C.: U.S. Government Printing Office, 1986.

U.S. Department of Health and Human Services, National Center for Health Statistics. "Mortality," *Vital Statistics of the United States*, vol. 2, part A., p. 51. Washington, D.C.: U.S. Government Printing Office, 1991.

U.S. Department of Labor, Women's Bureau. *20 Facts on Women Workers*, no. 90–2. September 1990.

Wallis, Claudia. "The Nuclear Family Goes Boom!" *Time*, Fall 1992, pp. 42–44.

Weaver, Vanessa J., and Jan C. Hill. *Smart Women, Smart Moves*. New York: American Management Association, 1994.

"What Does Family Mean?" *American Demographics*, June 1992, p. 3.

Work/Family Directions, Inc. *Recommitting the Work Force: Maximizing Employee Contribution in an Environment of Constant Change*. Boston, 1995.

Resources

American Society of Association Executives, The ASAE Building, 1575 I Street, NW, Washington, DC 20005–1168.

Bureau of National Affairs, Inc., 1231 25th Street, NW, Washington, DC 20037.

CoHousing. The Journal of the CoHousing Network, P.O. Box 2584, Berkeley, CA 94702.

Frye, June, M.D., Director of the Sleep Disorder Center at the Medical College of Pennsylvania in Philadelphia.

Hayes, Christopher, Ph.D., National Center for Women and Research, Long Island University.

Hughes, Don, Credit Counseling Services of Southwest Florida, Naples, Fla.

The Joint Custody Association. James Cook: (310) 475–5352.

Kropf, Marcia, Ph.D., vice president of Catalyst, a women's issues research organization, New York, N.Y.

National Association for the Self-Employed, 2121 Precinct Line Road, Hurst, TX 76054.

National Center for Health Statistics (NCHS), Washington, D.C.

National Men's Resource Center, San Francisco, Calif. Gordon Clay: (415) 453-2839.

Network of Small Businesses, 5420 Mayfield Road (#205), Lyndhurst, OH 44124. Financial assistance for new or expanding businesses.

New Ways to Work, 149 Ninth Street, San Francisco, CA 94103. Specialists in flexible management and flexible work options.

The Partnership Group, Inc., 840 West Main Street, Lansdale, PA 19446: (215) 362-5070. A family resource service for employers, employees, and their families.

Small Business Administration, Director of Business Development Publications, Box 1000, Fort Worth, TX 76119.

Superintendent of Documents, U.S. Government Printing Office, Washington, DC 20402-0001: (202) 783-3238. *Handbook for Small Business* contains descriptions of federal programs that assist small businesses, and directions on where to get more information.

U.S. Chamber of Commerce, 1615 H Street, NW, Washington, DC 20062.

Whipple, Beverly, Associate Professor at Rutgers University's College of Nursing.

Women's Bureau, U.S. Department of Labor, Office of the Secretary, Washington, DC 02010: (202) 523-8916.

Work and Family Connection, Inc., Minnetonka, Minn. *Work & Family Newsbrief.*

Index

accountability, 27
Acock, Alan C., 17–18
action steps, 82–84
adaptability, 141, 147
advisory team, 188
approval, need for, 47
avoidant couples, 96
awareness groups, 16–17

Bardwick, Judith, 102, 159
behavioral styles, 96–98, 107–108, 142–149
blame others/fight style, 119
blame self/give in style, 120
Bly, Robert, 36
boundary setting, 27–29, 131–134
Boyett, Joseph, 163
brainstorming, 92
bridge building, 127–129
Brown, Peter, 34
burnout, 102
    preventing, 106–108, 113–115
business partnership
    ending, 196–197
    at home, 193–196
    management problems of, 190–192
    personal issues and, 188–189
    power plays in, 188
    relations in, 192–193
    starting, 186
    structure of, 186–188
    vision for, 189–192
business trips, 181

career challenges, 5–7
    management of, 153–167

career goals, 208–217
Catalyst, 166
chain of command, 157
challenge, identifying, 90–91
Chilcoat, Howard D., 130
child care, 11–12
    on-site, 166
children, 10–12, 129–131, 135
    responsibility of, 169, 170–171
clam up/withdraw style, 120–121
Clary, Mike, 160
co-dependency, 25–27
community housing, 170–171
commuter marriage, 175, 177–178
compulsive worker, 208, 209–211
confidant, partner as, 198–199
confrontation avoidance, 201–203
Conn, Henry, 163
content plateauing, 160
contingency fund, 9
contingent employment, 163
control formula, 122–123
co-preneurs, *see* business partnership
cost/benefit analysis, 95
"crab" syndrome, 84–85

Daddy track, 36
data gathering, 91–92
daytimers, 110–111
decision making
    behavior in, 96–98
    values in, 94–96
defensive behavior, 134
    avoidance of, 119–121
defensive reactions, interrupting, 121–123

delayed gratification, 73–74
Demo, David H., 17–18
devaluing partner, 59–60
disagreement, 118, 123–129
disapproval of partner, 61
disconnection, causes of, 58–64
discounting partner, 60–61
disorganization, 109
disrespect of partner, 62
distract/make nice style, 119–120
dominance of partner, 59
double-bind messages, 38
dual-income relationship, 4

enabling partner, 199–201
energetic behavior, 147
energy, stress as, 101–103
essential activities, 9–10
ex-spouses, 11

Fair Pay Act, 20
family
    extended, 12–13
    multifaceted, 11
    sense of, 129, 134
    separation from work, 21–25
family business, 185–197
Family Leave Act, 12
Farrell, Warren, 32
Feinschreiber, Robert, 32
fence mending, 127–129
filing procedure, 112–113
fire in belly, 155–156
flexible workplace options, 160–166
flexiplace, 164–165
flextime, 160, 163–164, 167
flipping schedules, 181–182
free-lancing, 166

Gallows Transaction, 63
gender differences, 33–35
goals
    mutual, 64
    realistic, 66
    success of, 67
Gottman, John, 96
guilt, 13–14, 131–132

help, requesting, 125–126
HELP confrontation system, 124–125

helping/hindering analysis, 140–141
home
    bringing work, 206–207
    businesses, 193–196
household chores, 17–18, 21–23
Hull, Raymond, 159

imbalance in partnership, 58–59
imposter syndrome, 49
indifference toward partner, 59
intimacy, maintaining, 211–213

job
    goals for, 138–140
    reasons for working at, 140–141
    redesign of, 162–163
job sharing, 165–166

Kent, Margaret, 32
key result areas (KRAs), 78, 81
Kropf, Marcia, 20–21

Laikin, Alan, 158
Landrum, Gene, 169
life, enjoying, 208–217
lifestyle, reassessing, 115–116
limit setting, 131–134
love, unconditional, 130

magic rescuer, 24–25
male bashing, 40
male/female teams, 182–183
marriage counseling, 215
Mead, Margaret, 153
men
    anger of, 31–33
    as partners, 19–20
    perception of women by, 38–40
    perspective of, 31–41
men's movement, 36–38
mentor, 154–155, 191
mentoring, 21
methodical behavioral style, 147
mission statement, 80
mixed messages, 37–38
money conflicts, 7–9, 33–34

Naples phenomenon, 173
negativity habit, 52
Nesbitt Trend Letter, 163

night work, 181–182

objectives, 83
  setting of, 80–82
office party rules, 203
office romances, 204
Olmsted, Barney, 163
one-night stands, 204–205
options, development of, 54–55
organizing strategies, 108–113

paperwork, 111–112
parent
  effectiveness training of, 130
  loving, 127–129
partnership, 27–29
  in achieving success, 198–207
  balancing careers in, 171–172
  critical issues of, 168–184
  failure of, 56–70
  management support of, 160–163
  objectives of, 80–82
  self-worth and, 42–55
  success of, 73–87
  trailer, 176–177
  working together, 185–197
partnership agreement, 187–188
pay self first, 197
Perfect Worthless Syndrome, 208–209
personal preference profile, 142–148
personal relationship, 208–217
personal resources, 141–142
Peter, Laurence J., 159
Peter Principle, 159
planning, 74, 77–78, 85
  key points of, 86–87
plateauing trap, 159–160
powerlessness
  feeling of, 153–154
  habit of, 50–51
Preateau Principle, 81
premarital/postmarital agreements, 75–77
pressure, working under, 101–103
priorities, 64–69
private time, 205–206
problem analysis, 90–94, 96–98
problems, as challenges, 89
problem-solving skills, 116

quality time, 10

relationships
  different perceptions of, 57
  system for approaching, 69–70
relocation, 174–176
resistance, overcoming, 127
responsibility, 64–66
  personal, 153, 199–201
role definition, 21
role expectations, 23–24
role-playing, 44–45
rules of game, 156–159

scapegoating, 201–203
self-esteem, 25–26
  definition of, 44–45
  high, 52–53
  low, 53–55
  role of, 42–55
self-management, 121–123
self-sabotage, 49–52
self-talk, 64
sex
  avoidance of, 209–211
  scheduling of, 213–215
  versus sleep, 216
sexual harassment, 32
situational analysis, 79–80
sleep, lack of, 216
Small Business Administration, 186
SMART objectives, 81–82
Smith, Suzanne, 163
social functions, 203
sole proprietorship, 187
sounding board, 199
  no-risk, 191
Steinem, Gloria, 26
Steiner, Claude M., 63
stress
  signs of, 107
  working for you, 100–117
stressors
  eliminating, 105–106
  emotional, 102
  identifying, 103–104
  internal *vs.* external, 104–105
structural plateauing, 159–160
success
  barriers to, 45–47
  partnership in, 198–207

support, gaining, 118–135
SWOT chart, 79

TEAM relationships, 149
time management, 158, 206–207
  in working couple, 9–10
tough behavior style, 146–147
transitional male, 35–36
travel
  job-related, 178–181
  with member of opposite sex, 182–183
turned-on people, 137–138

unconditional acceptance, 56–57

vacation time, 195–196
validation, 57
values, 46
  in decision making, 93–96
  hierarchy of, 48–49
victimization, 50–51

wage gap, 20
win/lose situations, 113–114
women
  attitudes of, 26–27
  men's perception about, 38–40
  outearning spouses, 172–174
  perception of, 18–19
  perspective of, 16–30
  supporting family, 173
workaholism, 208, 209–211
work-family separation, 21–25
working
  importance of, 137–138
  for self, 136–149
working couple
  building plan for, 74, 77–78
  challenges to, 3–15
  critical issues of, 168–184
  personality differences of, 191–193
working mothers, 17
Workplace 2000 (Boyett and Conn), 163